Y0-BRT-465

Bullet-Proof Logos

creating great designs which avoid legal problems

edited by
David E. Carter

with an introduction by
James R. Higgins
trademark attorney

production and layout
Alan York
Christa Carter
Kristin J. Back

book design
Suzanna M.W. Brown

Bullet-Proof Logos

First published in 1999 by Hearst Books International.
Now published by HBI,
an imprint of HarperCollins Publishers
10 East 53rd Street
New York, NY 10022-5299

ISBN: 0688-16926-0

Distributed in the U.S. and Canada by
Watson-Guptill Publications
770 Broadway
New York, NY 10003-5299
Tel: (800) 451-1741
(732) 363-4511 in NJ, AK, HI
Fax: (732) 363-0338

Distributed throughout the rest of the world by
HBI, an imprint of HarperCollins Publishers
10 East 53rd Street
New York, NY 10022-5299
Fax: (212) 207-7654

Printed in Hong Kong by Everbest Printing Company through Four Colour Imports, Louisville, Kentucky.

Designer's Worst Nightmare: You get a phone call from a once-happy client who is now shouting into the phone. "We're being sued!! The logo you designed infringes on the design of another company! The letter from their lawyer says 'cease and desist immediately.' They want us to take down the signs, destroy all letterheads, and anything else that has that logo!"

This scenario is enough to bring otherwise strong-willed designers into a cold sweat. Lawsuits and court battles over logo designs weren't what we had in mind when we became graphic designers.

The reality is, this Worst Nightmare happens all the time. And it's never fun. Except maybe for the lawyers.

I had one "infringement" experience many years ago, and even though I have tried to block it from my memory, it still haunts me. I have had this book in mind for years. There are some ways that knowledgeable design firms approach identity creation that will help to make a logo "bullet-proof," or pretty much immune from lawsuits over infringement.

When I started working on the book, I asked my friend and trademark attorney, Jim Higgins, to give me some guidelines on the book. The use of "secondary devices" was a result of those early discussions. When the book was completed, he wrote the introduction for me.

My special interest is in the creation of great logos; Jim's area of expertise is in keeping clients out of "legal hot water." The purpose of this book is to help you do both: create great logos while knowing when (and why) to take certain creative approaches that avoid problems.

If this book prevents you from getting even one letter or phone call from one upset client, or one plaintiff's attorney, it will be worth many times what you paid for it. That's why we did the book.

David E. Carter

Bullet-Proof Logos: Logo Law 101

by James H. Higgins, Jr.
Trademark Attorney

I chose my wife, as she did her wedding gown,
not for a fine glossy surface, but such qualities as would wear well.
—The Vicar of Wakefield© 1766

When I was asked to write the introduction for the latest book of my friend and client, David Carter, I was—and am—flattered and honored, for I have watched David's reputation grow over the years we have worked together. To convey my thoughts as a trademark lawyer in this latest publication in David's body of work, one can hardly find better advice in choosing a logo than the above suggestion from the venerable English author Oliver Goldsmith (1728-1744). If one designs a logo with "such qualities as would wear well", those qualities will satisfy both the marketing and legal aspects of a logo.

No doubt, perhaps even just moments prior to reading this book, you will have been presented with a host of logos that continue to "wear well", long after they have been created. Quality logos are all around every aspect of our lives—the "Louisville Slugger in an oval" of Hillerich & Bradsby Co, the "walking fingers" of the Yellow Pages, the fanciful "Golden Arches M" of McDonald's Corporation, the "GE" script-in-a-circle of General Electric Company, the yellow and green "jumping deer" of John Deere, Inc., the "three As in an oval" of the American Automobile Association, the famous Mercedes "star" of Mercedes Benz Werks AG, the "cover the earth" logo of Sherwin-Williams Company, the yellow and black "K-Kodak" label of Eastman Kodak Co., the left-handed script of "Holiday Inn", the roof design superimposed over "Pizza Hut" of Tri-Con Global Restaurants, Inc., the famous "Coca Cola" ribbon script of Coca Cola Corporation, and countless others. And, even though there is no image presented with the above logos, I am confident that each and every reader can visualize the logo's appearance.

Also, note that all of these logos conjure up the identity of the owner without naming the full name of the corporation that owns/uses the logo. This is another quality of a good logo that "wears well". The logo becomes an instant reminder—and constant salesman—for the company, often without formally naming the company.

With this book, David Carter will teach you how to design a logo that will have the prospect of "wearing well". But before you begin to learn how to design a logo for your business, take a moment to review the legal framework within which logos operate.

Legally, a logo is a trademark or service mark[1], which is defined as "any word, symbol or device, or combination thereof, which is used to **identify** and **distinguish** one's goods or services from those of one's competitors." A logo, then, is a "symbol" in the eyes of the trademark laws; if the logo is combined with words or letters, that is a "combination" mark.

Because the trademark laws govern logos, it is helpful to appreciate some principles of trademark law so you can make the most effective use of your logo.

These logos for three different companies show the potential problems of trademark confusion. It's more than just a communications problem, it can be a costly legal problem.

Priority of Use

Under the trademark laws of the United States, "first in time is first in right." This means, generally, that the first person to use a particular mark (whether a logo, or a word mark or a combination mark) has certain legal rights to the mark. The first user is called the "senior user"; the senior user's rights are called *common law* rights. Common law rights arise upon use, even without a formal registration (more on registration later). Common law rights, however, extend only to the boundaries of the user's actual trade area.

Trade Area and the Junior User

The trade area of common law rights exists only to the extent of actual, regular business under the mark/logo. The extent of actual business is called "penetration"—isolated or token sales do not establish penetration. Thus, if the senior user does business under the logo only in certain counties of a state, that is the extent of common law rights—plus a reasonable zone of expansion, depending on recent history of business under the mark. If a second person (called the "junior user") were to start operating under a similar logo outside of that trade area, the senior user's common law rights may not reach far enough to enjoin the junior user. This might be true even if the competitor were to open in another part of the same state. Thus, under the common law of trademarks and logos, it is possible to have more than one company using the mark/logo. This is called the concept of the remote junior user, and obviously, such a situation is to be avoided if possible.

Effect of Federal Registration

While trademark rights accrue on use, those rights can be enhanced substantially by obtaining federal registration. A federal registration preempts further uses of the mark or logo and in effect gives the senior user a *nationwide* trade area, even if there is no actual usage yet in a part of the country. Federal registration, then, can avoid the problem of the remote junior user. However, federal registration operates prospectively only, and cannot affect pre-existing common law rights.

The Single Source Rule

USA trademark law is founded on the concept that a mark or a logo is supposed to identify a "single source" for the particular goods or services to the relevant class of consumers. Thinking back to the famous logos listed at the beginning of this introduction, it is seen that these logos fit the "single source rule" quite nicely. It should also be seen that the "remote junior user" situation is not in harmony with the "single source rule." That is why federal registration is often so important to achieve the full goal of a logo (or any other mark).

Hierarchy of Trademark Distinctiveness

In the context of a trademark's (or a logo's) legal mission to *identify* and *distinguish* the owner's goods or services from his competitors, certain words are more capable of distinguishing than others. Thus, it is important to know the "hierarchy of trademark distinctiveness", as follows:

TYPE	EXAMPLE(S)	DEFINITION	PROTECTIBILITY
generic	car, bank, lawyer, etc. (nounal use)	states a "thing"	not a mark; never protectible
descriptive	**Honey Roast Peanuts (no)**	**mark *immediately***	
surname	**McDonalds® (not at first)**	***conveys* the goods**	**Protectible only after**
geographic	**Bluegrass (no)**		**"Secondary Meaning"**
laudatory	**Super, Mega (no)**		**(5 year use or much $$$)**
suggestive	Skinvisible® surgical tape Playboy® magazine L'eggs® hosiery	requires *imagination* to connect mark and goods	immediately on use
arbitrary	**Greyhound® bus lines** **Apple® computers**	**mark has no connection to goods**	**immediately**
coined	EXXON® gasoline XEROX® photocopiers KODAK film	made up term	immediately

Note that proper trademark use is always as an *adjective*, never as noun; if you use a mark as a noun, it could be termed generic and not protectible. Another lesson of the "hierarchy" is, choose at least a suggestive mark, so it is immediately protectible. If you choose a descriptive mark, you could have problems (ask the folks at Honey Roast Peanuts, who created a market but couldn't protect it).

Likelihood of Confusion

The touchstone of legal liability under USA trademark law (and the trademark laws of many other countries) is the "likelihood of confusion" (LOC) standard—if an appreciable percentage of relevant consumers are likely to be confused as to the source of the goods or services (keeping in mind the "single source" concept), then the senior user can enjoin the junior user's use of the mark/logo. Determination of LOC involves consideration of multiple factors, including

- the similarity of the marks as to their sight, sound and/or meaning;
- the similarity of the goods or services on which the marks are used;
- evidence of actual confusion, if any;
- the channels of trade in which the goods or services operate;
- the degree of overlap of respective consumers;
- the manner in which the marks are promoted;
- the degree of sophistication of the relevant consumers;
- the possibility of expansion by the senior user; and
- the good faith exhibited by the junior user.

The list is non-exhaustive, and analysis is much more than mere "factor counting." No single factor is dispositive. In fact, often one or two factors dominate the analysis. It is not necessary to show actual confusion. The test, after all, is *likelihood* of confusion. In addition, there is no protection afforded an "innocent" infringer; even if the junior user did not know about the senior user's mark, if the factors indicate LOC, the junior user can be enjoined from using the mark.

Effective Selection of a "Bullet Proof" Logo

While there can be no total legal guarantee, if you follow two steps in selecting a logo, your chances of creating/selecting a truly "bullet proof" logo will be maximized. First, the logo must fulfill the "identify" and "distinguish" requirements of the legal definition, so the mark/logo will pass legal muster.

On the "identify" portion of the legal definition, this means that the design component must be more than simple squares or circles or triangles (which of course are in common usage). Also, avoid choosing words of a composite mark that are descriptive of the goods or services (such as "Honey Roast Peanuts"). In other words, the logo design and the word(s) must have enough "pizazz" to *identify* your company as the *single source* of the goods or services offered by your company. One advantage to a logo design is that it can add distinctiveness to an otherwise unprotectible word. For example, the distinctive logo-style of LITE beer by Miller Brewing Company has been held protectible, whereas the word "Lite" was not. However, note that only the logo itself is protectible; that is why every other brewery is able to offer a competing "Lite" (or "Light") beer. This may not satisfy everyone's marketing needs.

As for the "distinguish" portion of the legal definition, the logo (both the design and any word used) must be differentiated from pre-existing logos so as to avoid confusion (LOC). This is best accomplished by a trademark search, which costs between $150 and $500 (1999 pricing). A search can identify existing logos that might conflict with the chosen logo. One search would be required to search for words of a composite mark, and a separate search would be necessary for the design component of the logo. Not only can a search identify problems with the chosen mark/logo, but the fact that a search was conducted will demonstrate good faith when the LOC factors are considered. No trademark or logo search is perfect, however, because even unregistered marks and logos (which can be quite difficult to locate) have legal rights. However, if a search of proper scope is conducted, the amount of risk will be substantially mitigated.

During this selection phase, an experienced trademark attorney can be helpful. The attorney can advise whether the selected mark/logo will qualify under the "identify" portion of the legal definition, and also whether the mark is distinctive enough to satisfy the "distinguish" requirement to avoid LOC with any pre-existing mark or logo. The best time to deal with logo problems is during this pre-selection phase, when there is no real investment yet in the logo.

In the pages which follow, David Carter divides his technique for designing logos into three classifications, [1] Name in Type; [2] Name in Modified Type; and [3] Name in Type With Secondary Device. It is seen that importance of the design component increases in each class.

The "Name in Type" class is basically a word mark without much design, so the word itself must supply the required legal distinctiveness. Here, the most important trademark concept to apply is found in the "hierarchy"—you need to select a word that is protectible in and of itself. In the "Name in Modified Type" class, the ornateness of the type can add legal distinctiveness, but it is still important to choose a protectible name (recall the "Lite" beer example, above). Finally, for the "Name in Type With Secondary Device" class, David Carter's suggested use of a "secondary device" adds even more distinctiveness (and therefore more protectibility) to the chosen mark/logo.

If you choose your name following the above principles of trademark law (including consulting with an experienced trademark attorney), then blend that choice with the teachings in this, David Carter's latest book, you will be well on your way to creating and adopting a "bullet proof" logo, one which will serve as an instant identifier of, and constant salesman for, your company.

James R. Higgins, Jr. is a registered patent attorney with over 20 years experience in trademark matters. His office is located at 401 South Fourth Avenue - Suite 2500, Louisville KY 40202. Phone (502) 584-1135; fax (502) 561-0442; e-mail jhiggins@middreut.com. Mr. Higgins' comments are general in nature only, and are not legal advice. For legal advice, consult with an experienced trademark lawyer. Kentucky law requires the following statement—**THIS IS AN ADVERTISEMENT**.

[1] A "trademark" is used for goods, such as baseball bats or cameras. A "service mark" is used for services such as restaurant or travel planning services. The law protects trademarks and service marks equally.

Name in type

The logos on this page are essentially company names set in type. The power of the design comes through consistent use, not creativity.

SONY®

BOEING

CASIO®

CHANEL

Name in modified type

The logos here get their uniqueness through some modification of the name set in type. This style is more distinctive than simply using a standard typeface; a corporate "personality" can be communicated through the type modification.

COMPAQ

radius™

Microsoft®

EATON

Canon

Name in type with secondary device

These logos have been further embellished by a "secondary visual device." This gives the logo even more distinctiveness while avoiding some of the potential problems that exist for logos which are completely composed of a graphic design. The fact that the type, not the secondary graphic device, is the primary element makes it more difficult to legally challenge "secondary device logos."

Bullet-proof logos: a portfolio of design excellence

The rest of the book is composed of logos which can be classified in one of the three design categories discussed earlier. For each logo shown, the design firm is listed.

Client: *Allen and Sons*
Designer: **ZGraphics, Ltd.**
East Dundee, Illinois

Client: *Sazaby, Inc.*
Designer: **Matsumoto Incorporated**
New York, New York

Client: *Learning Curve*
Designer: **Liska + Associates**
Chicago, Illinois

Craftsummer

Client: *CraftSummer, Miami University*
Designer: **Five Visual Communication & Design**
West Chester, Ohio

Client: *Charles Industries*
Designer: **Blevins Design**
Elmhurst, Illinois

JODIE DAY

Client: *Jodie Day*
Designer: **DotZero Design**
Portland, Oregon

GUIDANT

Client: *Guidant*
Designer: **Lippincott & Margulies**
New York, New York

Client: *Artists Garden*
Designer: **Denise Kemper Design**
Wadsworth, Ohio

Client: *WTVP Channel 47-Public Television*
Designer: **Simantel Group**
Peoria, Illinois

Client: *Medcor*
Designer: **Lipson•Alport•Glass & Associates**
Northbrook, Illinois

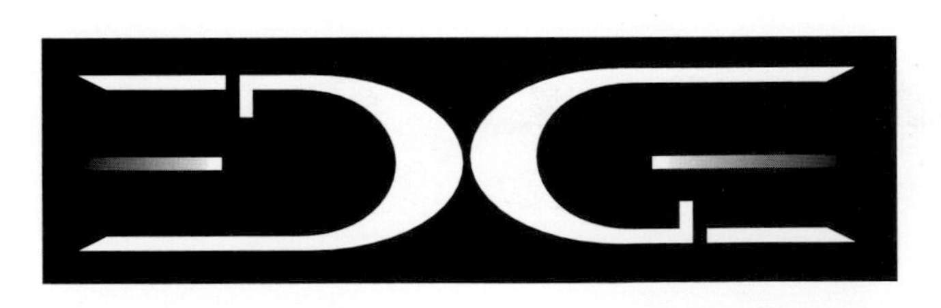

Client: *Edge*
Designer: **McGrath Design**
Albuquerque, New Mexico

Baskin 31 Robbins

Client: *Baskin Robbins*
Designer: **Lippincott & Margulies**
New York, New York

The St Paul

Client: *The St. Paul*
Designer: **Lippincott & Margulies**
New York, New York

NYNEX

Client: *Nynex*
Designer: **Lippincott & Margulies**
New York, New York

Client: *Tenneco*
Designer: **Lippincott & Margulies**
New York, New York

ecomat

Client: *Ecofranchising, Inc.*
Designer: **Stephen Loges Graphic Design**
New York, New York

PetOvat!ons

Client: *Petovations, Inc.*
Designer: **Graphica, Inc.**
Miamisburg, Ohio

|m|a|h|a|r|a|m|

Client: *Maharam*
Designer: **Matsumoto Incorporated**
New York, New York

WORLDESIGN

Client: *Worldesign Foundation*
Designer: **Matsumoto Incorporated**
New York, New York

Client: *National Pedal Sport Association*
Designer: **The Brothers Bogusky**
Miami, Florida

Client: *Hotel Triton/Kempton Hotel Group*
Designer: **Hunt Weber Clark Associates**
San Francisco, California

NOVACOR

Client: *Novacor*
Designer: **Burson Marstellar/Joe Miller's Company**
Santa Clara, California

Client: *Shop Channel*
Designer: **Pittard Sullivan**
Culver City, California

Client: *The Sci-Fi Channel*
Designer: **B.D. Fox & Friends, Advertising**
Santa Monica, California

Client: *CNS*
Designer: **Yamamoto Moss**
Minneapolis, Minnesota

Client: *Nickelodeon*
Designer: **Yoe! Studio**
Peekskill, New York

extreme(e)
audio

Client: *extrem(e) audio*
Designer: **Simantel Group**
Peoria, Illinois

Client: *Skyline Enterprises, Inc.*
Designer: **Westhouse Design**
Greenville, South Carolina

AC DATA SYSTEMS

SURGE SUPPRESSION SOLUTIONS

Client: *A.C. Data Systems*
Designer: **John Stribiak & Assoc.**
Palos Hills, Illinois

Client: *Hedge & Co. Inc.*
Designer: **Ford & Earl Assoc.**
Troy, Michigan

OMAN

Client: *Oman*
Designer: **Liska + Associates**
Chicago, Illinois

Client: *Little Kids, Inc.*
Designer: **Creative Vision Design Co.**
Providence, Rhode Island

Marzetti®
Since 1896

Client: *T. Marzetti Company*
Designer: **The Chesapeake Group, Inc.**
Cincinnati, Ohio

Client: *KMC Telecom*
Designer: **Emphasis Seven Communications, Inc.**
Chicago, Illinois

Client: *aire design company*
Designer: **aire design company**
Tucson, Arizona

Client: *Hitachi Data Systems*
Designer: **HDS Marcomm**
Santa Clara, California

Client: *Circle K - Mexico "Taquiza"*
Designer: **David Brewster Design**
Denise Kemper Design
Wadsworth, Ohio

Client: *Zeta4*
Designer: **The Brothers Bogusky**
Miami, Florida

Client: *N.E. Place/Matthews Media Group, Inc.*
Designer: **Alphawave Designs**
Burlington, Vermont

Client: *Grainger*
Designer: **Liska + Associates**
Chicago, Illinois

MOSAIC™

Client: *Frasier Paper Company (Mosaic)*
Designer: **Lipson·Alport·Glass & Associates**
Northbrook, Illinois

AMERICAN

CREW

Client: *American Crew*
Designer: **Liska + Associates**
Chicago, Illinois

Client: *Ko-Thi Dance Company*
Designer: **Becker Design**
Milwaukee, Wisconsin

Case study #1: Dog Eat Dog

In November 1998, Lycos, the highly successful internet search engine, was sued for trademark infringement by Labrador software. Labrador's complaint was based on Lycos' use of a labrador retriever as a logo in a $25 million dollar ad campaign. Labrador already uses a lab as a logo.

Lycos chose its new logo to symbolize that Lycos was good at "retrieving" information on the internet.

Labrador Software was founded in 1997 and its first product was called Labrador E-Retriever. The firm was concerned that the Lycos' Labrador Retriever logo design was in conflict with the Labrador Software's name and logo.

At press time, the outcome of the suit is uncertain, but, both firms are spending money on lawyers, not to mention executives' time that could be devoted to strategic planning, not managing a lawsuit.

The object of creating a "bullet-proof" logo is not to win lawsuits, but to *avoid* them.

Client: *Grainger*
Designer: **Liska + Associates**
Chicago, Illinois

Client: *Calypso Imaging*
Designer: **AERIAL**
San Francisco, California

Client: *DigiTech, Inc.*
Designer: **Westhouse Design**
Greenville, South Carolina

Client: *Rivery*
Designer: **RBMM/The Richards Group**
Dallas, Texas

Client: *Horticulture Design*
Designer: **Liska + Associates**
Chicago, Illinois

Client: *Gateway International Business Center*
Designer: **Westhouse Design**
Greenville, South Carolina

Client: *Chicago Mercantile Exchange*
Designer: **Liska + Associates**
Chicago, Illinois

EATON

Client: *Eaton*
Designer: **Lippincott & Margulies**
New York, New York

Comerica

Client: *Comerica*
Designer: **Lippincott & Margulies**
New York, New York

PRIMERICA

Client: *Primerica*
Designer: **Lippincott & Margulies**
New York, New York

Client: *Hartmarx*
Designer: **Lippincott & Margulies**
New York, New York

DOMAIN
ENERGY

Client: *Domain Energy (Tenneco)*
Designer: **Lippincott & Margulies**
New York, New York

ENRON
CORP

Client: *Enron Corporation*
Designer: **Lippincott & Margulies**
New York, New York

Client: *Handok*
Designer: **Lippincott & Margulies**
New York, New York

Client: *Yoshiki Yamauchi*
Designer: **LDW**
Los Angeles, California

Client: *GQC Holdings, Inc.*
Designer: **Russell Leong Design**
Palo Alto, California

Client: *Honeysweet International*
Designer: **Thibault Paolini Design**
Portland, Maine

Client: *Benson & Hedges*
Designer: **Liska + Associates**
Chicago, Illinois

Client: *Lipson·Alport·Glass & Associates*
Designer: **Lipson·Alport·Glass & Associates**
Northbrook, Illinois

Client: *Internet Dynamics, Inc.*
Designer: **Simantel Group**
Peoria, Illinois

experian

Client: *Experian (TRW)*
Designer: **Lippincott & Margulies**
New York, New York

Client: *Humana*
Designer: **Lippincott & Margulies**
New York, New York

SCANA

Client: *Scana*
Designer: **Lippincott & Margulies**
New York, New York

Client: *Flagstar*
Designer: **Lippincott & Margulies**
New York, New York

FLAGSTAR

Client: *Alchemy*
Designer: **Bremmer & Goris Comm.**
Alexandria, Virginia

Client: *Hallmark Cards, Inc.*
Designer: **Steel Wool Design**
Tulsa, Oklahoma

Client: *Imation Corporation*
Designer: **Larsen Design + Interactive**
Minneapolis, Minnesota

Client: *Alchemy*
Designer: **Bremmer & Goris Comm.**
Alexandria, Virginia

Client: *Hallmark Cards, Inc.*
Designer: **Steel Wool Design**
Tulsa, Oklahoma

Case study #2: NBC Logo

On January 1, 1976, NBC introduced a new stylized "N" logo to replace its ubiquitous peacock design. Within hours, the network was stunned to discover that its new logo was virtually identical to that of the Nebraska Television Network. (See both logos at right.) The result: embarrassed NBC officials had to "buy" their logo from Nebraska.

NBC eventually dropped its stylized "N" logo, and returned to its peacock roots, with a modified version of the peacock. The original NBC peacock (before the "N") and the current logo are shown below.

Client: *Samsung*
Designer: **Lippincott & Margulies**
New York, New York

Client: *Roadway "caliber"*
Designer: **Lippincott & Margulies**
New York, New York

Client: *Conoco "breakplace"*
Designer: **Lippincott & Margulies**
New York, New York

ACCU COLOR

Client: *AccuColor*
Designer: **Liska + Associates**
Chicago, Illinois

Client: *Coregis*
Designer: **Lipson·Alport·Glass & Associates**
Northbrook, Illinois

radius™

Client: *Radius*
Designer: **Mortensen Design**
Mountain View, California

NAVCONTROL
MARINE ELECTRONICS

Client: *Navcontrol Marine Electronic*
Designer: **Callery & Company**
Patchogue, New York

Client: *JNANA Technologies Company*
Designer: **Burnett Group**
New York, New York

Caffé á Roma™

Client: *Caffé á Roma*
Designer: **The Weber Group Inc.**
Racine, Wisconsin

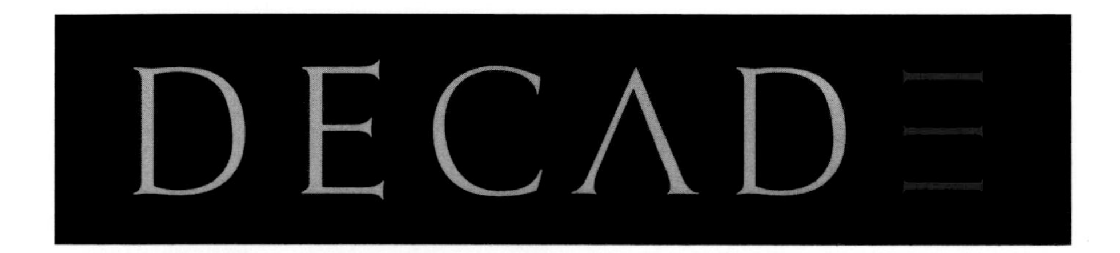

Client: *Episcopal School of Dallas*
Designer: **RBMM/The Richards Group**
Dallas, Texas

Client: *Jim Henson Productions*
Designer: **Yoe! Studio**
Peekskill, New York

Client: *The Tai Ping Yang - Westin Shanghai*
Designer: **Hansen Design Company**
Seattle, Washington

Client: *Michael Bonilla Illustration*
Designer: **Graphica, Inc.**
Miamisburg, Ohio

Client: *Fresh Squeezed Design*
Designer: **Fresh Squeezed Design**
Fargo, North Dakota

Client: *Miller Brewing Co.*
Designer: **Yoe! Studio**
Peekskill, New York

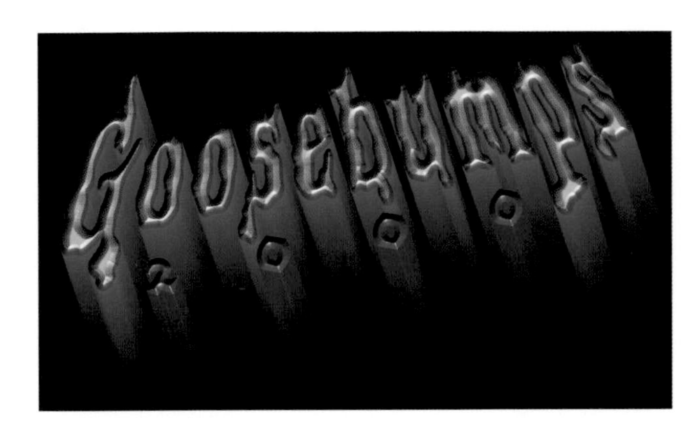

Client: *Parachute Press*
Designer: **Yoe! Studio**
Peekskill, New York

FREE INFO

Client: *GTE*
Designer: **Sibley/Peteet Design**
Dallas, Texas

Client: *Bridges International Repertory Theatre*
Designer: **Hansen Design Company**
Seattle, Washington

LONG
SHOT

Client: *Long Shot*
Designer: **Hansen Design Company**
Seattle, Washington

Client: *Newquest Technologies*
Designer: **Richards & Swensen, Inc.**
Salt Lake City, Utah

Client: *Lucy's Laces*
Designer: **Gill Fishman Associates, Inc.**
Cambridge, Massachussetts

LUCY'S LACES

NOVALIS™

Client: *Novalis International Limited*
Designer: **Albert•Bōgner Design Communications**
Lancaster, Pennsylvania

LIGHTHOUSE

Client: *Lighthouse Advertising (self promotion)*
Designer: **Lighthouse Advertising & Design, Inc.**
Santa Clara, California

CHEROKEE
COMMUNICATIONS, INC.

Client: *Cherokee Communications*
Designer: **Zoe Graphics**
Pennington, New Jersey

YOU ONLY LIVE TWICE

GOLDFINGER

THUNDERBALL

LIVE and LET DIE

DIAMONDS ARE FOREVER

THE MAN WITH THE GOLDEN GUN

MOONRAKER

THE LIVING DAYLIGHTS

OCTOPUSSY

LICENCE TO KILL

THE JAMES BOND 007™ COLLECTION

(opposite)
Client: *MGM/UA Home Video*
Designer: **B.D. Fox & Friends, Advertising**
Santa Monica, California

Client: *Doosan*
Designer: **Lippincott & Margulies**
New York, New York

Client: *FMC*
Designer: **Lippincott & Margulies**
New York, New York

Case study #3: Budget

When Budget Rent-a-Car updated its logo, it started with a type-only design (shown right). The type was changed slightly, but the major change was to add a "secondary" device under the logo. The new design is shown below.

By going from one "bullet-proof" logo to another, Budget was following guidelines to avoid creating a new design that would potentially infringe on that of another company.

Client: *Rite Hite*
Designer: **Becker Design**
Milwaukee, Wisconsin

Client: *Glade*
Designer: **Lipson•Alport•Glass & Associates**
Northbrook, Illinois

Client: *VIDA*
Designer: **Rousso & Associates**
Atlanta, Georgia

Client: *Datascope, Corp.*
Designer: **AERIAL**
San Francisco, California

Client: *Pacific Beach House, Inc.*
Designer: **AERIAL**
San Francisco, California

Beach House

Client: *Phoenix Network*
Designer: **AERIAL**
San Francisco, California

PhoenixNetwork.

CITYPLACE

Client: *Southland Corporation*
Designer: **RBMM/The Richards Group**

Client: *Cactus Cafe*
Designer: **Mark Palmer Design**
Palm Desert, California

Client: *H2 Oh*
Designer: **RBMM/The Richards Group**
Atlanta, Georgia

Client: *Reunion Arena*
Designer: **RBMM/The Richards Group**

Client: *Salus Media*
Designer: **AERIAL**
San Francisco, California

Client: *Association for Women in Communications*
Designer: **Louisa Sugar Design**
San Francisco, California

DIVERSITY

Client: *Crossroads Global Crafts*
Designer: **Simantel Group**
Peoria, Illinois

CROSSROADS

Client: *Interactive*
Designer: **Vaughn/Wedeen Creative**
Albuquerque, New Mexico

INTERACTIVE

Client: *Netscout Software*
Designer: **Gill Fishman Associates, Inc.**
Cambridge, Massachussetts

NetScout®

Client: *Stahl Design, Inc.*
Designer: **Stahl Design, Inc.**
Indianapolis, Indiana

StahlDesign

Client: *Paul Allen & Associates ©1998*
Designer: **Richards & Swensen, Inc.**
Salt Lake City, Utah

Client: *Dunn Communications*
Designer: **Richards & Swensen, Inc.**
Salt Lake City, Utah

Case study #4: Texaco & CalTex

A logo designer working on a project for a client in the petroleum field might look at these two identities and assume that using a star and a circle would be perfectly fine. After all, the designer reasons, "Texaco and CalTex both use a circle and a star, and if two big companies are using logos that are fairly similar, then what would it matter if there was one more firm with the same concept?"

However, upon further investigation, the designer would discover that CalTex is a corporate "relative" of Texaco. In the end, using a star and a circle for a petroleum-related firm could be very costly.

Client: *Lily's alterations*
Designer: **Ramsden Design**
Houston, Texas

THE SNORING
INSTITUTE

Client: *Weiss, McCorkle & Mashburn*
Designer: **Cornerstone**
Baltimore, Maryland

Client: *Sinogen*
Designer: **Artemis**
Palo Alto, California

S I N O G E N

Client: *Arrow Electronics Unlimited*
Designer: **Waters Design Associates, Inc.**
New York, New York

Client: *Mutual Life Insurance Company of New York*
Designer: **Waters Design Associates, Inc.**
New York, New York

Client: *Computer Power Inc.*
Designer: **The Design Shop**
Glen Ridge, New Jersey

Client: *Search Alliance*
Designer: **Cornerstone**
Baltimore, Maryland

SearchAlliance

Client: *Digital Imaging Group*
Designer: **CookSherman, Inc.**
San Francisco, California

Client: *Impact Unlimited*
Designer: **AERIAL**
San Fransico, California

Client: *AG Heinze*
Designer: **Mark Palmer Design**
Palm Desert, California

Client: *Spiegel, Inc.*
Designer: **Liska + Associates**
Chicago, Illinois

Client: *The Child Care Company*
(provider of medical supplies for children)
Designer: **Paganucci Design, Inc.**
New York, New York

Case study #5: Compaq

Compaq Computer's old logo used an underline as a graphic "secondary device."

When the logo was updated, the line was removed, and the name in type was the essential logo.

The design got its distinctiveness from the stylized Q. Interestingly, in many print ads and TV commercials, Compaq uses the Q alone, even though the company name's initial is "C".

Client: *Fraze Pavilion*
Designer: **Nova Creative Group, Inc.**
Dayton, Ohio

Client: *Axis*
Designer: **Lomangino Studio, Inc.**
Washington, D.C.

Client: *Glo's Broiler*
Designer: **Jeff Fisher LogoMotives**
Portland, Oregon

Client: *Frank Duca Press*
Designer: **John Langdon Design**
Philadelphia, Pennsylvania

Client: *Nortel (Northern Telecom)*
Designer: **Dean Corbitt Studio**
Dallas, Texas

Client: *The Reel Scoop*
Designer: **Jeff Fisher LogoMotives**
Portland, Oregon

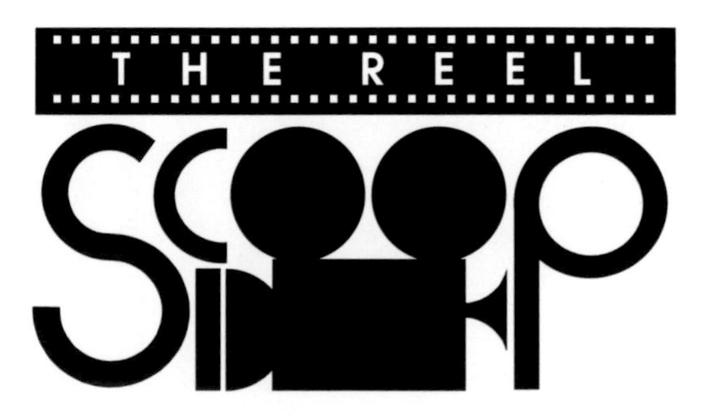

Client: *Integraphics*
Designer: **Cathey Associates, Inc.**
Dallas, Texas

Client: *Dansk*
Designer: **Graphic Design Continuum**
Dayton, Ohio

Client: *Real empreendimentos*
Designer: **RTKL Associates Inc**
Baltimore, Maryland

SHOPPING24

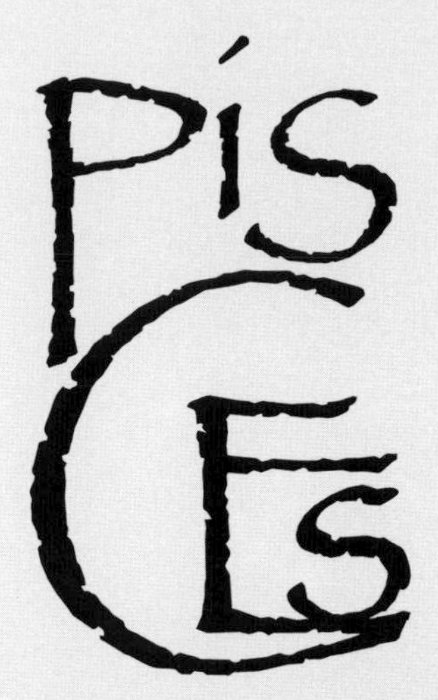

Client: *Pisces Jewelry*
Designer: **Simantel Group**
Peoria, Illinois

Client: *RX Choice*
Designer: **Kilmer & Kilmer**
Albuquerque, New Mexico

RxCHOICE

Client: *ROCK N JAVA CAFE*
Designer: **Creative Link Studio, Inc.**
San Antonio, Texas

Client: *The Loop Corporation*
Designer: **Hansen Design Company**
Seattle, Washington

Client: *Health Exchange*
Designer: **Lebowitz/Gould/Design, Inc.**
New York, New York

id´i·om

Client: *Idiom*
Designer: **AERIAL**
San Francisco, California

Client: *Bremer Wedding Ring Gallery*
Designer: **Simantel Group**
Peoria, Illinois

Client: *Hallmark Cards, Inc.*
Designer: **Hallmark Cards, Inc.**
Kansas City, Maryland

POLARIS
VENTURE PARTNERS

Client: *Polaris Venture Partners*
Designer: **Hansen Design Company**
Seattle, Washington

Client: *The Cathedral of Hope, Dallas Texas*
Designer: **Sibley/Peteet Design**
Dallas, Texas

Anschell

Client: *Anschell*
Designer: **Bob Rankin Design**
Bellevue, Washington

CONNECT®

Client: *Connect*
Designer: **Studio Archetype**
San Francisco, California

Client: *MFB International, LTD.*
Designer: **Rappy & Company, Inc.**
New York, New York

FCB ENERGY

Client: *FCB Energy*
Designer: **Crowley Webb And Associates**
Buffalo, New York

Client: *FirstBank Financial Corp.*
Designer: **Matrix International Assoc., Ltd.**
Denver, Colorado

1STBANK

Client: *Pro Tab, Inc.*
Designer: **Cathey Associates, Inc.**
Dallas, Texas

HI-TECH OIL COMPANY

PetroLink

Client: *Marketing Sciences America*
Designer: **Design Associates, Inc.**
Cleveland, Ohio

Client: *TTP Netherlands -via- Brems Eastman*
Designer: **David Lemley Design**
Seattle, Washington

Client: *Los Angeles Women's Foundation*
Designer: **Hershey Associates**
Santa Monica, California

Client: *U.S.-Japan Link, Inc.*
Designer: **Hiroshi Hamada Design Studio**
Santa Fe Springs, California

Client: *L'Ermite*
Designer: **Hiroshi Hamada Design Studio**
Santa Fe Springs, California

L'ERMITE
HANDCRAFTED GIFTS

Client: *Aquarium of Niagara*
Designer: **Crowley Webb And Associates**
Buffalo, New York

Client: *Plant Fantasies*
Designer: **DeMartino Design**
Mt. Kisco, New York

Client: *Buffalo In Bloom*
Designer: **Crowley Webb And Associates**
Buffalo, New York

Client: *Eight Hills Catering*
Designer: **Callery & Company**
Patchogue, New York

Eight Hills
CATERING

Client: *Rockingham Council of the Arts, Inc.*
Designer: **Seran Design**
Harrisonburg, Virginia

Client: *Safeway Security Systems*
Designer: **Callery & Company**
Patchogue, New York

Client: *Brothers Gourmet Coffees, Inc.*
Designer: **Robert W. Taylor Design, Inc.**
Boulder, Colorado

Case study #6: KFC

Kentucky Fried Chicken (now known as KFC) has a "bullet-proof logo" but it doesn't fit into any of the three categories shown in the opening of this book.

KFC's recipe (pardon the pun) for creating a legally distinctive logo goes back to the firm's founder: Col. Harlan Sanders. By using the Colonel's face (and Colonel tie) as the dominant graphic feature, a singularly distinctive logo is created. The blue graphic is essentially a "secondary device."

There are a number of memorable logos that use a "character" as the dominant feature. Pillsbury's "Poppin Fresh," The Jolly Green Giant, and the Morton's Salt umbrella girl are examples of how firms use a well-known character (real or created) to forge the company's identity.

Client: *Tarjac, Inc.*
Designer: **In House Graphic Design, Inc.**
Waterloo, New York

Client: *Dr. Pepper*
Designer: **Rousso+Associates, Inc.**
Atlanta, Georgia

Soccer
Pepper

Client: *Roehm Renovations*
Designer: **Simantel Group**
Peoria, Illinois

Client: *I.B. Goodman Company*
Designer: **DesignCentre**
Cincinnati, Ohio

Client: *A&M Records*
Designer: **Lorna Stovall Design**
New York, New York

ROXY LOPEZ

Client: *Fanta*
Designer: **Back Yard Design**
New York, New York

pop life

Client: *Liollio Associates*
Designer: **Rousso+Associates, Inc.**
Atlanta, Georgia

Client: *Catholic Charities Foundation*
Designer: **Crowley Webb And Associates**
Buffalo, New York

Client: *The Nasdaq Stock Market*
Designer: **Enock**
New York, New York

THE NASDAQ STOCK MARKET℠

NASDAQ®

Client: *Resurrection Health Care & Hope Cancer Care Network*
Designer: **Emphasis Seven Communications, Inc.**
Chicago, Illinois

Client: *CheckFree Corporation*
Designer: **Internal Creative Department**
Norcross, Georgia

ONE
PLUS

Client: *Gulf & Western*
Designer: **Tom Fowler, Inc.**
Stamford, Connecticut

Client: *Infinet Incorporated*
Designer: **Cathey Associates, Inc.**
Dallas, Texas

Client: *The Kroger Company*
Designer: **DesignCentre**
Cincinnati, Ohio

Client: *Brasizzle*
Designer: **Fleury Design**
Huntington Station, New York

Client: *Julians*
Designer: **Cisneros Design**
Santa Fe, New Mexico

JULIANS
ITALIAN BISTRO

Client: *Hitachi Data Systems*
Designer: **HDS Marcomm**
Santa Clara, California

Client: *Turner Martin*
Designer: **Sam Smidt**
Palo Alto, California

Client: *Axxys Technologies, Inc.*
Designer: **Cathey Associates, Inc.**
Dallas, Texas

Client: *Matrix International Associates, Ltd.*
Designer: **Matrix International Associates, Ltd.**
Denver, Colorado

Client: *Merrill Lynch*
Designer: **DeMartino Design**
Mt. Kisco, New York

Client: *LensCrafters*
Designer: **DesignCentre**
Cincinnati, Ohio

LENSCRAFTERS®
VISION

Client: *Data Downlink*
Designer: **Enock**
New York, New York

data downlink

Client: *Contours Salon & Day Spa*
Designer: **Ritz Henton Design Group**
Essex, Connecticut

SALON & DAY SPA

FRESHWATER
exporters, l.l.c.

Client: *Freshwater Exporters*
Designer: **Oakley Design Studios**
Portland, Oregon

Client: *Greater Buffalo Partnership*
Designer: **Crowley Webb And Associates**
Buffalo, New York

Client: *Duo Delights*
Designer: **Lambert Design Studio**
Dallas, Texas

Sweet Sinsations

Client: *Postrio Restaurant/Kimpton Hotel Group*
Designer: **Hunt Weber Clark Associates**
San Francisco, California

Client: *Cadence Design Systems*
Designer: **Joe Miller's Company**
Santa Clara, California

timeout

Client: *Leadership Buffalo*
Designer: **Crowley Webb And Associates**
Buffalo, New York

Client: *Diane Tutch*
Designer: **Jeff Fisher LogoMotives**
Portland, Oregon

Case study #7: NCR

NCR had a basic logo, with distinctive initials set into blocks (top example). As time changed, NCR kept the blocks, but changed the style of lettering. When yet another logo update was undertaken, NCR went to a stylized graphic (example at bottom left). That's when the problems began. Gartner Group Inc. sued, claiming that the new NCR logo infringed on its design. In the end, NCR wound up still using the logo. That's not the issue, though. The whole idea of creating a "bullet-proof" logo is not to win law suits—but to avoid them.

Client: *Playwrights Horizons*
Designer: **Straightline International**
New York, New York

playwrights horizons

Client: *Unifications*
Designer: **Cathey Associates, Inc.**
Dallas, Texas

Client: *CCG Meta Media, Inc.*
Designer: O&J Design, Inc.
New York, New York

LIFESPAN

Client: *Lifespan*
Designer: **Tharp Did It**
Los Gatos, California

ResourceNet

Client: *ResourceNet Communications Inc.*
Designer: **TRIAD, INC.**
Larkspur, California

Client: *U.S. Department of Energy*
Designer: **Apex Technology**
Alexandria, Virginia

Client: *PR Newswire/Source Communications*
Designer: **DeMartino Design**
Mt. Kisko, New York

Client: *Suncast*
Designer: **Visual Marketing Associates**
Dayton, Ohio

Client: *Rimsat Ltd.*
Designer: **Emphasis Seven Communications, Inc.**
Chicago, Illinois

Client: *Cisneros Design*
Designer: **Cisneros Design**
Santa Fe, New Mexico

CISNEROS
D E S I G N

Client: *Raging Rivers Water Park/Grafton, Illinois*
Designer: **Kochan & Company**
St. Louis, Missouri

Client: *Steuben Child Care Project*
Designer: **Michael Orr + Associates, Inc.**
Corning, New York

THE BREWERY

Client: *The Brewery*
Designer: **Design Ranch**
Iowa City, Iowa

Case study #8: Ryder

The old Ryder Truck Rental logo was simply name in type. The capital letters made the name stand out a little, but it was not particularly distinctive, nor was it memorable.

When Ryder redesigned its logo, the first change was to go from all caps to caps and lower case type. The most apparent change was the introduction of a strong "secondary device" which gives the design a sense of motion, and also increases its memorability.

Client: *Crowley Webb And Associates*
Designer: **Crowley Webb And Associates**
Buffalo, New York

Client: *Seattle Men's Chorus*
Designer: **Jeff Fisher LogoMotives**
Portland, Oregon

PHILANDROS

Client: *Action Floor Systems*
Designer: **Blevins Design**
Elmhurst, Illinois

Client: *Andrée Light Options*
Designer: **O&J Design, Inc.**
New York, New York

Light Options

Client: *Global Village*
Designer: **Belyea Design Alliance**
Seattle, Washington

Global Village
GLASS STUDIOS

Client: *BellSouth*
Designer: **Young & Martin Design**
Atlanta, Georgia

Client: *Altair*
Designer: **Hunt Weber Clark Associates**
San Francisco, California

Client: *World Variety Produce*
Designer: **Bryan Friel Studio**
Long Beach, California

Client: *The University of Akron School of Art*
Designer: **Herip Design Associates**
Peninsula, Ohio

Client: *Little Treasures Child Care Center*
Designer: **Trudy Cole-Zielanski Design**
Churchville, Virginia

Client: *Imagenation*
Designer: **Young & Roehr Advertising**
Portland, Oregon

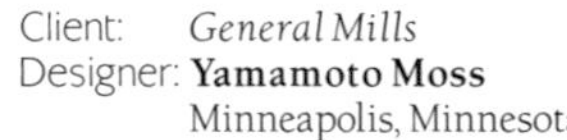

Client: *General Mills*
Designer: **Yamamoto Moss**
Minneapolis, Minnesota

Newventures

Client: *Brothers Gourmet Coffees, Inc.*
Designer: **Robert W. Taylor Design, Inc.**
Boulder, Colorado

Fairwinds®

Client: *W.R. Grace Building Products*
Designer: **Doerr Associates**
Concord, Massachusetts

Client: *Joan Jenkins*
Designer: **Musikar Design**
Rockville, Maryland

Client: *Kelvin Construction Company*
Designer: **Niedermeier Design**
Renton, Washington

KELVIN

Case study #9: Transamerica

Transamerica had a very modern, very 70s, logo design that was quite recognizable. The design was also one that could be on the plaintiff's side in any number of infringement actions. When the firm modernized its design, a complete overhaul of the identity was done.

The new design used the world-famous Transamerica tower in San Francisco as the identity. Surveys have shown that the building is one of the most recognized anywhere—it often appears in the skyline of movies shot in The City.

The result is a design that does double duty for the company. It functions in ads as well as tourist and entertainment features. The design is so distinctively theirs that it is also "bullet proof."

TRANSAMERICA

SM

Client: *Red Monkey Ads & Ideas*
Designer: **Oakley Design Studios**
Portland, Oregon

Client: *Tect Products Inc.*
Designer: **DeMartino Design**
Mt. Kisco, New York

Client: *KEZK-FM/St. Louis*
Designer: **Kochan + Company**
St. Louis, Missouri

I Believe In
SAINT LOUIS

Client: *United Nations*
Designer: **UN - Design Studio**
New York, New York

Stop Crime!

Client: *Kite Fitness*
Designer: **bonatodesign**
Berwyn, Pennsylvania

Client: *Shark Courier Service*
Designer: **DeMartino Design**
Mt. Kisco, New York

CAF

Client: *Chicago Advertising Federation*
Designer: **Lipson• Alport•Glass & Associates**
Northbrook, Illinois

Client: *Laser Impact, Inc.*
Designer: **Wet Paper Bag Graphic Design**
Fort Worth, Texas

Client: *Pihas, Schmidt & Westerdahl Advertising*
Designer: **Phillips Design**
Tampa, Florida

Client: *United Nations*
Designer: **Kelleher Design**
New York, New York

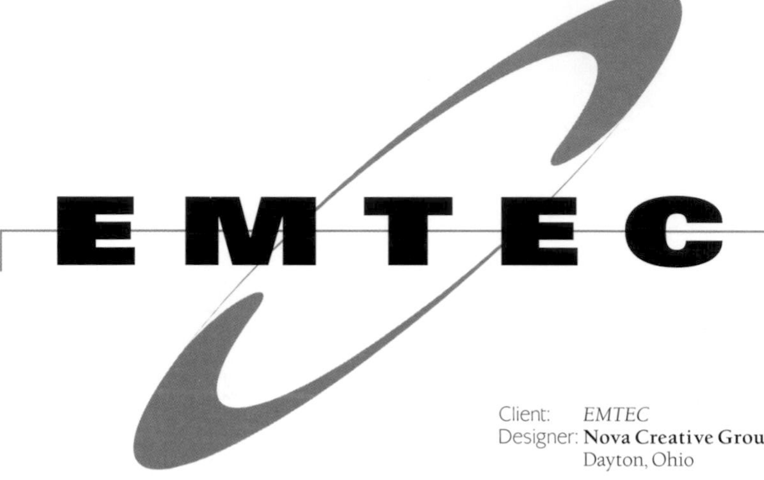

Client: *EMTEC*
Designer: **Nova Creative Group**
Dayton, Ohio

ECHO
interactive
INCORPORATED

Client: *ECHO interactive*
Designer: **The Rittenhouse Group**
Milwaukee, Wisconsin

Client: *Terra Nova restaurant & bakery*
Designer: **aire design company**
Tucson, Arizona

Client: *Executive Car Buying Services*
Designer: **Callery & Company**
Patchogue, New York

Client: *Tatra Enterprises*
Designer: **Callery & Company**
Patchogue, New York

Client: *Tony's Pizza Service*
Designer: **Rapp Collins Communications**
Minneapolis, Minnesota

Client: *Family Place*
Designer: **Lambert Design Studio**
Dallas, Texas

Client: *Coral Way Village*
Designer: **The Brothers Bogusky**
Miami, Florida

Client: *CDK Contracting Company*
Designer: **Kilmer & Kilmer**
Albuquerque, New Mexico

Client: *Eugene/University Music Association*
Designer: **Jeff Fisher LogoMotives**
Portland, Oregon

Client: *Junior League of Portland*
Designer: **Jeff Fisher LogoMotives**
Portland, Oregon

Client: *Jeff Maul*
Designer: **Jeff Fisher LogoMotives**
Portland, Oregon

Client: *John Stribiak & Associates*
Designer: **John Stribiak & Associates**
Palos Hills, Illinois

LEXINGTON
PHYSICAL
THERAPY

Client: *Lexington Physical Therapy*
Designer: **Kirby Stephens Design, Inc.**
Somerset, Kentucky

Client: *Laser Solutions*
Designer: **Nealy Wilson Nealy, Inc.**
Indianapolis, Indiana

Client: *Spokane Convention & Visitors Bureau*
Designer: **Klundt Hosmer Design Assoc.**
Spokane, Washington

The TEXAS Triangle

Client: *The Texas Triangle*
Designer: **Sibley/Peteet Design**
Dallas, Texas

Client: *Applied Energy Group*
Designer: **Coleman Design Group, Inc.**
Washington, D.C.

Client: *Finalé Dessert Cafe*
Designer: **Stahl Design Inc.**
Indianapolis, Indiana

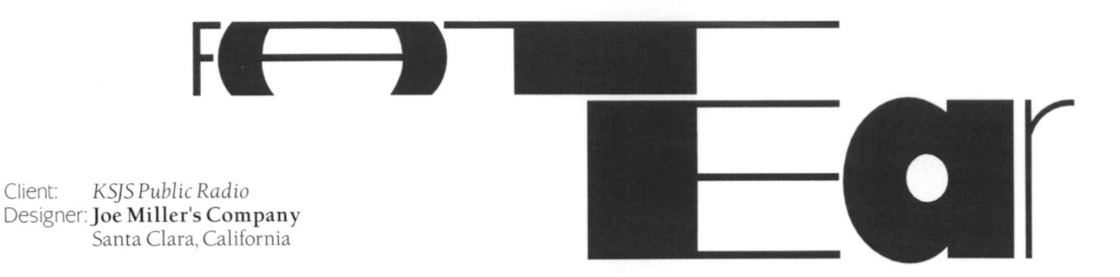

Client: *KSJS Public Radio*
Designer: **Joe Miller's Company**
Santa Clara, California

Case study #10: Moore Business Forms

Moore Business Forms had a distinctive "abstract" logo (often referred to by insiders as "the inverted jock strap"). When the identity was updated, the abstract gave way to a modified type design.

While we don't know the rationale for the actual change, we can speculate on the results.

Having an "abstract" mark which might be easily infringed requires constant vigilance, with attorneys writing letters to those whose trademarks might be considered "too close" to the firm's design. By going to a modified type design, the need for warning letters is reduced considerably. The end result is a savings in legal costs for the firm.

Client: *Whitman Walker Clinic*
Designer: **Musikar Design**
Rockville, Maryland

Client: *ASMC*
Designer: **Elliott Van Deutsch**
Falls Church, Virginia

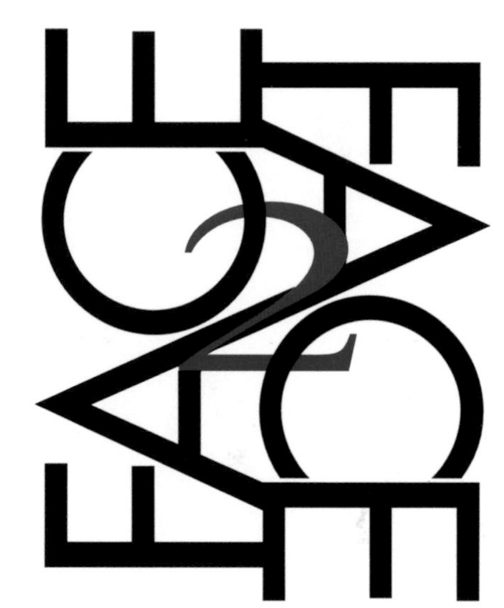

Client: *Flat Creek Skillet Lickers/Bruce Keedy*
Designer: **Whitney Design Works**
St. Louis, Missouri

The Flat Creek Skillet Lickers

Client: *Tech Source*
Designer: **Shields Design**
Fresno, California

TECHSOURCE
THE MAC SUPERSTORE

Client: *Our House at the Beach*
Designer: **DeMartino Design**
Mt. Kisco, New York

OUR HOUSE
AT THE BEACH
LAKE HOUSES

Client: *Ultimate Burrito*
Designer: **Jeff Fisher LogoMotives**
Portland, Oregon

FLEXPOINT

Client: *Luminet*
Designer: **Sibley•Peteet Design**
Dallas, Texas

Client: *Mercruiser*
Designer: **SHR Perceptual Management**
Scottsdale, Arizona

Client: *Dover Partners Inc.*
Designer: **Nova Creative Group, Inc.**
Dayton, Ohio

DOVER
PARTNERS, INC.

Client: *Bobolinks*
Designer: **DeMartino Design**
Mt. Kisco, New York

Client: *Milburn Peat Co.*
Designer: **Schlatter Design**
Battle Creek, Michigan

green
thumb

Client: *Digital Controls Corp.*
Designer: **Rousso + Associates, Inc.**
Atlanta, Georgia

BLIPCLIP

Client: *Taber Pontiac*
Designer: **Rousso + Associates, Inc.**
Atlanta, Georgia

Client: *Barry's Barber Shop*
Designer: **Simantel Group**
Peoria, Illinois

Client: *Nelson*
Designer: **Design North**
Racine, Wisconsin

Client: *Harrigan's Grill*
Designer: **Sibley/Peteet Design**
Dallas, Texas

Client: *Communiqué*
Designer: **AERIAL**
San Francisco, California

Communiqué

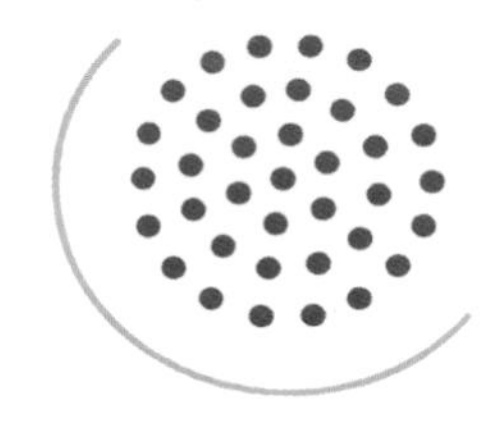

Communications
Etiquette
Training

Client: *Hotel Bohéme*
Designer: **AERIAL**
San Francisco, California

Client: *Advanced Concepts*
Designer: **MCD**
Redondo Beach, California

Client: *Abacus*
Designer: **Graphic Design Continuum**
Dayton, Ohio

Client: *Stage Directions Magazine*
Designer: **Angela Jackson**
North Highlands, California

STAGE
DIRECTIONS

Client: *Vintage*
Designer: **Kelleher Design**
New York, New York

ViNTaGe

Client: *CEL Technologies*
Designer: **Design North**
Racine, Wisconsin

Client: *Zymark Corporation*
Designer: **LMImage**
Boston, Massachusetts

Client: *SONAE*
Designer: **RTKL Associates** Inc.
Baltimore, Maryland

GAIASHOPPING

Client: *Wet Paper Bag Graphic Design*
Designer: **Wet Paper Bag Graphic Design**
Fort Worth, Texas

Wet Paper Bag

Client: *A&H Lithoprint*
Designer: **Blevins Design**
Elmhurst, Illinois

a&h

Client: *New Mexico Lottery*
Designer: **Kilmer & Kilmer**
Albuquerque, New Mexico

Client: *Carmen Schleiger*
Designer: **Jeff Fisher LogoMotives**
Portland, Oregon

Case study #11: Ten Thousand Diamonds

Got a good idea for a logo that is diamond shaped? For starters, keep in mind that there are more than 10,000 *registered* trademarks with a diamond shape. (Not to mention all the others that are *not* registered.

Below is a nice abstract design set on a diamond base. But, if you are intent on using the diamond background, keep all the cautions you have read in this book in mind.

A much better solution is to use the diamond as a "secondary device" and put the name in a distinctive typeface, as Skil has done.

Client: *Contract Attorneys*
Designer: **Jeff Fisher LogoMotives**
Portland, Oregon

CONTRACT ATTORNEYS

Client: *Natrol*
Designer: **Gauger & Silva**
San Francisco, California

Client: *Nottingham Properties*
Designer: **RTKL Associates Inc.**
Baltimore, Maryland

Client: *One Source Communications, Inc.*
Designer: **Cathey Associates, Inc.**
Dallas, Texas

OneSource
Communications, Inc.

SCULPTURE

Client: *Chip Williams*
Designer: **Wet Paper Bag Graphic Design**
Fort Worth, Texas

Client: *ImageWare Software*
Designer: **Triad, Inc.**
Larkspur, California

Client: *Kathy Magner*
Designer: **PLA**
Issaquah, Washington

Client: *Hitachi Data Systems*
Designer: **HDS Marcomm**
Santa Clara, California

Client: *U.S. Department of Energy*
Designer: **APEX Technology**
Alexandria, Virginia

EM PLUGGED IN

EM's GUIDE TO UPCOMING TRAINING COURSES SEPTEMBER 1996

Client: *Philip Morris*
Designer: **Weiss/Watson**
Mt. Kisco, New York

PROFITRAK

Client: *City Laundry Northwest*
Designer: **Jeff Fisher LogoMotives**
Portland, Oregon

Client: *Ridgetop*
Designer: **Jeff Fisher LogoMotives**
Portland, Oregon

RIDGETOP

Client: *Constitution Bank*
Designer: **John Langdon Design**
Philadelphia, Pennsylvania

Client: *Emerging Business Internet Exchange*
Designer: **bonatodesign**
Berwyn, Pennsylvania

Case study #12: Signature as logo

John Hancock and Lord & Taylor have a unique—and powerful—way to establish "bullet-proof" logos.

The John Hancock insurance company uses a variation of the famous (some would say flamboyant) signature which appears on the Declaration of Independence. (The signature has been modified several times over the years.)

Lord & Taylor, a major department store group, has used a "handwritten" logo very effectively for a number of years.

Both logos are "bullet proof."

Client: *AMA Purchase Link*
Designer: **Lipson·Alport·Glass & Associates**
Northbrook, Illinois

AMA PurchaseLink[sm]

Client: *Radio Shack*
Designer: **Lambert Design Studio**
Dallas, Texas

SHACKrap

Client: *Microsoft Corporation*
Designer: **RossWest Design**
Issaquah, Washington

Client: *Telco Systems*
Designer: **Media Concepts Corporation**
Assonet, Massachusetts

microFOX

Client: *Novaworks*
Designer: **Enock**
New York, New York

NOVAWORKS
Get system-ready

Client: *M & M Precision Systems*
Designer: **Nova Creative Group, Inc.**
Dayton, Ohio

Client: *Orion Pictures*
Designer: **B.D. Fox & Friends, Advertising**
Santa Monica, California

Client: *20th Century Fox*
Designer: **B.D. Fox & Friends, Advertising**
Santa Monica, California

HOME ALONe

Client: *Hawkeye Food Systems Inc.*
Designer: **Design Ranch**
Iowa City, Iowa

Client: *Einstein*
Designer: **Design North**
Racine, Wisconsin

einstein
personal communications

Client: *SAVATAR, Inc.*
Designer: **Joyce Designs**
Brookline, Massachusetts

Client: *Fratello's Italian Cafe*
Designer: **RossWest Design**
Issaquah, Washington

Client: *Phoenix Partners*
Designer: **Straightline International**
New York, New York

comunica
LEARNING PARTNERS, INC.

Client: *Comunica*
Designer: **Cisneros Design**
Santa Fe, New Mexico

DRUMS ALONG THE ROCKIES

Client: *The Blue Knights Drum & Bugle Corps*
Designer: **Matrix International Assoc., Ltd.**
Denver, Colorado

Case study #13: Importance of category

The issue of exactly "what is trademark infringement?" is not always simple.

The "product category" is often the difference between blatant infringement and a logo that can be used.

If Haro Designs were in any petroleum-related business, Chevron would likely have a major complaint, but by being in a distinctly different product category, the rules change.

When in doubt, consult your friendly trademark attorney.

POWER
GAMES

Client: *New Mexico Lottery*
Designer: **Kilmer & Kilmer**
Albuquerque, New Mexico

Client: *Triangle Productions!*
Designer: **Jeff Fisher LogoMotives**
Portland, Oregon

Client: *Shukovsky English Entertainment*
Designer: **Enock**
New York, New York

Client: *United States Academic Decathalon*
Designer: **Point Zero Design**
Marina Del Rey, California

USAD

Client: *U.S. Forest Service*
Designer: **Jeff Fisher LogoMotives**
Portland, Oregon

Client: *Infinitech, Inc.*
Designer: **AKA Design, Inc.**
St. Louis, Missouri

Client: *Critical Path*
Designer: **Addis Group**
Berkeley, California

CriticalPath[SM]

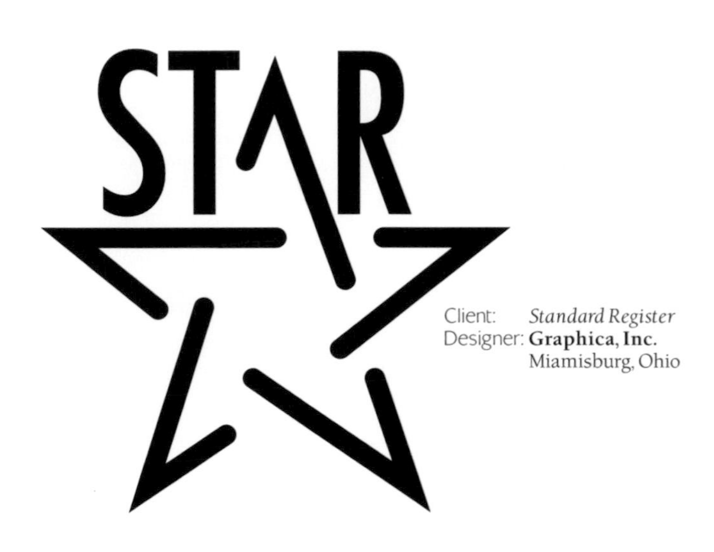

Client: *Standard Register*
Designer: **Graphica, Inc.**
Miamisburg, Ohio

Client: *Exposition Services, Inc.*
Designer: **Berry Design, Inc.**
Alpharetta, Georgia

Client: *Innerspace Industries*
Designer: **Shields Design**
Fresno, California

Client: *Checkfree Corporation*
Designer: **Internal Creative Department, CheckFree Corporation**
Norcross, Georgia

Client: *General Signal Networks Tautron*
Designer: **Cole Design Group**
Collinsville, Connecticut

Client: *Personal Care Group*
Designer: **Zunda Design Group**
South Norwalk, Connecticut

Client: *Hershey Chocolate USA*
Designer: **Zunda Design Group**
South Norwalk, Connecticut

Client: *Trend-Lines, Inc.*
Designer: **Berni Design**
Greenwich, Connecticut

Client: *Entryon*
Designer: **Hansen Design Company**
Seattle, Washington

Client: *Arachnid Design*
Designer: **Stephanie Cunningham**
Ft. Lauderdale, Florida

Client: *The Learning Company*
Designer: **Addis Group**
Berkeley, California

REEL CITY
PRODUCTIONS

Client: *Reel City Productions*
Designer: **Addis Group**
Berkeley, California

Occupational
HealthSource

Client: *Nix Health Care System*
Designer: **DiBaggio Design**
San Antonio, Texas

Client: *ATCC (American Type Culture Collection)*
Designer: **Stephen Loges Graphic Design**
New York, New York

Client: *Metasys*
Designer: **Steve Thomas Marketing Communications**
Charlotte, North Carolina

METASYS

Client: *Dreyer's*
Designer: **Axion Design, Inc.**
San Anselmo, California

Client: *Big Deahl*
Designer: **Mires Design, Inc.**
San Diego, California

Client: *Memtek*
Designer: **Axion Design, Inc.**
San Anselmo, California

Client: *Bell-Carter Foods*
Designer: **Addis Group**
Berkeley, California

Client: *Bullseye*
Designer: **Gunnar Swanson Design Office**
Duluth, Minnesota

Bullseye

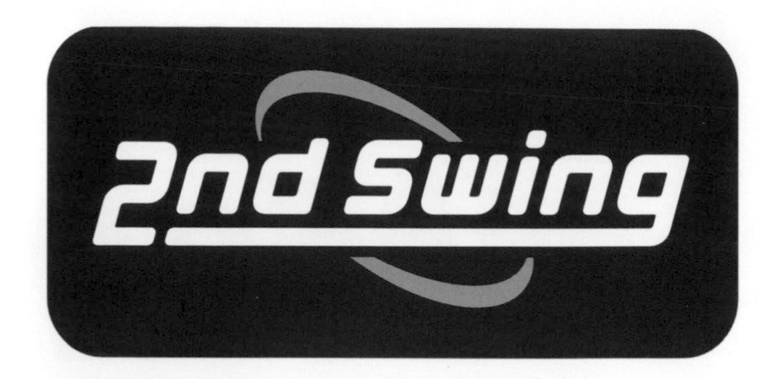

Client: *Sara Lee*
Designer: **Axion Design, Inc.**
San Anselmo, California

Client: *2nd Swing*
Designer: **Parachute, Inc.**
Minneapolis, Minnesota

Case study #14: Lines as design devices

The "modified type" style of logo design frequently uses one or more reverse (negative space) lines on the type. There are numerous examples of this style in this book, and this is an excellent starting point for creating a "bullet proof" logo.

When creating a design with this style, open your mind to different ways to apply the lines. The AEI logo uses a diagonal line very effectively, while TRW has a line weaving its way through the letters to create a distinctive design.

Client: *Cafe Toma*
Designer: **Bruce Yelaska Design**
San Francisco, California

Client: *Clorox*
Designer: **Axion Design, Inc.**
San Anselmo, California

Client: *California Center for the Arts*
Designer: **Mires Design**
San Diego, California

CAPITOL RISK CONCEPTS

Client: *Capitol Risk Concepts, Ltd.*
Designer: **Lee Communications, Inc.**
Pound Ridge, New York

Client: *Franzia*
Designer: **Axion Design, Inc.**
San Anselmo, California

Client: *Darwin Asset Mamagement*
Designer: **Lee Communications, Inc.**
Pound Ridge, New York

Client: *Imagemaker Salon*
Designer: **Tim Celeski Design**
Seattle, Washington

IMAGEMAKER

Client: *Chesebrough-Pond's*
Designer: **Hans Flink Design Inc.**
New York, New York

Client: *The Invisions Group*
Designer: **The Invisions Group**
Bethesda, Maryland

THE
INVISIONS
GROUP

Client: *R.J.R. Foods, Inc.*
Designer: **Dixon & Parcels Associates**
New York, New York

Knowledge
Action
Performance

Client: *Ernst & Young—Stanford Project*
Designer: **McKenzie & Associates**
San Francisco, California

Client: *Bayer Corporation*
Designer: **Hans Flink Design Inc.**
New York, New York

Client: *Mars, Inc.*
Designer: **Dixon & Parcels Associates, Inc.**
New York, New York

Client: *Yia Yia's Eurobistro, PB&J's Restaurants*
Designer: **EAT Advertising & Design**
Kansas City, Missouri

Client: *Hershey Chocolate USA*
Designer: **Zunda Design Group**
South Norwalk, Connecticut

Client: *Superior Brands, Inc.*
Designer: **Dixon & Parcels Associates**
New York, New York

Client: *Tocqueville Asset Management*
Designer: **Lee Communications, Inc.**
Seattle, Washington

Client: *Polaris Venture Partners*
Designer: **Hansen Design Company**
Seattle, Washington

Client: *Nike—Official Brand*
Designer: **David Lemley Design**
Seattle, Washington

OfficialBrand

Client: *The Fairchild Corporation*
Designer: **Lee Communications, Inc.**
Pound Ridge, New York

Client: *Bailey Design Group, Inc.*
Designer: **Transcore**
Plymouth Meeting, Pennsylvania

TRANSCORE

Client: *WavePath Information Arts Inc.*
Designer: **Beggs Design**
Palo Alto, California

Client: *Active Voice*
Designer: **David Lemley Design**
Seattle, Washington

Client: *Vantive*
Designer: **Beggs Design**
Palo Alto, California

grider
+ CO

Client: *Grider and Company P.A.*
Designer: **Gardner Design**
Wichita, Kansas

Client: *B-WILD*
Designer: **David Lemley Design**
Seattle, Washington

d
M

Client: *Design Milwaukee*
Designer: **Planet Design Company**
Madison, Wisconsin

Client: *Walcav Seafoods Ltd.*
Designer: **Faine/ Oller Productions, Inc.**
Seattle, Washington

Case study #15: Rectangle with lines

The difficulty of coming up with a great logo design *that will clear for national use* is demonstrated here.

Take the concept of "a rectangle with diagonal lines." There might be some great designs that could come out of this general concept, but if the goal is to create a truly "bullet-proof" logo, it might be good to avoid that general concept altogether.

Unless, of course, you want to get letters from Novell and Venture.

These two designs are both outstanding. But...they have pretty well staked out the "rectangle with diagonal lines" territory with a "keep out" sign.

Client: *Aldus*
Designer: **David Lemley Design**
Seattle, Washington

Client: *Nike Boyswear*
Designer: **David Lemley Design**
Seattle, Washington

Client: *Lenscrafters*
Designer: **DesignCentre**
Minnetonka, Minnesota

Teleforum

Client: *NYNEX*
Designer: **Enock**
New York, New York

CardScan

Client: *Corex Technologies*
Designer: **Gill Fishman Associates, Inc.**
Cambridge, Massachusetts

vertical reality

Client: *Novellus Systems, Inc.*
Designer: **Larsen Design + Interactive**
Minneapolis, Minnesota

SPORTSWOMAN

The Magazine for Women in Sports

Client: *Sports Woman Inc.*
Designer: **Faine / Oller Productions, Inc.**
Seattle, Washington

NEW FOXBORO

Client: *New Foxboro*
Designer: **TGD Communications, Inc.**
Alexandria, Virginia

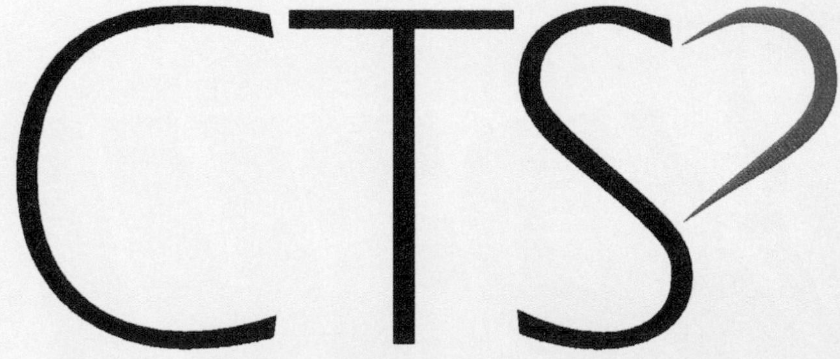

Client: *Cardio Thoracic Systems*
Designer: **The Graphic Expression, Inc.**
New York, New York

Client: *Lifetime TV*
Designer: **Eskil Ohlsson Assoc. Inc.**
New York, New York

TRUST
WARE®
PROVIDING THE INTELLIGENT ADVANTAGE

Client: *Sungard AMS*
Designer: **Premier Solutions Ltd.**
Malvern, Pennsylvania

Client: *HQ Percussion*
Designer: **Whitney Design Works**
St. Louis, Missouri

MATRIX

Client: *New York Women in Communications*
Designer: **Glamour Magazine Promotions**
New York, New York

Case study #16: Lucent Technologies

When Lucent Technologies was formed as an evolution of "Bell Labs," the firm emerged with a logo design that was so distinctive, so cutting edge, it was literally "bullet-proof" because there was absolutely nothing like it up to that time.

Created by the design firm of Lippincott & Margulies, this logo is immediately recognizible since it is so unlike what a logo is supposed to be.

Note: This type of solution is not for amateurs or for the weak of heart. It's very difficult to break new ground in logo design. If you decide to go this route, be prepared to do a lot of research to make sure that you aren't the *second* one to get this idea. With that warning, see cases 17, 18, & 19.

Lucent Technologies
Bell Labs Innovations

Client: *IN vision ltd.*
Designer: **Premier Solutions**
Malveren, Pennsylvania

Client: *Danmar and Associates*
Designer: **aire design company**
Tucson, Arizona

Client: *Wise Solutions, Inc.*
Designer: **Edward Walter Design**
New York, New York

CALIFORNIA

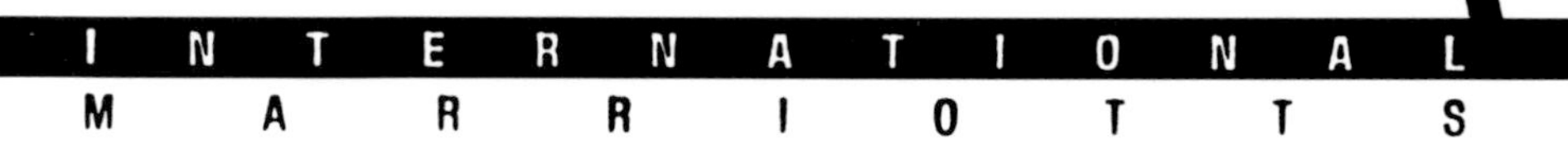

Client: *Marriott-San Francisco*
Designer: **Winni Lum Design +**
San Francisco, Calfornia

Client: *R.O.I. Marketing*
Designer: **Silverman Group, Inc.**
New Haven, Connecticut

FIRSTAIR

Client: *First Air*
Designer: **Spencer Zahn & Associates**
Philadelphia, Pennsylvania

Client: *Fair Acres Shopping Center*
Designer: **Dotzler Creative Arts**
Omaha, Nebraska

Client: *Brooklyn Information and Culture*
Designer: **Nestor Stermole Visual Communication Group**
New York, New York

Client: *Spotlight Apparel*
Designer: **Silverman Group, Inc.**
New Haven, Connecticut

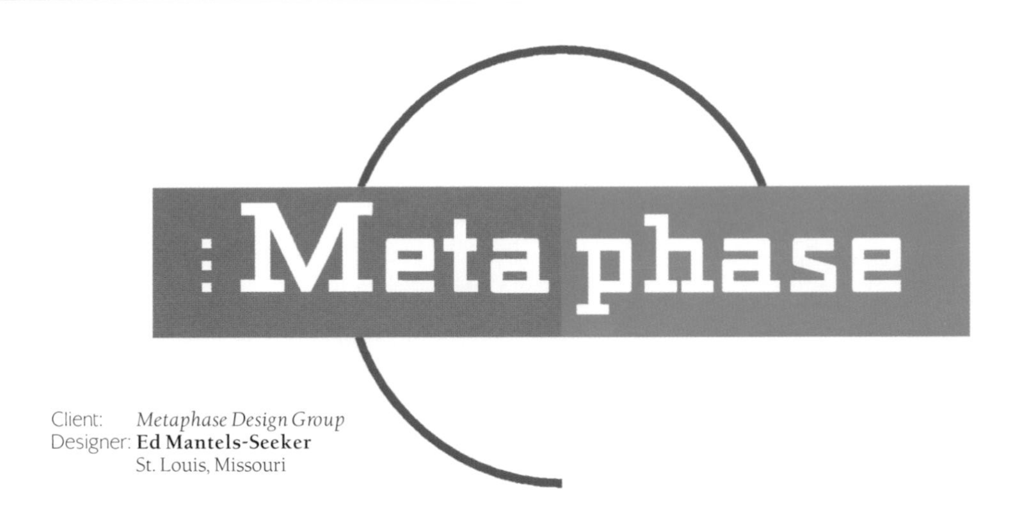

Client: *Metaphase Design Group*
Designer: **Ed Mantels-Seeker**
St. Louis, Missouri

Client: *Alpha 1 Services*
Designer: **Vance Wright Adams & Associates**
Pittsburgh, Pennsylvania

Client: *Edocs*
Designer: **McNulty & Co.**
Thousand Oaks, California

Client: *Taylor Guitars*
Designer: **Mires Design, Inc.**
San Diego, California

Case study #17: Logo Breakthroughs

There is a great deal of potential marketing power in having a highly recognizable logo such as Lucent Technologies (Case study 16). Therefore, designers should (and will) continue to seek ways to break new ground in search of a cutting-edge design that will still be likely to avoid legal problems.

The logo shown at left is a typical "basic" design; there is little to set it apart from the pack. But starting with that design, then applying a filter from the software program Adobe Photoshop and the result might be something like the design at right.

Is it "bullet-proof?" Perhaps. The real purpose of this is to start you thinking about ways to break design barriers and come up with a truly innovative design.

Client: *Lincoln Design*
Designer: **Lincoln Design**
Eugene, Oregon

Client: *Comprehensive Health Education Foundation*
Designer: **Rick Eiber Design (RED)**
Preston, Washington

Client: *Big NS Studios*
Designer: **Phoenix Creative**
St. Louis, Missouri

Client: *Federal Data Corporation*
Designer: **Macvicar Design & Communications**
Arlington, Virginia

Client: *John Boone*
Designer: **Waters Design Associates Inc.**
New York, New York

Client: *Fairmont-Masons*
Designer: **Winni Lum Design +**
San Francisco, California

hoglezoo

Client: *Hogle Zoo*
Designer: **Mortensen Design**
Mountain View, California

PHASE OUT

Client: *Target*
Designer: **Pedersen Gesk**
Minneapolis, Minnesota

Priority

Client: *Priority Mortgage*
Designer: **Gardner Design**
Wichita, Kansas

david's limited

Client: *David's Limited*
Designer: **Frank D'Astolfo Design**
New York, New York

Client: *Accelerated*
Designer: **Hansen Design Company**
Seattle, Washington

Client: *Schwan's Sales Enterprises / USA Cup*
Designer: **Rapp Collins Communications**
Minneapolis, Minnesota

Client: *Scitex Sphere*
Designer: **Pittard Sullivan**
Culver City, California

Client: *Heirlooms, INC.*
Designer: **The Wecker Group**
Monterey, California

Wells Fargo Bank

Client: *Wells Fargo Bank*
Designer: **Morla Design**
San Francisco, California

Client: *The Johnson Group*
Designer: **MacVicar Design & Communications**
Arlington, Virginia

Client: *SoapToons*
Designer: **McNulty & Co.**
Thousand Oaks, California

Client: *Chingones*
Designer: **Mires Design, Inc.**
San Diego, California

Client: *Avid Associates*
Designer: **Upland Advtg. & Design**
West Stockbridge, Massachusetts

LOCUST VALLEY
CEMETERY

Client: *Locust Valley Cemetery*
Designer: **Guarino Graphics, Ltd.**
Glen Cove, New York

Client: *The Food Group*
Designer: **Mires Design, Inc.**
San Diego, California

Case study #18: Quest for the unique

The tools able to fulfill the desire to have a design that's really unique can begin inside Adobe Photoshop. The program already has a number of high-powered "filters." In addition, you can buy a large number of other "plug-in" filters that will allow you to create a huge number of visual effects that will let you create highly unusual—possibly totally unique—designs that will represent the client well. Below are two more versions of the same logo we saw in the last case study.

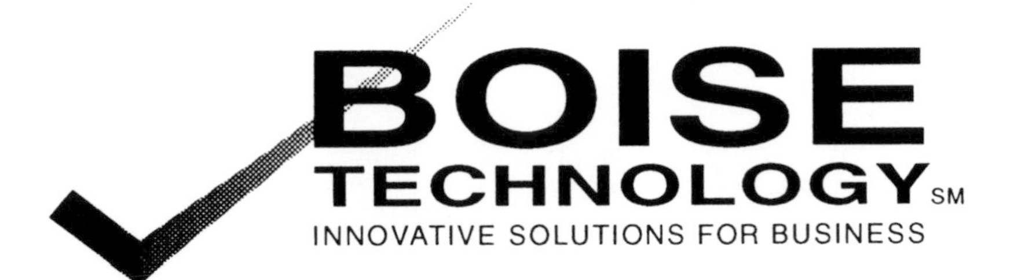

Client: *Boise Cascade Office Products*
Designer: **JOED Design Inc.**
Elmhurst, Illinois

Client: *Vitality Plus*
Designer: **Art 270, Inc.**
Jenkintown, Pennsylvania

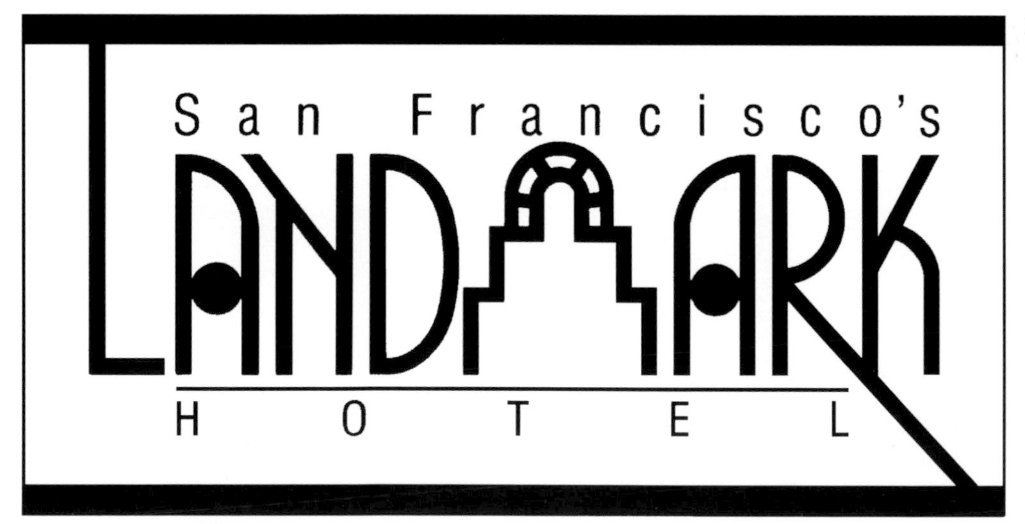

Client: *Marriott Hotel- S.F.*
Designer: **Winni Lum Design +**
San Francisco, California

LYNX

SERVICES FROM PPG

Client: *PPG*
Designer: **Vance Wright Adams & Associates**
Pittsburgh, Pennsylvania

Client: *Northhampton Peanut Company, Inc.*
Designer: **Berni Design**
Greenwich, Connecticut

AMERITRADE®

Clearing Services for the Securities Industry

Client: *AmeriTrade*
Designer: **Dotzler Creative Arts**
Omaha, Nebraska

Eddie Jazz™

Client: *Eddie Jazz*
Designer: **Polloni Design**
Raleigh, North Carolina

MALLET

Client: *Mallet and Company Inc.*
Designer: **Frank D'Astolfo Design**
New York, New York

Client: *Warner Bros. Records*
Designer: **Lorna Stovall Design**
New York, New York

Client: *Shawnee Mills*
Designer: **Sibley/Peteet Design**
Dallas, Texas

DELTA
TOXICOLOGY

Client: *Delta Toxicology*
Designer: **Rick Eiber Design (RED)**
Preston, Washington

Client: *Waters Design Associates*
Designer: **Waters Design Associates Inc.**
New York, New York

Client: *St. Patrick's Center*
Designer: **McDermott Design**
St. Louis, Missouri

Client: *Vertical Records*
Designer: **Joseph Rattan Design**
Plano, Texas

CONNECTICUT
GRAND OPERA & ORCHESTRA

Client: *Connecticut Grand Opera & Orchestra*
Designer: **Tom Fowler, Inc.**
Stamford, Connecticut

HEART & SOUL

Client: *Heart & Soul*
Designer: **Sibley/Peteet Design**
Dallas, Texas

Client: *Tom Fowler, Inc.*
Designer: **Tom Fowler, Inc.**
Stamford, Connecticut

Client: *Alexis Gill Inc.*
Designer: **INC 3**
New York, New York

ALEXISGILL
Transformation Through Learning

Client: *Nextec Applications Inc.*
Designer: **Mires Design, Inc.**
San Diego, California

Hospital
and Health
Center

Client: *Children's Hospital*
Designer: **CWA, Inc.**
San Diego, California

TailWind

Client: *Nike*
Designer: **David Lemley Design**
Seattle, Washington

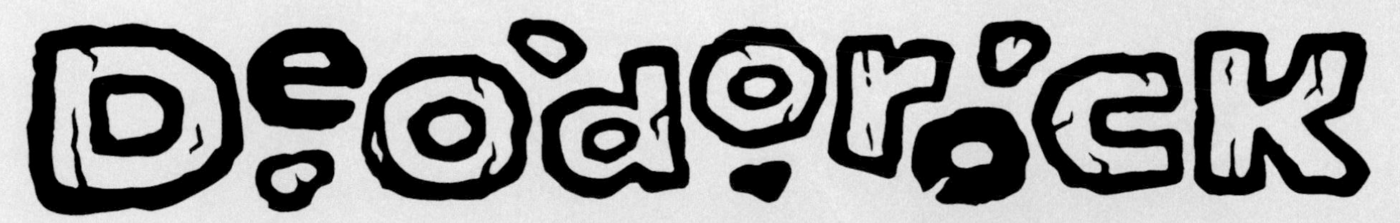

Client: *Life Style Products, Inc.*
Designer: **Rapp Collins Communications**
Minneapolis, Minnesota

Client: *Mary Kay*
Designer: **Edward Walter Design**
New York, New York

ONE
OF
THOSE
DAYS

Client: *One Of Those Days*
Designer: **Frank D'Astolfo Design**
New York, New York

Client: *The Madeira School*
Designer: **MacVicar Design & Communications**
Arlington, Virginia

Client: *Allied Domecq Retailing USA*
Designer: **Design Forum**
Dayton, Ohio

Case study #19: Cutting Edge?

Here are a few more examples of ways to use Adobe's Photoshop's filter feature to create highly unusual graphics.

Once you have a design you believe is "cutting edge," it is always a good idea to have an attorney do a check for any designs that might present a legal problem.

Client: *Java Joes*
Designer: **Sayles Graphic Design**
Des Moines, Iowa

Client: *Bristol-Myers Squibb*
Designer: **Designation Inc.**
New York, New York

APROVEL

VECTOR PROPERTIES™
Value-Directed Services

Client: *VECTOR PROPERTIES*
Designer: **Polloni Design**
Raleigh, North Carolina

Client: *Collinsville Area Recreation District*
Designer: **AKA Design, Inc.**
St. Louis, Missouri

Client: *Loomis, Fargo & Co.*
Designer: **The Focus Group**
Houston, Texas

Mac's Place

Client: *Mac's Place*
Designer: **Tim Celeski Studios**
Seattle, Washington

Portfolio™

Client: *Eastman Kodak Company*
Designer: **Forward Design**
Rochester, New York

Client: *Eight O'Clock Coffee*
Designer: **Words and Pictures**
Park Ridge, New Jersey

Client: *Yanke Bionics Inc.*
Designer: **Minx Design**
Akron, Ohio

YankeBionics INC.

CUSTOM FOOT ORTHOTICS

Kodak

WRITABLE CD

Client: *Eastman Kodak Co.*
Designer: **Forward Design**
Rochester, New York

Client: *Jerry Mesmer*
Designer: **Tim Kenney Design Partners**
Bethesda, Maryland

Advideo

Client: *Reeves Video Tape Corp.*
Designer: **Eskil Ohlsson Assoc. Inc.**
New York, New York

Client: *Zaroff's Delicatessen Restaurant*
Designer: **The Spangler Design Team**
St. Louis Park, Minnesota

McABEE BEACH
Cafe

Client: *McAbee Beach Cafe*
Designer: **The Wecker Group**
Monterey, California

1 of the Girls

Client: *Atlantic Records*
Designer: **Lorna Stovall Design**
New York, New York

Client: *Casa De Mio*
Designer: **Gardner Design**
Wichita, Kansas

Client: *Electronic Security & Communications Corp.*
Designer: **INC 3**
New York, New York

VectorVision
CORPORATION

Client: *Vector Vision Corporation*
Designer: **Hedstrom/Blessing, Inc.**
Minneapolis, Minnesota

Client: *Little City Restaurant*
Designer: **Bruce Yelaska Design**
San Francisco, California

SCACCHI

Client: *Scacchi Shoes*
Designer: **Louis & Partners**
Bath, Ohio

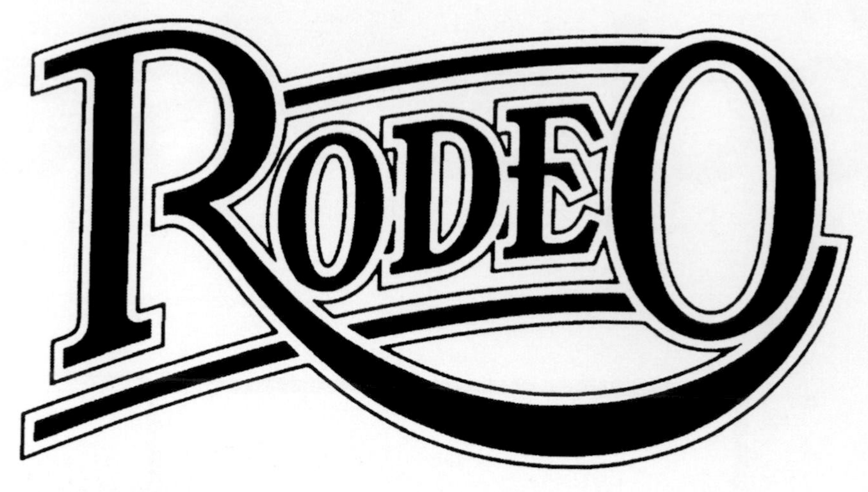

Client: *Rodeo Bar & Grill*
Designer: **Lance Anderson Design**
Dunsmuir, California

Client: *CIMS- BMS Computer Inc.*
Designer: **Business Graphics Group**
Pleasanton, California

Client: *CheckFree Corporation*
Designer: **CheckFree Corporation**
Norcross, Georgia

INFOVUE™

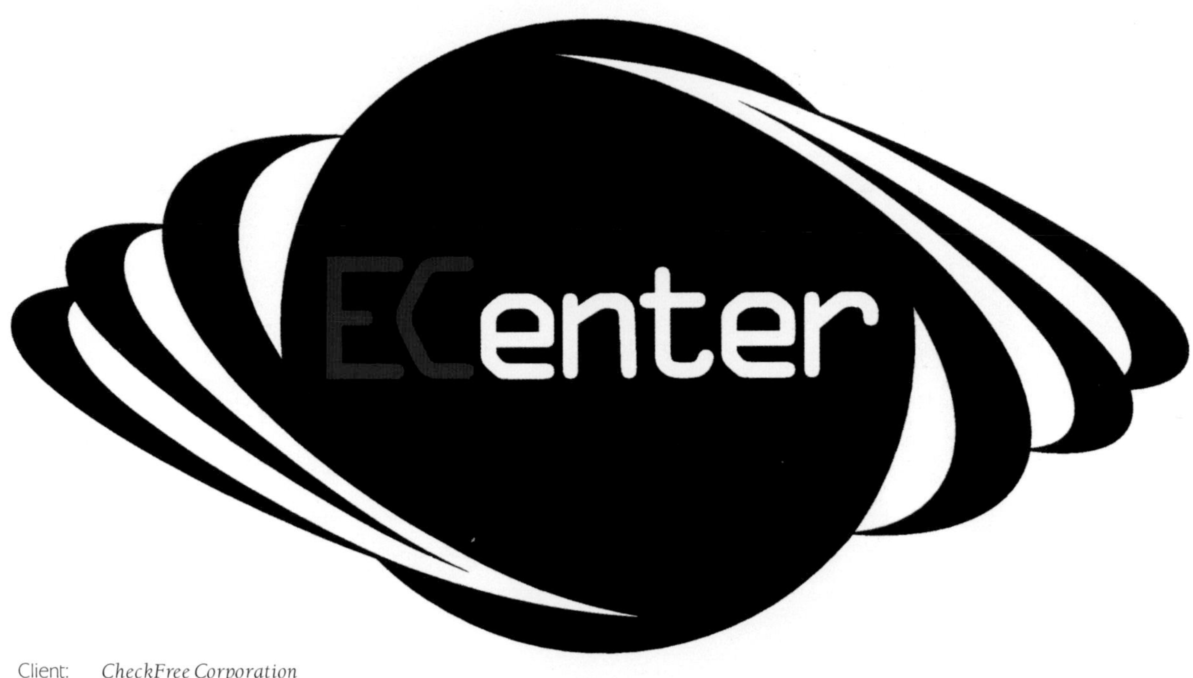

Client: *CheckFree Corporation*
Designer: **CheckFree Corporation**
Norcross, Georgia

Client: *El Mirasol Villas*
Designer: **Edward Walter Design**
New York, New York

REPORT MANAGER™

Client: *CheckFree Corporation*
Designer: **CheckFree Corporation**
Norcross, Georgia

Client: *Robinson Knife Company*
Designer: **Michael Orr & Associates Inc.**
Corning, New York

Client: *Amster Yard*
Designer: **Amster Yard**
New York, New York

AMSTER YARD

Textiles

Client: *Gene Small Textiles*
Designer: **Diane Kuntz Design**
Santa Monica, California

STONE
BROOK
FARMS

Client: *Stone Brook Farms*
Designer: **Edward Walter Design**
New York, New York

Client: *Be Bopp-a-Latte Cafe'*
Designer: **David Lemley Design**
Seattle, Washington

Client: *Hedstrom Corporation*
Designer: **Axis Design Communications, Inc.**
Highland Park, Illinois

Client: *Benchmark Communications*
Designer: **Macvicar Design & Communications**
Arlington, Virginia

Client: *Taylor's Cafe and Taproom*
Designer: **Frank D'Astolfo**
New York, New York

EQWEST SM

Client: *EQWEST*
Designer: **Philip Quinn & Partners**
Redwood City, California

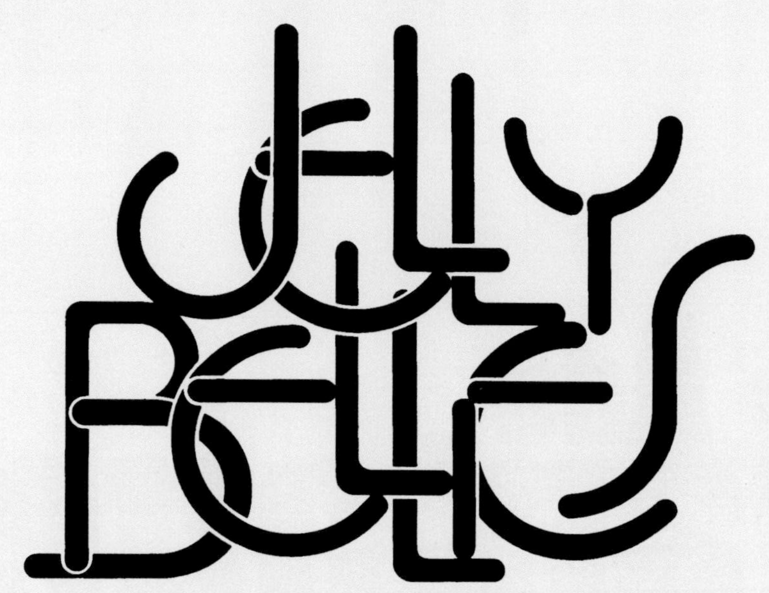

Client: *Jelly Bellies*
Designer: **Hershey Associates**
Santa Monica, California

Client: *Nat. Assn. of Vascular Access Networks*
Designer: **Philip Quinn & Partners**
Redwood City, California

THE NO MAINTENANCE PETS

flappers

Client: *Gregory Toys*
Designer: **Richards & Swensen, Inc.**
Salt Lake City, Utah

Add Vantage™

Client: *Sungard AMS*
Designer: **Premier Solutions** LTD.
Malvern, Pennsylvania

FORUM™

Client: *CheckFree Corporation*
Designer: **CheckFree Corporation**
Norcross, Georgia

Client: *The Center of Contemporary Arts*
Designer: **Phoenix Creative**
St. Louis, Missouri

Client: *Gateway Resources*
Designer: **Gunnar Swanson Design Office**
Duluth, Minnesota

Client: *Ames Business Services*
Designer: **Polloni Design**
Raleigh, North Carolina

Client: *Dallas Society of Visual Communications*
Designer: **Swieter Design U.S.**
Dallas, Texas

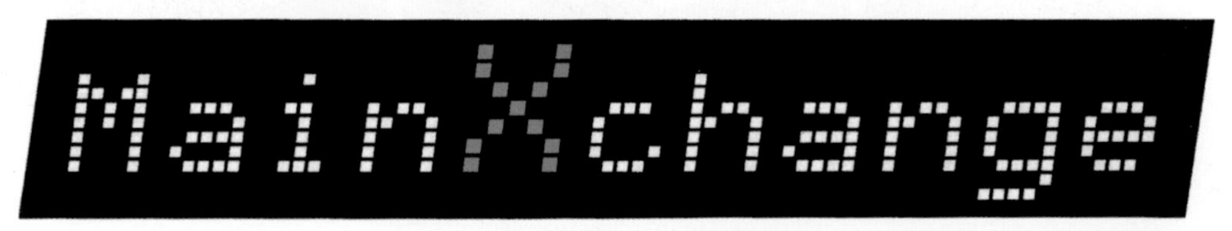

Client: *Main Exchange*
Designer: **Grafik Communications, Ltd.**
Alexandria, Virginia

AccSys
INC.

Client: *ACCSYS*
Designer: **The Majestic Group, Inc.**
Indianapolis, Indiana

Client: *St. Louis Music*
Designer: **Phoenix Creative**
St. Louis, Missouri

LOFFLER

Client: *Loffler Business Systems*
Designer: **Larsen Design + Interactive**
Minneapolis, Minnesota

MAESTRO
MEDIA

Client: *Eastman Kodak Co.*
Designer: **Forward Design**
Rochester, New York

Client: *Applied Derbigum Contractors- Owens Corning Fiberglas*
Designer: **Lesniewicz/Navarre**
Pittsburgh, Pennsylvania

EPVA
ACTION

Client: *Eastern Paralyzed Veterans Association*
Designer: **Frank D'Astolfo**
New York, New York

Client: *Preptech*
Designer: **McElveney & Palozzi Design Group, Inc.**
Rochester, New York

SKIN SENSUALS™

Client: *Skin Sensuals*
Designer: **Forward Design**
Rochester, New York

EASTMANOR
TRANSITIONAL CARE

Client: *East Manor Transitional Care*
Designer: **The Weber Group Inc.**
Racine, Wisconsin

Client: *Barnhill & Associates*
Designer: **Robert Meyers**
Communication Design & Planning
Pittsburgh, Pennsylvania

Client: *National Telephone Cooperative Association*
Designer: **Coleman Design Group, Inc.**
Washington, D.C.

The Voice of Rural Telecommunications

FOODINI'S™

ESCAPE FROM COOKING!

Client: *Chevron Products USA*
Designer: **Design Forum**
Dayton, Ohio

Client: *Bush Furniture*
Designer: **Forward Design**
Rochester, New York

Hardee's®

Client: *Hardee's*
Designer: **Lippincott & Margulies**
New York, New York

Client: *Pompeii Ristorante*
Designer: **Belyea Design**
Seattle, Washington

POMPEII
RISTORANTE

Case study #20: A personal experience

A few years ago, I was an "expert witness" in a trademark infringement lawsuit filed by the owner of a small business against a competitor. After watching the billable hours multiply beyond control, I called the attorney who had retained my services.

"I could settle this whole thing in twenty minutes," I said.

"How?" the attorney asked.

"Get both parties in a room, show them a couple of new logos which would be 'next step' designs for each firm—designs that would no longer be in conflict with each other."

"Hmmm," the lawyer said.

"Then I would explain to each of them that the money being spent on legal fees would be much better spent on marketing."

The attorney had no response. I resigned from the case a few minutes later, and vowed never again to be an "expert witness." I stand firm in my belief that it's better to avoid trademark suits than to win them.

*Mr. Higgins was NOT the attorney in this case.

INDEX

DESIGNERS

CLIENTS

ČESKOSLOVENSKÁ MUZEA V PŘÍRODĚ

ČESKOSLOVENSKÁ MUZEA V PŘÍRODĚ

Vydavateľstvo Osveta Martin
Nakladatelství Profil Ostrava
1989

ISBN 80-217-0039-4

Chráníme odkaz minulosti

Proměny přírody a společnosti zákonitě vedou k zániku hodnot platných a důležitých v našem nedávném životě. Tyto hodnoty – některé předměty denní potřeby, výrobní nástroje, umělecká díla anebo jen proklamované ideje, společenské poměry, některé živočišné a rostlinné druhy a také funkční vztahy mezi těmito sférami – povětšině mizí beze stopy a po krátkém či delším čase opustí i naši paměť. Avšak některé minulé děje, věci a myšlenky dále uchováváme. Uchováme je jako svědectví o minulém životě, jako svědectví nadále společnosti potřebné. Proto se na přání dávných vládců uchovávaly záznamy o posloupnosti panujícího rodu, o vítězných a ztracených bitvách, o udatnosti, slávě i zradě, o vůli bohů i o činech vykonavatelů této vůle. O věhlas této pompy usilovalo pero dějepisce i básníka i štětec malířův. Prostý lid ukládal svoji paměť a moudrost do pověstí, balad a přísloví, předávaných z pokolení na pokolení. K takovému dědictví patřila i dřevěná židle s basreliéfem, znázorňujícím čin lidového hrdiny.

S péčí o zanikající hodnoty přírody i lidské společnosti se setkáváme až koncem 18. století a zejména v 19. století. Byl to čas encyklopedistů a později čas Darwinova učení o vývoji a selekci druhů, čas průmyslové revoluce, čas nové společnosti, která se nemohla obejít bez rozvoje vědy a kultury, sloužící k prosazení jejich ekonomických i politických cílů.

V tomto tvůrčím a rozporuplném ovzduší, v kterém se zákonitě zrodilo Marxovo a Engelsovo učení o dialektice a historickém materialismu, se stále naléhavěji prosazují názory o nutnosti uchování mizejících hodnot lidského ducha a přírody. Posléze vznikají i instituce sloužící tomuto záměru. Archívy, knihovny a galérie se už neomezují jen na službu světským a církevním feudálům, rodí se nová kulturní instituce – muzeum. Ve svých počátcích byla plně poplatná romantismu, který ovládl naši kulturu a vědu nejméně do sedmdesátých let minulého století. V muzeích se shromažďovaly především věci starobylé, cenné a zvláštní – umělecká díla, předměty a písemnosti historické ceny a také cizokrajné zvláštnosti. Ostatně nebylo jich mnoho. U nás patří k nejstarším muzea v Praze, v Brně a v Opavě.

Moderní názor na běh světa a na poslání vědy a kultury se v našich muzeích začíná uplatňovat až v osmdesátých a především až v devadesátých letech minulého století. Nové expozice podávají přehled o nerostech, rostlinách a živočiších, národopisné expozice se pokoušejí o obraz tradiční kultury našeho lidu. Vývojové hledisko se však prosazuje jen ojediněle. V dokumentaci i v expoziční technice sehrává důležitou roli fotografie, později i zvukový záznam a film.

Stále se hledají nové formy prezentace i vědeckého využití. Vznikají botanické a zoologické zahrady, kde jsou uchovávány vzácné nebo zánikem ohrožené druhy. Jako vyšší forma tohoto záměru jsou o několik desítek let později zakládány přírodní rezervace s ohroženými botanickými i živočišnými druhy. K této úrovni a formě ochrany zanikajících hodnot patří i památkové rezervace, včetně chráněných území lidového stavitelství. Předností rezervací je uchování původních hodnot v původním prostředí. Pokud takové prostředí již neexistuje nebo nelze zajistit jeho uchování, nebo není organizátorům dostupné, přistupují k rekonstrukci adekvátního prostředí, vytvářejí je tedy uměle. To je případ tzv. safari, území uzpůsobeného pro volný život exotické zvěře. Do této kategorie patří i národopisná muzea v přírodě.

Národopisné muzeum v přírodě je netradiční muzejní expozicí, kterou tvoří seskupení lidových staveb a jiných předmětů, dokládajících způsob života lidu, snesených z vymezeného území na jedno místo, nejčastěji do volné přírody nebo do parku, tedy do prostředí více nebo méně podobnému místu, odkud byla stavba převezena.

Národopis a lidové stavitelství

Způsob bydlení prostého lidu – se vším, co k bydlení patří – studuje vědní disciplína, zvaná etnografie; v minulosti se více užívalo domácího názvu národopis. Etnografie nepatří k oborům s dlouhou tradicí. Vznikla až koncem 18. století jako důsledek prosazení ideologie nového společenského řádu, kapitalismu. Objektem etnografického studia se stal prostý lid, jeho způsob života, jeho práce, myšlení, jeho umění.

Když se vrátíme k počátkům tohoto oboru, tedy na konec 18. století, marně budeme hledat téma lidové stavitelství. A nejinak tomu bylo téměř po celé století devatenácté. Český a slovenský národopis se stal významnou složkou národního obrození a ve shodě s politickými a kulturními záměry tohoto hnutí se zaměřil především na lidovou slovesnost. Sbírky lidových písní, historických balad, přísloví, pohádek a pověstí, shromažďované velkými osobnostmi kulturních dějin našich národů, jako byli Dobrovský, Jungmann, Kollár, Šafařík, Čelakovský a později Erben, měly prokázat odvěkou existenci osobité národní poezie i vlastní národní kultury, srovnatelné s kulturou vyspělých evropských národů. V pohádkách, poezii a mýtech se hledala duše této kultury, duše národa.

O materiální stránku života lidu se národopis začal zajímat až v polovině 19. století. I v tomto případě stojí u zrodu tohoto zájmu velké osobnosti české kultury – Josef Mánes a Božena Němcová.

Od vzniku oboru uběhlo nejméně sto let, než se jeho zájem obrátil k lidovému stavitelství. K prvním pracím tohoto druhu patří studie Aloise Jiráska a mladého Zdeňka Nejedlého o názvosloví české chalupy. Pokud jde o technickou dokumentaci staveb, tu patří přední místo slovenskému architektu Dušanu Jurkovičovi. To mluvíme o devadesátých letech minulého století, tedy o čase, kdy na severu Evropy vznikala první muzea v přírodě. Řekněme rovnou, že naše etnografie se nestala vůdčí silou v prosazování myšlenky muzea v přírodě; vytvořila pouze teoretické předpoklady k jeho vzniku.

Národopis a muzeum

Dalo by se předpokládat, že myšlenka muzea v přírodě uzrála na půdě muzejní. Tento předpoklad, jak uvidíme dále, platí jen do určité míry.

Až do šedesátých let minulého století není lidová kultura ve sbírkách evropských muzeí téměř vůbec zastoupena. Etnografické sbírky v muzeu v Kodani z roku 1807 a ve Štýrském Hradci z roku 1811 jsou pouhou výjimkou. Pokud se v muzeu přece jen něco z lidové kultury uchovalo, dokládalo to pouze sváteční nebo výjimečnou stránku života lidu. Tato skutečnost do značné míry vyplývá z romantizujícího zaměření tehdejšího národopisného bádání. Výjimku tvoří sběry, které shromáždily expedice ke kulturám mimoevropským, jak tomu bylo až do šedesátých let minulého století v Moravském (tehdy Františkově) muzeu v Brně.

Ke změně tohoto stavu dochází v Evropě v sedmdesátých a osmdesátých letech, u nás – snad opět s výjimkou Brna – nejméně o jedno desetiletí později. Děje se tak v čase vítězné konjunktury kapitalismu, jehož záměrům se podřizuje věda i kultura. Nové vědecké směry, zejména pak pozitivismus, tvrdě odmítají romantismus ve všech jeho podobách. Prvořadým úkolem etnografie se má stát komplexní poznání současného života lidu, tedy především jeho všedního života, poznání jeho kladných i záporných stránek.

Sběry muzeí se v tom čase velmi podstatně rozšiřují o doklady života a práce lidu. Vznikají etnografické sbírkové fondy, prvá oddělení etnografie v muzeích a první etnografická muzea.

Zakladatelem prvního samostatného národopisného muzea byl Artur Hazelius. Jeho zásluhou vzniklo ve Stockholmu v letech 1872 a 1873 Nordiska Museet, zaměřené na lidovou kulturu celé Skandinávie. Ve střední a východní Evropě se založení etnografických oddělení v muzeích pojí s pozdějšími letopočty: Olomouc 1883, Moskva 1885, Poznaň 1894, Lvov 1895, Vídeň 1869 a Praha 1896, pokud jmenujeme velká celonárodní muzea. Mnohem výraznější zastoupení však národopis získal ve sbírkách nově zakládaných muzeí regionálních. Pokud jde o nový pohled na lid, často zůstalo pouze u návrhu na komplexní dokumentaci způsobu života lidu; v expozicích nadále ještě převažovaly atraktivní předměty – kroje a lidové umění.

Národopisné sbírky a expozice v muzeích se staly druhým významným předpokladem vzniku muzeí v přírodě.

Světové výstavy a idea muzea v přírodě

Velmi významnou a doposud málo doceněnou roli při vzniku muzeí v přírodě sehrály velké výstavy, především výstavy světové a jubilejní. Jejich organizátoři – politici, průmysloví podnikatelé a velké osobnosti kultury – patřili k nejprogresívnějším složkám tehdy úspěšného kapitalistického řádu, k průkopníkům moderního životního stylu a k propagátorům rozvoje vědy a kultury.

Vše započalo na první světové výstavě v Londýně 1851, kde byly vystaveny modely lidových staveb z různých končin světa. Na světové výstavě v Paříži v roce 1878 se pokročilo dále. Artur Hazelius, budoucí zakladatel prvního muzea v přírodě na světě, tu vystavil skutečný interiér skandinávské jizby. Vynikal precizností a věrohodností. Jednotlivé předměty této expozice měly vytvořit dokonalou představu o způsobu života, neměly to být pouze atraktivní kusy nábytku sestavené a vybrané podle estetických kritérií. V duchu dobové módy oživil interiér figurínami ve vesnických krojích. Skandinávskému interiéru v Paříži úspěšně konkurovali především Holanďané. Jejich jizba z Hindeloope byla sevřena čtyřmi stěnami (ta skandinávská jen třemi), vcházelo se do ní dveřmi, takže iluze opravdovosti byla dokonalá.

Příčinu vzniku takových expozic však nehledejme pouze v úsilí o věrnou dokumentaci způsobu života, jako tomu bylo u Hazelia. Interiér jizby častěji sloužil jako atrakce, navazující na oblibu panoptik a panorámat nejrůznějšího druhu, včetně figurín, dokreslujících atmosféru dramatického výjevu. Ostatně figurín se užívalo v muzeích v přírodě ještě v našem století a v muzeích v expozicích interiéru ve Spojených státech při nich setrvávají doposud.

Zatímco na londýnské výstavě byly k vidění pouze modely staveb a na pařížské výstavě interiéry lidových domů, pátá světová výstava, která se konala ve Vídni už v roce 1873, představila návštěvníkům jako své dvacáté oddělení skupinu skutečných lidových staveb z několika evropských zemí. (Dodejme ještě, že se tu představila také lidová domácí a řemeslná výroba a že zejména Morava zde byla zastoupena velmi reprezentativně.) Záměr vystavovatelů nesouvisel ani s muzeem, ani s etnografií. Chtěli návštěvníky poučit, jak účelně a vkusně stavět. Vesměs šlo o kopie, podle jednoho pramene přenesli sem také originály. Tři z obytných domů byly vybaveny nábytkem a vším domácím nářadím a jedna usedlost byla trvale obývána selskou rodinou.

Tehdejší Uhry byly ve Vídni zastoupeny dřevěným kostelem, usedlostmi z oblasti Szeklerů a sedmihradských Sasů, domy maďarského a rumunského rolníka a také domem chorvatským a slovenským; žili prý v nich, zřejmě jen po krátkou dobu, celé rodiny, pocházející z míst původu stavby. Na výstavě stál ještě panský (asi bojarský) dům z Moskvy, horská usedlost tyrolská, dům z Alsaska-Lotrinska, alpská salaš z okolí Salcburku, švédský statek, rakouská vesnická škola a polský dům z Haliče, krytý slámou.

Pokud se budeme zajímat o zmíněný dům ze Slovenska, zjistíme, že šlo ve skutečnosti o dům z německé obce Gajdel v Nitranské župě; dnes se obec jmenuje Kľačno a patří do okresu Prievidza. Dům byl roubený, jednopatrový a na vídeňském výstavišti jej jako věrnou kopii ze smrkových trámů postavil tesař Anton Steinhübel ze sousední Tužiny. Interiér byl vybaven původním nábytkem a jinými předměty, které darovali obyvatelé tehdejšího Gajdla.

Po Vídni se s lidovými stavbami setkáváme na výstavách v Amsterodamu roku 1883, v Krakově roku 1887, ve Lvově 1894 a ještě i na jiných výstavách a při jiných příležitostech. Vyvrcholením této aktivity se stala Národopisná výstava českoslovanská, která se konala v Praze v roce 1895. Obšírněji o ní pojednáme o kus dále.

Po Praze následovala velká mileniální výstava v Budapešti v roce 1896 s domy ze všech zemí tehdejšího Uherska. V témže roce se uskutečnila etnografická výstava v Rize, konaná u příležitosti desátého všeruského archeologického kongresu. Tato lotyšská výstava nás zajímá ze dvou důvodů. Potěší nás, že její organizátoři zcela záměrně navázali na úspěch pražské výstavy, a překvapí nás cílevědomé úsilí organizátorů o oživení expozice. Tajemník přípravného výboru M. Skruzitis pobýval tři týdny v Praze na podzim roku 1895 a obeznámil se s výstavou i všemi aktivitami, zejména s programy regionálního folklóru. Jeho rádcem se stal náš Lubor Niederle. Do Rigy si kromě poznatků odvezl i vzory figurín užívaných v Praze. Středem výstavy se staly dvě staré tradiční usedlosti a jeden nový dům, dokumentující lotyšskou současnost. K usedlostem patřily stodoly, chlévy, studny a zahrádky s květinami a léčivými bylinami. Figurín v lotyšských krojích bylo využito k zobrazení konkrétních pracovních i slavnostních situací, jako je mlácení obilí, zpracování lnu, ale i tradiční svatba: v domě bohatého sedláka sedělo u prostřeného stolu devatenáct svatebních hostů. Návštěvníkům výstavní vesničky se nabízela jídla tradiční lotyšské kuchyně.

Charakter a osud výstav v Praze, v Rize a Budapešti byl v mnohém podobný. Na rozdíl od expozic lidového stavitelství na světových výstavách v sedmdesátých a osmdesátých letech měly vyhraněný, převážně odborný ráz a velmi výrazně ovlivňovaly rozvoj národopisu ve svých zemích. Také jejich konec je příznačný. Jejich tvůrcové usilovali o jejich delší trvání i po skončení výstavy. Bylo to úsilí marné, ale pochopitelné. Vždyť v jejich době již byla na světě první muzea v přírodě.

Z prehistorie skansenů

Snad bude vhodné připomenout, že kopie lidových domů se stavěly dokonce už v 18. století, a to jako stylová kulisa pro nejrůznější kratochvíle panstva – pro bukolické hry a selanky v klasicistním a rokokovém duchu. Staly se součástí zámeckých parků a slohových zahrad. K nejznámějším atrakcím tohoto druhu patřil park Petit Trianon a také Chantilly u Paříže z konce 18. století. V téže době bychom mohli navštívit kuriózní scenérii v parku královského zámku v dánském Fredensborgu s šedesáti kamennými postavami v lidových krojích. Tato originální expozice v přírodě přivedla Švýcara K. V. von Bonstettna k myšlence – v té době stejně originální – založit zahradu se stavbami primitivních evropských národů – Laponců, Islanďanů a jiných. Aniž to tušil, vznikla právě v jeho hlavě už roku 1790 idea expozice lidových staveb v přírodě, snad prvá na světě.

Artur Hazelius

Ale ani našemu panstvu nebyly podobné romantické kratochvíle cizí. Z kroniky obce Sklenova se dovídáme o slavnosti ve „valašském“ stylu, která se konala v roce 1822 nebo o rok později na počest návštěvy olomouckého arcibiskupa knížete Rudolfa. Na louce poblíže Hukvald postavili celou salaš a úřednictvo a sloužící, odění ve valašský šat, tam vykonávali práci pastevců – pásli stádo a vyráběli sýr.

Jiného charakteru je přesun dřevěného kostela od jezera Vang v Norsku do Bierutowic ve Slezsku, pokud víme nejdelší transport lidové stavby vůbec. Stalo se tak v létě roku 1842 a jen přesun po moři a po řece Odře trval dva měsíce.

Muzeum v přírodě a Skansen

Čas muzeí v přírodě dozrál v osmdesátých a devadesátých letech minulého století. Nezávisle na sobě nebo jen v malé závislosti vznikla tehdy ve třech skandinávských zemích a také jinde v Evropě se usiluje o totéž. Opomeneme skandinávský spor o prioritu a rozhodneme se pro švédský Skansen. Nezvolíme je pro superlativy pojící se k tomuto „divu světa“ – nejstarší, největší, nejatraktivnější a nejnavštěvovanější, ale proto, že okolnosti jeho vzniku mnohé vysvětlují.

Vydejme se tedy do Stockholmu sedmdesátých let minulého století. Setkáme se tam s dr. Arturem Hazeliem, čtyřicátníkem, původně učitelem švédského jazyka a literatury, v čase naší návštěvy již známým vlastivědným pracovníkem, zakladatelem prvního národopisného muzea (1872–73). Jemu přikládáme prvenství v prosazování nového způsobu prezentace lidové kultury. Usiloval o vystavení věcí v jejich původních funkčních a prostorových vazbách, což je doposud v muzeologii myšlenka zcela aktuální. Hazelius vystavuje lidový interiér v Paříži a ve svém Nordickém muzeu předvádí v roce 1874 expozici bydlení Laponců: v sále muzea postavil kožené stany, vybavil jejich interiér a doplnil figurínami v kroji. (Tento typ expozice je ostatně ve Skandinávii doposud v oblibě; viz národní muzeum v Oslo.)

K muzeu v přírodě zbýval už jediný krok. Hazelius prý tímto směrem vykročil už v roce 1885. Trvalo však ještě šest let, než bylo dne 11. října 1891 otevřeno první muzeum v přírodě na světě. Stalo se tak ve Stockholmu, v jeho výletní části Djurgården, v prostoru bývalé královské obory, na návrší zvaném Skansen, což česky znamená hradby. Názvu skansen se po čase začalo v některých zemích střední a východní Evropy užívat jako synonyma muzea v přírodě.

Stockholmský Skansen (Stiftelsen Skansen) se stal logickým dovršením Hazeliových záměrů o zpodobnění způsobu života muzejními prostředky. Řídil se devízou

Skansen Stockholm – 1891

1/ Lapská chýše
2/ Chlév pro soby

3/ Lapská komůrka na zásoby

„poznej sama sebe“, tedy sama sebe jako jedné složky rodného kraje, lidu tohoto kraje, podmínek k životu. V duchu této koncepce usiloval Hazelius o komplexní ztvárnění lidové tradice, o tzv. živé muzeum, naplněné prací, uměním a obyčeji. Nelze ovšem nevidět, že vedle obavy o osud zanikajícího lidového stavitelství se motivací jeho úsilí stal dozajista pannordický patriotismus, podporovaný vládnoucími místy, především samotnou královskou rodinou.

V roce 1899 navštívil stockholmský Skansen F. A. Šubert, ředitel Národopisné výstavy československé a spiritus agens ideje národopisného muzea v přírodě v Praze. Poznejme tedy Skansen v jeho začátcích očima našince; šlo o první fundovanou zprávu o Skansenu, o zprávu, která ovlivnila vývoj této ideje u nás.

Šuberta zaujaly všechny formy oživení. Zúčastnil se lidové slavnosti, na kterou přišlo 30 000 návštěvníků. Na planince upravili místo pro tanec, nedělnímu výletu stockholmské rodiny posloužila stylová restaurace. Ve Skansenu stály nejen obytné domy, ale celé dvory vybavené zemědělským nářadím. V domech hořel oheň a u stolu jako by při různých pracích seděly figuríny v krojích. V osadě Laponců bydlela ve stanu skutečná „lapská“ rodina a pečovala o stádo sobů. Jinde tkala u stavu stará žena a v horském salaši se zpracovávalo čerstvě nadojené mléko. Před poštou stály poštovní vozy se zápřahem.

Opusťme Šuberta a přesuňme se o osmdesát let dopředu, kdy ve Skansenu pobýval pisatel těchto řádků. To již Skansen patřil k největším kulturním a turistickým atrakcím na světě a jeho návštěvnost přesáhla dva milióny v jediném roce. Přibylo staveb i aktivit všeho druhu, a ty opět nejvíce zaujaly. Každodenně tam vystupovala folklórní skupina, během roku se okázale slavila Lucie, pořádal se vánoční jarmark, o Valpurgině noci se tančilo při ohních, o Jáně se stavěly máje. Z interiérů zmizely figuríny, na druhé straně přibylo řemeslníků, lidových umělců i prostých venkovanů. Zkušenému oku však neujde, že s rychlým zánikem tradičního způsobu života jejich místa často zastupují mladí lidé, kteří se starému řemeslu naučí na umělecké škole. Ve Skansenu si sami pečou tradiční druhy chleba a v zimě předvádějí ukázky tradičního stolování, spojeného s ochutnávkou. V salaši, kterou navštívil i Šubert, nás pozdraví hospodyně v kroji, návštěvníkovi podá placku z hrubé mouky. (Hospodyně mluví dokonale anglicky.) Ze všech druhů aktivity je sestaven roční plán. Například v týdnu práce se lnem najdeme u rybníčků, vodních stoup a mlýnců na patnáct žen a mužů, ovládajících tradiční techniku. Mlýny a jiné technické stavby na vodní pohon stojí v jedné řadě na svahu, prudce spadajícím k mořskému zálivu. Kola mlýnů a stoup jsou poháněná vodou z malého rybníčka, spojeného mohutným potrubím s hladinou moře.

Za Šubertovy návštěvy tu ještě nestála městská čtvrť – s bankou, spořitelnou, kavárnou a spoustou obchodů. Hojně navštěvovaným místem se stala sklárna. Před očima návštěvníka se tam tvaruje sklo a návštěvník si je může zakoupit ještě teplé; na jeho přání upraví tvar, dekor i barvu skla.

Některé atrakce však náš návštěvník přijímá se smíšenými pocity. Smíří se se zoologickou zahradou, neboť tu chovají pouze skandinávskou zvířenu, hůře přijme sortiment desítek obchůdků poplatný více komerci než kultuře a v žádném případě se nesmíří s dětskými koutky a rybníčky v Disney-stylu.

Skandinávské prvenství a vzor pro Evropu

Nejméně tři velká skandinávská muzea v přírodě zpochybňují prvenství stockholmského Skansenu. Nikdo však nepochybuje o prvenství skandinávských muzeí v přírodě v rámci Evropy a celého světa a také o tom, že právě tato muzea se stala vzorem pro ostatní Evropu.

V Oslo o takovém muzeu rozvažovali už v roce 1881, ne-li dříve. Také zde přála této myšlence samotná královská reprezentace. Již v roce 1883 stály na královském majetku ve čtvrti Bygdøy stavby z několika oblastí Norska a také středověký kostelík. Roku 1902 bylo Norsk Folkemuseum zpřístupněno veřejnosti. Může se pochlubit skvosty skandinávské architektury: roubenými stavbami ze 13. až 16. století, uchovanými ve vynikajícím stavu.

K nejstarším a nejlepším muzeím v přírodě na světě patří i jiné norské muzeum, jehož počátky se kladou k roku 1887. V podhorském městě Lillehammeru je tehdy začal stavět lékař Anders Sandvig. Při výstavbě muzea, a ta trvala celých šest desítek let, uplatnil důsledné evoluční hledisko jak při výběru staveb, tak i při jejich umístění v muzeu. Doložil vývoj domu od nejprimitivnějších forem k náročným, rozsáhlým stavbám a svůj záměr podpořil podklady sociálními a ekologickými.

Vybudování tohoto muzea, nazvaného dnes na počest jeho tvůrce Sandvigske

Samlinger, představuje významný počin na cestě k vědecky podloženému obrazu minulé společnosti, k uplatnění muzea v přírodě jako specifické formy vědecké dokumentace.

Kodaňská národopisná výstava v roce 1879 prý přivedla Bernharda Olsena k založení velkého celodánského muzea v přírodě v Lyngby v Kodani, otevřeného v roce 1901. Dnes nás toto muzeum upoutá zejména ukázkami tradičního zemědělství. Dánsko má však nesporný primát v zobrazení městské kultury. Zasloužil se o to všestranný podnikatel Petr Holm, který v druhém desetiletí našeho století započal budovat v samém středu města Aarhus starou městskou čtvrť (Den gamle By), tedy její rekonstrukci. Úzké uličky, kanály a mosty, honosné stavby měšťanů a obchodníků a početné dílny řemeslníků vytvářejí přesvědčivou atmosféru života města v minulém století.

Podobné originální postavení přiznáme finskému městu Turku, v kterém od třicátých let našeho století vyrůstalo muzeum řemesla, městská ulice s nejméně třiceti řemesly. Celonárodní finské muzeum v přírodě vznikalo od roku 1909 pod Helsinkami, na mořské výspě zvané Seurasaari.

Dominující postavení skandinávských skansenů vyplývá i z jejich počtu: ze stovky muzeí v přírodě, založených do konce světové války, jich celé čtyři pětiny vznikly ve Skandinávii.

V ostatních evropských zemích zůstalo v 19. století jen u úmyslu a nanejvýše u projektu. Už v roce 1888 zamýšlel polský profesor Ignac Baranowski umístit tatranské muzeum do jedné goralské usedlosti in situ a – jak jsme již vzpomenuli – o uchování národopisných dědinek na výstavě marně usilovali v Praze, Rize a Budapešti.

Nejinak to skončilo v Holandsku, kde byli k realizaci nejblíže. Na výstavě v Amsterodamu, konané v roce 1883 a zaměřené v duchu státní politiky na koloniální země, stálo asi dvacet staveb z různých částí Indonésie. Po skončení výstavy byly roku 1885 přeneseny do města Leide jako základ trvalé expozice; udržely se tam pouze do roku 1903. Ale již roku 1912 vzniká u Arnhemu velké celoholandské muzeum, dnes Het Nederlands Openluchtmuseum s osmdesáti objekty: patří k nejnavštěvovanějším na světě a je dostupné pouze lodí.

Z ostatních míst jmenujme lotyšskou Rigu (1924), náš Rožnov (1925) a velké celonárodní muzeum vesnice (Muzeul satului) v Bukurešti, reprezentující všechny rumunské regiony, muzeum vystavěné podle projektu sociologa Dumitra Gustiho. Až před druhou světovou válkou vzniklo první muzeum v přírodě v Anglii, a to na ostrově Man. Počítá osm hospodářských usedlostí in situ včetně hektarů polí a luk a dokládá dosud živou keltskou tradici.

Deklarace o muzeích v přírodě, teoretická východiska

Po přestávce vynucené válkou a poválečnou obnovou dochází ve většině evropských států k intenzívnímu zájmu o ochranu lidového stavitelství. Byl vyvolán rychlým zánikem těchto staveb a také změnou politického klimatu: ve většině zemí se péče o lid a jeho tradice stává významnou součástí státní politiky (země socialistického tábora) nebo součástí programu silných pokrokových stran.

Na valném shromáždění Mezinárodní rady muzeí (ICOM) při UNESCO v Ženevě roku 1956 dochází k rozhodnutí o podpoře výstavby muzeí v přírodě. Šlo o kvalitativní změnu v postoji k těmto muzeím, do té doby muzejními orgány často přehlíženým. Na základě této iniciativy se o rok později schází ve čtyřech skandinávských městech první mezinárodní konference o muzeích v přírodě a jedná o principech jejich výstavby.

Diskuse na této konferenci i na dalších akcích Svazu evropských muzeí v přírodě, který vznikl o několik let později, měla vést k nové teorii muzeí v přírodě. Ta Hazeliova již nedostačovala, navíc její romantismus a patriotismus často sklouzl k nostalgii a k nepravdivé a podbízivé atraktivnosti, mnohdy spojené i s komerčností. Diskutovalo se především o dvou teoretických přístupech. Ten první zastávali pracovníci památkové péče. Lidový dům je pro ně především hmotným dokladem o uměleckých schopnostech a technické dovednosti lidových tvůrců, v druhé řadě je důležitým komponentem krajiny. Proto prosazují uchování staveb na místě (in situ) pokud možno nejdéle a s jejich přivezením do Skansenu, který má mít především záchrannou funkci, se smiřují až tehdy, když již jiná možnost nezbývá. Obvykle se staví též proti oživování expozic a proti jiným formám aktivit.

Zatímco první směr zdůrazňoval původnost, druhý směr akcentoval komplexnost. Zastávali jej etnografové a zejména etnografové pracující v muzeu. Lidový dům a lidové stavitelství chápali jako jednu složku lidové kultury, z hlediska muzejního jako sbírkový předmět. Přenesení staveb do muzea, jejich výběr a rozestavení vytváří předpoklad pro pravdivé zobrazení minulého života. Ve způsobu jeho zobrazení však nebylo jednoty. Ve shodě s praxí muzejních expozic převládalo hledisko typologické, tj. řazení objektů podle vývojových a regionálních typů. (Vzpomeňme, že tento záměr realizoval Sandvig už na počátku století.) Za progresívnější přístup plně využívající specifiky muzeí v přírodě považujeme vytváření modelových situací, odpovídajících skutečnosti z hlediska výběru staveb a jejich vzájemných sociálních a výrobních vazeb. Takzvané oživení muzea ukázkami výrobních, uměleckých a obyčejových aktivit je logickým dovršením tohoto záměru.

Deklarace o muzeích v přírodě z roku 1957, která je výsledkem této diskuse, moudře a prozíravě usměrnila tendence v této oblasti. Stanovila, co patří a nepatří do skansenu, vyslovila se k tak zvanému oživování muzea i k otázce kopií a rekonstrukcí, odsoudila komerčnost i kýč.

Velký ohlas Deklarace vyplynul z aktuálnosti tohoto tématu ve všech evropských zemích. Dochází k mohutné vlně zakládání muzeí v přírodě na celém světě. V současnosti víme o dvou tisících muzeí tohoto typu a jejich počet stále vzrůstá.

Muzea v přírodě v socialistických státech

Deklarace o muzeích v přírodě našla příznivou odezvu zejména v zemích tábora socialismu. Jako důsledek socializace zemědělství a také zvýšené životní úrovně tam lidové stavby rychle zanikaly. Ve většině těchto zemí bylo na co navázat. V Polsku stála sice jen čtyři nevelká muzea, ale Rumunsko se chlubilo velkým reprezentačním muzeem v Bukurešti, Československo mělo svůj Rožnov a v Sovětském svazu se myšlenka skansenů vlivem skandinávského sousedství nejdříve uchytila v pobaltských republikách.

Dnes víme nejméně o devadesáti muzeích v přírodě v Sovětském svazu. Po dlouhých letech diskuse si vydobyly pevné místo v systému ochrany památek, ale i v kulturním životě státu. O obtížném prosazování myšlenky skansenu svědčí muzeum v Kiži na Oněžském jezeru v Karélii, zpřístupněné v roce 1961. O výběru staveb rozhodovala jejich historická hodnota a též míra ohrožení v terénu. Tak se sem svezly

1/ Szentendre – Maďarsko

2

3

2/ Lublin – Polsko

3/ Nowogród nad Lomżą – Polsko

především dřevěné církevní stavby z 18. a 19. století, později též obydlí, sýpky, mlýny aj. Převážilo zde hledisko památkové péče, sledující pouze ochranu stavební a umělecké hodnoty díla.

Zvláštní druh muzeí v přírodě vznikl v místech, spojených s pobytem velkých osobností sovětské historie. Patří k nim muzeum v obci Šušenskoje, v místě Leninova sibiřského vyhnanství. Vedle dvou domků, v kterých Lenin nuceně přebýval, tam stojí dalších třicet usedlostí; deset jich sem přenesli, dvacet zůstalo na původním místě. Muzeum bylo zpřístupněno v roce 1970. Podobně je koncipováno i muzeum ve vsi Michajlovskoje pod Pskovem, tedy v místě Puškinovy deportace, a muzeum v Irkutsku, dokládající vyhnanství „děkabristů“ v roce 1825.

Z významných sovětských muzeí v přírodě jmenujme běloruský skansen u Minska, gruzínský u Tbilisi, velké severské muzeum v přírodě u Archangelska s osmdesáti objekty ze 16. až 19. století, a také východosibiřský skansen v lokalitě Ulan-Ude u Bajkalu se třemi sektory, dokumentujícími způsob života Burjatů, Evenků (Tunguzů) a sibiřských Rusů.

Po Pobaltí se v nedlouhé historii sovětských skansenů nejvýrazněji prosazuje Ukrajina, kde napočteme patnáct rezervací lidové architektury a deset muzeí v přírodě, z nichž k nejznámějším patřila muzea ve Lvově a Užhorodě. V sedmdesátých letech, po celé desítce let diskusí, se však u Kyjeva začalo s výstavbou muzea s názvem Muzej narodnoj architěktury i byta Ukrajinskoj SSR, které co do promyšlenosti koncepce i co do terénních a materiálních podmínek patří k nejperspektivnějším muzeím v přírodě na světě.

Zabírá plochu 150 ha a je rozvrženo do šesti sektorů ukrajinských etnografických oblastí, jako jsou Podněpří, Polesí, Podolí a ukrajinské Karpaty. Ve výstavbě je i sedmý sektor, dokládající stavební kulturu a způsob života socialistického venkova.

Systematickým využíváním vědeckých poznatků se může pochlubit muzeum lidových technik v rumunském Sibiu. Je tematicky rozloženo do několika areálů podle účelu výroby; největší místo zabírají technická zařízení na přípravu stravy. V současnosti je v Rumunské socialistické republice nejméně dvacet skansenů.

K rychlému rozvoji muzeí v přírodě dochází v Maďarské lidové republice. Úspěšně zde vyřešili otázku transferu zděných staveb, které v maďarské nížině převládají. Z terénu přivážejí nejvýraznější stavební prvky (štít, okna, dveře, apod.), kdežto zděné části domu staví na místě. Takto vzniká od roku 1966 celomaďarské muzeum v přírodě v Szentendre u Budapešti, kde počítají se zastoupením deseti regionů. Výběr objektů se děje na základě velmi důkladné technické a etnografické dokumentace maďarské lidové kultury. Vysokou úroveň mají expozice interiérů v usedlostech, navozující konkrétní životní situaci (např. ráno v domě zemana). Výčet maďarských skansenů přesahuje číslo třicet.

V Polsku jich napočítáme již přes čtyřicet. Dominantní postavení si z nich udržuje Muzeum Budownictva Ludowego v Sanoku s širokým metodickým záběrem, zahrnujícím nejen Polsko, ale díky osobnosti Jerzyho Czajkowského celou východní Evropu. Samotné muzeum na řece Sanu se vyznačuje jednak typologickým přístupem, jednak úsilím o autentičnost staveb i všech vystavených předmětů. Z nejnovějších perspektivních skansenů jmenujme Muzeum Wsi Lubelskiej v Lublinu s vynikajícím exteriérem objektů, dokumentujícím všechny druhy rostlinné říše – druhy užitkové, okrasné i volně rostoucí, i způsob jejich obdělávání a zužitkování.

Významné místo v historii skansenů si vydobyla bulharská Etara (Eter) ležící na okraji města Gabrovo. Jde o rezervaci řemeslnické osady, která byla do původního stavu doplněna patnácti rekonstrukcemi domů. Dnes Etara počítá na padesát stavebních objektů s dílnami a především se šedesáti řemeslníky a lidovými umělci, kteří vyrábějí předměty denní potřeby, umělecké předměty i suvenýry. Patří k nejnavštěvovanějším muzeím v Evropě; počet návštěvníků se blíží k půl miliónu.

Západní Evropa a ostatní svět

Ze zemí západní Evropy má nesporné prvenství Německá spolková republika. Od přelomu století, kdy v severní části země došlo pod skandinávským vlivem k prvním pokusům, vzniklo tu osmdesát muzeí v přírodě. Jako první vzpomeneme porýnské muzeum v Kommern, které se stalo – zejména zásluhou dlouholetého prezidenta Svazu evropských muzeí v přírodě Adelharta Zippelia – neoficiálním celoevropským metodickým centrem. Skládá se ze čtyř areálů počítajících na sedmdesát objektů a jeho silnou stránkou jsou ukázky tradičního způsobu hospodaření, sadaření a chovu domácích zvířat.

Na přední místo v Evropě se prodírají dvě vestfálská muzea v přírodě, navzájem diametrálně odlišná: „selské“ muzeum v Detmoldu a „technické“ v Hagenu. Vznikla v šedesátých letech, obě vynikají technickou dokonalostí výstavby, což je u konstrukce hrázděných patrových budov velmi důležité. V detmolském muzeu se z původní stavby přivážely nejen trámy hrázděné konstrukce, ale také původní výplň z cihel.

Naproti tomu v Hagenu staví především rekonstrukce. Hlavní váhu přikládají technickému zařízení, které instalují s neobyčejnou důkladností tak, aby mohlo být kdykoliv uvedeno v chod. Předváděná technická zařízení představují historii techniky – od primitivních stoup po dokonalé stroje tovární výroby. Úzké údolí, ve kterém stojí muzeum, je přehrazeno několika vodními nádržemi, které zabezpečují dostatek vody pro tři desítky technických staveb na vodní pohon.

Z ostatních zemí západní Evropy určitě stojí za pozornost tři celonárodní muzea v přírodě – v rakouském Stübingu (1962), ve švýcarském Ballenbergu (1978) a konečně v belgickém Bokrijku (1958).

Pozornému čtenáři dozajista neujde, že směrem na sever muzeí v přírodě výrazně přibývá a že na jihu Evropy jich téměř není. Jakoby existovala jakási nepřímá úměra: čím řidší osídlení, tím hustější síť skansenů. Vždyť ve Skandinávii jich dnes napočteme na sedmnáct set a na ostatní Evropu jich zbývá jen tři sta. Vysvětlení je prosté: na jihu se stavělo především z kamení a hlíny a takové stavby se – na rozdíl od dřevěných staveb evropského severu – těžko přenášejí. Navíc se uchovávaly až do našeho věku v dobrém stavu a často se mění v památkové objekty chráněné na místě nebo v celé rezervace.

Právě v tomto prostředí vzniká nový perspektivní typ muzeí v přírodě, tzv. ekomuzea. Tato muzea ochraňují původní krajinu včetně původních obydlí, která taktéž zůstávají v původní tradiční podobě, a jejich obyvatelé vykonávají obvyklé tradiční práce. Taková muzea byla založena u města Bordeau v Gaskoňsku (1970) a na dalších sedmi místech. Ekomuzea se nevyhýbají ani starým památkám průmyslu, jako jsou sklárny a doly.

Idea ekomuzea získala své přívržence, a to nejen v zemích jižní Evropy (například v Jugoslávii), ale i v Sovětském svazu a Polsku, kde se tomuto typu podobá rozsáhlá chráněná oblast polských Tater, v které se nadále udržuje tradiční horské salašnictví.

Muzea v přírodě existují pochopitelně i mimo Evropu – v Asii, Africe, Americe i v Austrálii. Víme též, že jsou poplatná kulturnímu a politickému ovzduší té které země; například jihoafrické muzeum v přírodě, které vzniká poblíže Pretorie, nepočítá se stavbami původního afrického obyvatelstva a omezuje se pouze na stavby koloniální.

K velmi intenzívnímu rozvoji muzeí v přírodě dochází v posledních třech desetiletích ve Spojených státech. Od evropských skansenů se odlišují především svým komerčním zaměřením. Vstupné, suvenýry, vlastní restaurace a hotel, jsou hlavními zdroji příjmů. S tím souvisí i požadavek atraktivnosti expozic. Motivací mnoha skansenů jsou specifika národních skupin. A tak najdeme muzea s domky přesídlenců z Ukrajiny, z Polska a nejvíce ze Skandinávie. Jiným vděčným tématem je doba pionýrů – novoosídlenců, a také „zlatá horečka". Největší počet muzeí však zobrazuje americkou farmu, tedy činné hospodářství v tradiční podobě. (V roce 1966 započal venkovský učitel ve státě Georgia s akcí zvanou Foxfir. Pomocí ankety shromažďoval údaje o životě na farmách. Akce se rozrostla do nevídaných rozměrů a jejím výsledkem je také vznik několika muzeí.) Vděčným tématem je též americké město z konce minulého století, se vším, co k němu patří, tedy i s hotelem, poštou a domem lékaře. Věhlasným muzeem tohoto typu se stalo nově vystavěné město ve starém stylu, Williamsburg ve státě Virginia.

1

2

3

4

5

1/ Maria Saal – Rakousko
2/ Hagen – NSR
3/ Fagernes – Norsko
4/ Lillehammer – Norsko
5/ Arnhem – Holandsko

Národopisná výstava československá a jiné neuskutečněné projekty

Doložili jsme již, jaký význam měl pro vznik ideje muzea v přírodě příklad ze zahraničí. Nicméně rozhodující roli vždy sehrály domácí podmínky – politické a kulturní klima a jeho tendence. Živnou půdou pro vznik takové ideje se nejčastěji stal patriotismus v jeho početných formách. O dalším vývoji rozhodovala též úroveň a zaměření vědního oboru, nejčastěji národopisu, a příslušných kulturních institucí, ponejvíce tedy muzeí a orgánů památkové péče.

Tak tomu bylo také u nás, v Československu. Naše etnografie se lidovými stavbami začala zabývat v posledních dvou desítkách let minulého století a v tom čase se k materiální kultuře obrátila také pozornost našich muzeí, zejména nově zakládaných regionálních muzeí. Mnohdy však zůstalo pouze u záměru a muzejní sbírky stejně zůstaly u sváteční podoby lidové kultury.

Mnohem progresívněji než ve vědě a v muzeích je prezentováno lidové stavitelství a také lidová výroba a lidové umění na velkých výstavách – světových, jubilejních, celonárodních, dokonce i průmyslových, jejichž organizátory se stali političtí a ekonomičtí představitelé vedoucích radikálních sil buržoazie. Pokud se jejich iniciativa a ekonomika spojila s odborností, zaručenou znalci, došlo k překvapivým výsledkům. Národopis tak získal pozici pro velkorysou prezentaci a stal se dokonce objektem samostatných výstav.

Zrod myšlenky muzea v přírodě v Československu také souvisí s výstavou. Vše začalo na Zemské jubilejní výstavě, která se konala v roce 1891 v Praze. Pořadatelé tu dali vystavět „českou chalupu" a naplnili ji lidovými výšivkami. Šlo o velmi volnou a reprezentační rekonstrukci jizerského domu, o akci v duchu „českého svérázu", jehož představitelé programově usilovali o povýšení vybraných hodnot lidové kultury na kulturu národní. Dařilo se jim zejména v písni a tanci (Česká beseda), méně už v kroji a stravě.

Ohlas „české chalupy" na výstavě byl veliký. Už v čase konání jubilejní výstavy vyvstala myšlenka uspořádat Národopisnou výstavu československou. Autorství ideje výstavy přisuzujeme F. A. Šubertovi, řediteli Národního divadla v Praze. Jeho přičiněním se dne 28. července 1891 sešla ve velké zasedací síni staroměstské radnice řada vynikajících osobností české vědy a kultury a rozhodla o uspořádání výstavy. Dne 9. září bylo vydáno provolání k českému národu, sepsané Eliškou Krásnohorskou.

Příprava Národopisné výstavy československé svedla ke spolupráci významné představitele vědy, umělce a pracovníky kultury. Shodovali se na nutnosti opravdového poznání českého lidu, v názoru na využití získaných poznatků se však lišili. První skupina, zvaná „česká chalupa", do níž se seskupili především Alois Jirásek, Čeněk Zíbrt, Zikmund Winter a František Bartoš, usilovala o poznání patriarchální vesnice s cílem udržet všechny tradiční rysy selství a „češství"; jakékoliv narušení tohoto stavu považovali za ohrožení národní specifičnosti. K „české chalupě" mělo blízko hnutí „českého svérázu".

Druhá velká skupina, ke které patřili především Jan Jakubec, Václav Tille, Jiří Polívka, Jan Herben, Lubor Niederle a Otakar Hostinský, se vyznačovala novým přístupem k národní kultuře; její pracovní metodou se stal pozitivismus. V jeho duchu odsoudili romantismus, panslovanství a nekritické vlastenčení. O názorech této skupiny nechme promluvit Jana Jakubce:

„Těžiště našeho života lidového pošinulo se jinam. Duše lidu našeho mluví k nám více z jeho průměrného klopotného života rodinného, nežli ve vzácných chvílích slavnostních." A jinde: „My se hlásíme k těm upřímným vlastencům, kteří nedoufají, že by na dlouhou budoucnost mohl se udržeti samostatný kroj národní i ve prospěch národa si to ani nepřejí."

Tedy sbírati vše, podle Tilleho dokonce i údaje o zločinnosti a opilství. Roku 1893 založili stoupenci tohoto směru Národopisnou společnost českoslovanskou. Pro naši problematiku je významné, že členové společnosti, především pak Lubor Niederle, svým pojetím, na svou dobu moderním a pokrokovým, výrazně ovlivnili ideovou a odbornou podobu Národopisné výstavy českoslovanské.

Pražský výbor Výstavy poslal už koncem roku 1891 muzeím, obcím a především regionálním vlastivědným pracovníkům výzvu ke spolupráci a k zakládání krajinských výborů. Výsledek této iniciativy byl nečekaný. Ve třech následujících letech vzniklo více než dvě stě krajinských a místních výborů pro přípravu Národopisné výstavy v Praze. Tak byl vytvořen základ k systematické vlastivědné práci, koordinované pokyny, návody a dotazníky, posílanými z pražského centra. Usměrňovaly regionální pracovníky ke komplexnímu studiu a ke sbírání předmětů, dokumentujících život lidu a obsahovaly též výzvy k pořizování modelů lidových staveb a dokonce i k ochraně a získávání originálů.

V letech 1892 až 1894 se v českých zemích konalo 180 místních národopisných výstav; setkaly se s velikým ohlasem a významně podepřely pozice české národní kultury. Podnítily vznik mnoha muzeí a blahodárně ovlivnily jejich program sběrů a jejich demokratický ráz. V letech 1891 až 1894 vzniklo 34 muzeí a hned po výstavě dalších 19 muzeí.

Z krajinských výstav a krajinských výborů si více povšimneme vsetínské výstavy a práce tamního valašského výboru. Výběr není náhodný. Vsetínská výstava patřila k nejlepším a na půdě vsetínského výboru se rozhodlo o výstavbě valašské dědinky v Praze.

Na slavnostní zahájení Národopisné výstavy na Vsetíně dne 14. srpna 1892 se sjeli významní představitelé české vědy a kultury a vedoucí činitelé přípravného výboru pražské výstavy; ze Slovenska přijeli hosté v tak významném zastoupení, že se vsetínská výstava stala manifestací česko-slovenské jednoty.

Čtrnáct tříd nové vsetínské školy bylo naplněno předměty z celého Valašska. Převažovaly kroje, řemeslo a lidové umění. Nechyběl tu ani „valašský šenk" s Pelárovou „muzigou". „Mnozí návštěvníci, kteří začali prohlídku výstavy šenkem, se už zpravidla dál nedostali...", psalo se o výstavě.

V dějinách vývoje našich muzeí v přírodě má významné místo a časovou prioritu interiér valašské jizby, vystavený v jedné třídě. Měl malá okénka s květinami, byl vybaven originálním lidovým nábytkem a stála tu pec s kamnovcem i pecními vidlicemi. Předměty denní potřeby i umělecké předměty stály nebo visely na svém původním místě. Na stole byl svatební koláč, nad stolem visela dřevěná holubička, nad koutnicí byl upevněn dožínkový věnec a vedle něho obrázky na skle, nad ložnicí visel kolébač a nechyběla tu ani dřevěná stoupa a „choďák", prosté zařízení, s jehož pomocí se děti učily chodit. Pro dokreslení pravdivé atmosféry valašské jizby umístili sem i kozu a králíky, jak tomu bylo leckde na Valašsku v zimním čase. V síni před jizbou stály žrna, škopky, kadluby a jiné nářadí. O nedělích za stolem seděli a hráli cimbalista a houslista, jiný Valach strouhal šindel a Valaška předla.

Druhý den, v neděli, vyšel ze Vsetína průvod ven za město do volné přírody. Tři tisíce návštěvníků tam sledovaly svatbu z Valašské Polanky a dožatou z Hovězí. O kus dál postavili salaš, kde bača s Valachy prodával ovčí sýr. Hráli tu i muzikanti a „... hosté nešetřili grošů, házejíce je do cimbálu“. S podobným pojetím, zdůrazňujícím maximální úsilí o zpodobnění originálního prostředí, se snad setkáme jen ve stockholmském Skansenu, otevřeném jen o rok dříve. Jak velký krok dopředu nebo spíše vykročení zcela opačným směrem ve srovnání s „českou chalupou“ na Jubilejní výstavě!

Zatímco výstavní výbory v jiných krajích se omezily pouze na sběr předmětů pro pražskou výstavu a lidové stavitelství dokumentovaly v nejlepším případě modelem, ve Vsetíně se rozhodli, že v Praze postaví celou valašskou dědinku. Je to prý „... čest a povinnost naše“, prohlásil Karel Bubela (1844–1908), předseda výboru, jinak zemský poslanec a úspěšný podnikatel. Připomeňme, že k silné vsetínské trojce patřil ještě stavitel Michal Urbánek (1849–1923) a architekt Dušan Jurkovič, v té době zaměstnaný u Urbánka. Právě ten připravil výběr staveb a dohlížel na realizaci výstavby.

Na Slovensku se celonárodním centrem podobných snah stal Martin. Když tu v roce 1887 konal spolek slovenských žen Živena výstavu lidových výšivek, postavil Blažej Bulla na dvoře Paulínyho domu výstavní pavilón v duchu oravské architektury. Základní význam pro zrod myšlenky slovenského skansenu však měla – vedle působení skandinávského vzoru – až Národopisná výstava československá v Praze a její přípravné údobí. Setkáváme se v něm se jmény Andrej Kmeť, Pavel Socháň a jinými, rozhodující role však opět připadla Dušanu Jurkovičovi. Připravil projekt „gazdovstva“ z Čičman (stavbu realizoval architekt Makovec) a na výstavbu domu z Oravy osobně dohlížel; v Praze jej stavěli dva oravští tesaři.

Samotná Národopisná výstava československá se konala v letních měsících roku 1895 a navštívily ji více než dva milióny návštěvníků. Stala se manifestací hospodářské a kulturní vyspělosti národa a svým převážně demokratickým charakterem se stala také demonstrací politickou. Patří k největším akcím české kultury 19. století.

Ve výstavním paláci bylo vystaveno sedmnáct tisíc předmětů, dokumentujících způsob života lidu z Čech, Moravy, Slezska a Slovenska; většina exponátů dokládala spíše onu sváteční podobu života. Velké pozornosti se těšila slovácká „jízda králů“, která po demontáži výstavy byla přenesena do nového Národopisného muzea v Praze a zůstala tam až do roku 1960. Nechyběly ani „selské jizby“, interiéry lidových staveb z deseti míst Čech a Moravy. Hodnota jednotlivých expozic byla různá – od reprezentativních instalací „českého svérázu“ až po realisticky pojatou jizbu valašského pasekáře.

Nejpřitažlivější a nejpozoruhodnější částí výstavy se stala „výstavní dědina“. Emanuel Kovář, duše celé výstavy, vybral pro ni jedenáct typických staveb. Ve skutečnosti se jich tu však vystavělo nejméně dvakrát tolik. Z původního záměru ukázat, jak se dá bydlet, se stala významná národopisná akce. Realizace výstavby byla svěřena významným pražským architektům a stavebním firmám. Stavitelé se sice řídili dodanými podklady o jednotlivých domovních typech, velmi často však stavby poněkud idealizovali, zejména jejich dekor. V převážné většině případů šlo o rekonstrukci. Jen z dřevěného kostela z Podůlčan se sem přenesly některé části, bylo jich však užito u stavby kostela, který se nedržel žádného konkrétního vzoru. O užití původního stavebního dřeva se zmiňují i účty z výstavby valašské osady, a z jiných pramenů se dovídáme o přepravě valašské pily „jednošky“ a snad také zařízení „křiváčkářské“ dílny.

Kolem návsi s dřevěným kostelíkem se z jedné strany postavil dům od Břeclavi i s vinným sklepem, dále horácký statek od Velkého Meziříčí, hanácký statek od Litovle, slezský statek opavský a vedle něj těšínská chalupa z Orlové, dále vesnická kovárna a z moravské a slezské architektury se přešlo na Slovensko, zastoupené usedlostí z Oravy a „gazdovstvím“ z Čičman. Směrem k umělému rybníku stála ještě kopaničářská chalupa ze Starého Hrozenkova. Druhé části návsi, shromažďující stavby z Čech, vévodil český mlýn s jedním složením, za ním stál statek z okolí Petrovic na Milevsku, chalupa od Jaroměře, velký statek z okolí Hlinska, chodské stavení od Domažlic a konečně pojizerský statek z okolí Turnova. K tomu pražští „baráčníci“ postavili „českou rychtu“, stavbu v lidovém duchu. To vše se vystavělo v poměrně krátkém čase, v zimě a na jaře před výstavou. Fotografie z výstavy prozradí, že jednotlivé usedlosti byly stylově oploceny a najdeme tu i stylové brány a zahrádky s květinami a slunečnicemi.

Samostatnou část výstavní dědiny tvořila valašská osada. Její počátky hledejme na Vsetíně a především u Dušana Jurkoviče. Prostudoval a dokumentoval mnoho valašských staveb a z nich potom vybral kolekci, na svou dobu velmi originální. Nenajdeme v ní ani fojtství, ani selský statek, ani honosnou církevní stavbu, ale chalupu z horské osady, se zdůrazněním tradičních výrobních technik. Všechno postavili na Vsetíně a v okolních vsích Urbánkovi tesaři, poté se stavby rozebraly, naložily na vagóny a od časného jara 1895 je valašští tesaři v Praze stavěli. Na železniční zastávce v Růžďce se do vagónu naložilo originální složení vodní pily „valašky“, získané pro pražskou výstavu od mlynářů Stradějů z Bystřičky.

Na valašskou osadu zbylo na pražském výstavišti relativně nevýhodné místo – „nehostinný pahorek“, psalo se doslova. Valašským stavbám však plně vyhovovalo. Nakonec mezi nízkým smrčím stála salašnická koliba a košár, opodál skutečný milíř na dřevěné uhlí, z jezírka vytékal potůček k dokonalé valašské pile „jednošce“, ale ještě před ní vtékala z něj voda do napajedla, do koryta z vydlabaného kmene. Při potůčku u pily našel svoje místo i kotel na pálení slivovice. Po druhé straně osady stála „křiváčkárna“, tedy kovárna, přizpůsobená výrobě „křiváků“, primitivních nožů (kudel). Střed osady představovala chalupa „půlgruntového gazdy“ z Horního Vsacka, s velkým dvorem, s hospodářskými staveními.

Nejvěhlasnější stavbou celé „národopisné dědiny“ se stala hospoda Na posledním groši, kde vyhrávala Pelárova kapela. K hostům této hospody patřili Mikoláš Aleš, Svatopluk Čech, Alois Jirásek, Václav Rais, Jaroslav Vrchlický, Ignát Hermann, V. V. Štech, Jaroslav Kvapil a další. O oživení výstavy typickými ukázkami prací pečoval další vsetínský občan, tehdy student filozofie v Praze, Josef Válek, později významný vlastivědný pracovník. A tak tu pracoval a svoje výrobky prodával „křiváčkář“, ženy v pracovním oděvu předváděly běžné denní práce a k salaši patřilo i malé stádo ovcí a koz; snad tu prý též tesařský mistr Vincenc Drda řezal na pile desky.

Ve vývoji ideje muzea v přírodě zaujímá valašská osada na pražské výstavě velmi významné místo. Sociálním aspektem při výběru objektů, snahou o maximální pravdivost, byť šlo – až na pilu – jen o kopie staveb, a také úsilím o oživení expozice ukázkami tradičních prací v mnohém předčila projekty následujícího století, včetně jeho druhé poloviny.

1

Národopisná
výstava
Praha
1895

2

3

4

1/ Bohumír Jaroněk
2/ Turnovský statek
3/ Gazdovstvo čičmanské
4/ Nádvoří valašského statku

Pod dojmem velkého úspěchu „národopisné dědiny“ se brzy ozvaly hlasy, volající po jejím udržení natrvalo. Iniciátorem těchto snah byl opět F. A. Šubert. Podle něho výstavní „dědina“ v mnohém předčila stockholmský Skansen. Už v září 1895 svolalo kuratorium budoucího muzea národopisný sjezd, ze kterého povstala rezoluce, požadující „uchování výstavní dědiny i se skupinou valašskou“. Mělo o ni pečovat vznikající Národopisné muzeum československé.

Obtížná a zdlouhavá jednání byla zmařena špatným technickým stavem objektů. Nebyly stavěny na pevných základech a navíc stály na území, zaplavovaném při povodních. V roce 1899 navštívil výstavu architekt Josef Materna a podal veřejnosti zdrcující zprávu: většina objektů je napadena dřevokaznou houbou. (Valašská osada ve výčtu napadených objektů chyběla; snad to bylo pro její položení na pahorku.) A tak v roce 1901 neslavně skončily pokusy o první velké muzeum v přírodě ve střední Evropě. Většina trámů se prodala na palivové dříví, menší část jako stavební dříví.

V čase zániku výstavy získalo nově ustanovené Národopisné muzeum československé letohrádek v Kinské zahradě pod Petřínem. Právě tam měl vzniknout „národopisný sad“, kam by se převezlo alespoň to, co se ještě z „národopisné dědiny“ dalo zachránit. Z toho mála, co se převezlo, se dřevěný kostelík udržel jen do roku 1913, a tak tu zůstala

5

6

7

8

5/ Jaroměřská chalupa
6/ Kopaničářská chalupa
7/ Kovárna
8/ Kostel v československé vesnici

valašská zvonička od Vsetína, vyřezávaný kříž z Bojanovic u Hodonína a zděná boží muka ze Žižkova.

Naděje na vybudování velkého muzea v přírodě v Praze ožila v roku 1910 v souvislosti s návrhem na uspořádání Slovanské výstavy v Praze v roce 1914, později přesunuté na rok 1916. Součástí výstavy se měla stát „slovanská dědina", počítající padesát až osmdesát staveb jednotlivých slovanských národů – kopií, ale také originálů. Ideové zdůvodnění a výběr objektů vypracoval Lubor Niederle, který chtěl – v duchu své evoluční teorie o vývoji slovanského domu – doložit slovanskou jednotu a zároveň i specifičnost jednotlivých slovanských národů. Válka a poválečné uspořádání východní Evropy odsoudily i tento návrh do role nerealizovaných projektů. (Podobně ostatně dopadl i záměr Maďarů po milenijní výstavě v Budapešti v roce 1896.)

Centrální orgány nové republiky, myšlence muzea v přírodě příliš nepřály; převládalo spíše hledisko umělecko-historické školy, zdůrazňující péči o umělecké sbírky. Přesto se něco i v Praze podařilo. V roce 1929 se sem převezl a později i pod Petřínem postavil dřevěný kostelík karpatského typu z Medveďova u Mukačeva. V letech 1936 až 1938 byl konečně schválen návrh Drahomíry Stránské na zřízení národopisného muzea v přírodě v Praze. Návrh vycházel z územního hlediska, ze zastoupení jednotlivých stavebních typů z celého Československa. Ke kostelíku z Medveďova přibyl Joklův dům z Čičman, ale k jeho postavení a k realizaci muzea v přírodě už nedošlo; v tomto případě pro druhou světovou válku.

Mimopražským centrem snah o vybudování muzea v přírodě se stala východní Morava. Počátek těchto snah hledejme v mimořádném úspěchu Valašska na pražské výstavě v roce 1895. Začneme nerealizovanými návrhy.

Při příležitosti příprav na Výstavu Slovácka podal v roce 1912 profesor gymnázia v Uherském Hradišti Bohumil Fišer návrh na postavení „Slovácké vesnice". Realizace záměru byla zmařena válkou. Při stejné příležitosti, tedy při Výstavě Slovácka v roce 1937, předložil návrh na slovácký skansen v Uherském Hradišti Jan Húsek. O něco později přichází Antonín Václavík s myšlenkou postavit nevelký skansen Luhačovského Zálesí.

Nejblíže k realizaci měl projekt Bartošova národopisného muzea v přírodě vypracovaný advokátem Ladislavem Ruttem. K výstavbě bylo vybráno místo u Gottwaldova, na pomezí Hané, Slovácka a Valašska; tyto tři regiony měly tvořit náplň skansenu. Jednání o výstavbě, probíhající v letech 1937 až 1947, nakonec nebyla úspěšná.

Valašské muzeum v přírodě

Jeden projekt se však přece jen uskutečnil. Stalo se tak v Rožnově pod Radhoštěm, kde v roce 1925 vzniklo Valašské muzeum v přírodě jako jedno z prvních muzeí tohoto druhu ve střední Evropě.

Jeho vznik je svázán se jmény bratrů Jaroňků, Bohumíra (1866–1933) a Aloise (1870–1944). Pocházeli z Malenovic u Gottwaldova, z prosté rodiny, vyznačující se zájmem o umění a tvůrčí činnost všeho druhu. Jejich umělecká dráha byla velmi pestrá – malířství, keramika, gobelíny, umělecká i reportážní fotografie a také lidové umění. Zejména u Bohumíra se brzy setkáváme se zájmem o lidovou architekturu. Obdivoval se jí už jako mladý student při školních výletech z Nového Jičína do Štramberka. Jaroňkovo jméno nacházíme už na první schůzi krajinského výboru valašského. Nejméně dvakrát pobýval na Národopisné výstavě českoslovanské v Praze roku 1895; přijel tam z Budapešti, kde tehdy pracoval, i s velkou skupinou přátel. Po pražské Národopisné výstavě Bohumír navštívil i výstavu v Budapešti v roce 1896, kde také stála velká národopisná dědina a také tam usilovali o její udržení. Vše usměrnila cesta Aloise Jaroňka do skandinávských zemí v roce 1909. Navštívil muzea v přírodě Aarhusu v Dánsku, Bygdøy u Osla a Skansen ve Stockholmu. V tom čase se v mysli obou bratrů trvale uchytila myšlenka valašského muzea v přírodě. Inspirovalo je především malebné rožnovské náměstí, na kterém se uchovaly impozantní roubené patrové domy.

První projekt rožnovského skansenu, zpracovaný Bohumírem v roce 1913 jako temperová malba, měl šťastný osud. Na výstavě ve Vídni o něj projevil zájem sám následník trůnu a snad prý jeho přičiněním získal Rožnov 8 000 korun na zakoupení radnice, vystavěné v roce 1781. Významnou oporou všeho snažení Jaroňků se stal rožnovský muzejní spolek založený v roce 1911. To již byl nejvyšší čas k zásahu, neboť dřevěné domy na náměstí, patřící ponejvíce rožnovským měšťanům a obchodníkům, mizely jeden po druhém a místo nich se stavěly domy zděné. Stará radnice se měla přenést do městského parku jako základ muzea v přírodě. Nakonec zůstala na svém místě, ale už jako majetek muzejního spolku. Další plány přerušila válka.

K výstavbě muzea v přírodě došlo až za několik let po válce. Jaroňci a muzejní spolek pohotově využili příznivé atmosféry přípravy Valašského roku 1925 a navrhli a prosadili, aby se tyto velké národopisné slavnosti konaly už v areálu nového muzea v přírodě. V dubnu 1925 se začalo s demontáží radnice a v červenci, v čase konání Valašského roku, stály na mýtině v parku už dva velké domy – vedle radnice i měšťanský dům Billův z konce 17. století – a také několik staveb drobných – brána, zvonička, studna, včelín aj.

Na slavnostech Valašského roku vystupovalo na dva tisíce tanečníků, zpěváků a muzikantů z velkého počtu valašských obcí a jejich vystoupení, v kterém předvedli výroční i rodinné obyčeje, písně a tance, vážící se ke konkrétním slavnostním i pracovním událostem roku, zhlédlo více než dvacet tisíc návštěvníků. Valašský rok se stal významným předělem ve vývoji valašské lidové kultury. S plnou vážností a s podporou široké veřejnosti se zde prvně proklamovala a dokumentovala nutnost péče o lidovou kulturu, jejíž tradiční podoba rychle zanikala.

V tomto ovzduší se výstavba muzea dále úspěšně rozvíjela. Z náměstí se převezla Vaškova hospoda, stavba pocházející snad ze 16. století, další drobné stavby a významně se pokročilo ve sběru předmětů a ve vybavování interiérů. V tomto ovzduší Bohumír Jaroněk spřádá své vize „živého muzea". Prozrazují jakousi tvůrčí nespokojenost s dosavadní výstavbou.

Píše o tom: „Muzeum musí být živé a pravdivé. Jeho umístění do parku ho svírá. Nejsou zde potoky, louky, pole, ovocné stromy. O co lépe by muzeum vyhlíželo na pasece!"

Zájem představitelů státní a politické moci o rožnovský skansen a o lidovou kulturu však z roku na rok opadal a tento trend dovršila hospodářská krize. Kopie fojtství z Velkých Karlovic byla poslední stavbou Bohumírovy éry. Veřejnosti byla zpřístupněna v roce 1933, v roce jeho úmrtí.

Útlum stavební činnosti trval až do padesátých let. K jistému oživení došlo na počátku druhé světové války, kdy skupina tesařského mistra Michala Fabiana vystavěla podle dochovaných plánů kopii dřevěného kostela z Větřkovic u Příbora; originál vyhořel v roce 1887. Na náklady se složili rožnovští občané.

V roce 1953 přešlo Valašské muzeum do vlastnictví socialistického státu a na půdě Krajského muzea v Gottwaldově, jehož pobočkou se stalo, se rozhodlo o jeho dostavbě. Byla motivována především dvěma skutečnostmi. Jako důsledek industrializace kraje a zakládání JZD lidové stavby mizely po stovkách. Druhá skutečnost patří do oblasti ideové. Stavby rožnovského skansenu reprezentovaly pouze honosnou architekturu zámožné vrstvy obyvatel – měšťanů a vesnického fojta. Nový záměr akcentoval třídní a sociální hledisko: dostavba muzea měla dokumentovat život prostého obyvatele Valašska, jeho práci, umění, ale i sociální postavení.

Hledání optimální koncepce

V čase formování koncepce dostavby Valašského muzea se právě v Rožnově v roce 1958 sešla první celostátní konference o muzeích v přírodě a o ochraně lidového stavitelství. Zúčastnili se jí pracovníci památkové péče, muzeí, etnografové a architekti z mnoha vědeckých a kulturních institucí a vyslovili své názory, často dosti protichůdné.

Etnografové a pracovníci muzeí považovali muzeum v přírodě za expozici, specifickým způsobem zobrazující život lidu, zejména typy lidových staveb a způsob bydlení.

Pracovníci památkové péče zdůrazňovali především záchrannou funkci muzea v přírodě. Lidová stavba měla na svém původním místě zůstat co nejdéle a jen při jejím ohrožení se mělo rozhodnout o jejím převezení do záchranného regionálního skansenu; tam měly být stavby řazeny podle své funkce, měla tu tedy stát řada obytných domů, řada stodol, řada komor apod. Výjimečné postavení však mohly mít centrální skanseny český, moravský a slovenský a také Rožnov měl pokračovat v započatém směru.

Na konferenci byla po rušném jednání přijata koncepce prosazovaná pracovníky památkové péče. Záhy se však prokázala nereálnost požadavku udržet hodnotné lidové stavby na jejich původním místě. Z šesti tisíc lidových staveb vybraných pro ochranu in situ se jich každoročně několik set odepisovalo a u jiných se jejich okolí změnilo natolik, že právě ve skansenu našly vhodnější prostředí. K tomu ještě přistoupily obtíže s udržováním těchto staveb in situ a s jejich kulturním využitím. Nově vznikající regionální muzea v přírodě se naštěstí nikde nesmířila s funkcí skladu ohrožených staveb. Nedošlo ani k výstavbě centrálních reprezentačních skansenů u Prahy v údolí Šárka a v Brně pod hradem Veveří.

Vývoj na Slovensku měla usměrnit konference v Dolném Smokovci, která v mnohém navázala na konferenci rožnovskou. Nejvíce se tu mluvilo o třech skansenech – ve Vysokých Tatrách, u Demänovských jeskyní a v Martině. Skutečnost – až na poslední jmenované město – dopadla jinak.

V roce 1971 se ve Vysokých Tatrách sešla celoevropská konference ICOMOS, konference mezinárodní organizace, pověřené péčí o uchování lidového stavitelství. Závěry konference příznivě ovlivnily vývoj v našich zemích. Konference se vyslovila pro rozvoj muzeí v přírodě a podpořila požadavek, aby se pro přenesené stavby vytvořilo nebo našlo vhodné přírodní prostředí. V této souvislosti byla vyzvednuta funkce regionálních muzeí v přírodě.

V současnosti je výstavba našich muzeí v přírodě koordinována dvěma metodickými centry – rožnovským a martinským muzeem a také pracovní skupinou pro muzea v přírodě při československé sekci Mezinárodní komise pro studium lidové kultury v Karpatech a na Balkáně.

Nová česká muzea v přírodě

Šedesátá a sedmdesátá léta zbavila rožnovské muzeum přívlastku „ojedinělé“. Postupně vzniklo patnáct muzeí tohoto typu a v současnosti se zvažuje výstavba některých dalších. Jejich založení, správní a metodické zařazení a zejména jejich zaměření nebylo výsledkem realizace nějaké celostátní koncepce; takové hledisko chybělo. Tu záviselo především na iniciativě a možnostech tvůrců. Stavělo se podle rozdílných koncepcí, což přineslo i jeden klad: tato muzea se vyhnula stereotypu a představila lidovou kulturu z několika hledisek. Ta dvě základní – „památkářské“, zdůrazňující autentičnost, a etnografické, stavící na komplexnosti pohledu – se mísila v různých proporcích a někdy ani nezáleželo na firmě zřizovatele. Například koncepce výstavby muzea v Kouřimi, kterou realizuje Okresní muzeum v Kolíně, je bližší hledisku památkové péče než koncepce výstavby areálu lidových staveb Vysočina, jejímž garantem je Krajské středisko památkové péče a ochrany přírody v Pardubicích. Jistá živelnost se ostatně odráží i v nejednotných názvech nových muzeí v přírodě: národopisné muzeum, muzeum v přírodě, soubor lidových staveb a techniky, expozice lidové architektury, muzeum vesnice apod.

Na samém počátku jejich vzniku byla někdy jen myšlenka, jindy stará chalupa jako odkaz podobného záměru předků (Přerov nad Labem) nebo jen sbírka fotografií lidových staveb a snaha udržet je při životě (soubor staveb Vysočina).

Z českých muzeí má nejstarší tradici Polabské národopisné muzeum v Přerově nad Labem. Jeho počátky sahají až k Národopisné výstavě československé z roku 1895 a snad i k Zemské jubilejní výstavě v Praze v roce 1891. Věhlas těchto výstav vedl bývalého majitele přerovského panství, cestovatele a etnografa Ludvíka Salvátora Toskánského k svéráznému činu. Koupil bývalou panskou kovárnu, stojící uprostřed návsi, a dal ji přestavět na „staročeskou chalupu", a to zcela v duchu známé stavby stejného jména na Jubilejní výstavě. Vybavil interiér, přibyla studna, zvonička a dobový plot a tak vzniklo malé národopisné muzeum, zpřístupněné už v roce 1900.

Dnes se do Přerova nad Labem přenášejí chalupy, špýchary a jiné lidové stavby ze středního Polabí a k muzeu patří i některé původní usedlosti, které ve vesnici stály. Umístění muzea uprostřed vesnice má na jedné straně klad v návaznosti na urbanismus tradiční středočeské vsi, na druhé straně muzeu chybí místo pro další rozšíření.

Také v národopisném muzeu v Třebízi na Slánsku jsou základem objekty in situ, v tomto případě náves obce s rázovitým statkem Cífkovým a s rodným domem spisovatele Václava Beneše Třebízského, který je veřejnosti přístupný už od roku 1904.

Ještě více domů na původním místě najdeme v obci Vysočina, v osadě Veselý Kopec, která tvoří ještě s některými dalšími lokalitami základ chráněného památkového území, zvaného Soubor lidových staveb a řemesel Vysočina. V řídce osídleném podhůří Českomoravské vrchoviny jsou jednotlivé památkové lokality vzdáleny kus cesty od sebe. Vysočina se nejvíce blíží představě tzv. ekomuzea, kde se v původní podobě uchovává celá krajina a v ní i sídla obyvatel a jejich tradiční činnost.

O místo mezi muzei v přírodě se hlásí také Zubrnice, obec v okrese Ústí nad Labem, s památkovým areálem uprostřed obce a s tradiční železničkou.

Zcela jinak je koncipováno Muzeum vesnice v Kouřimi. Staví se na volné ploše, na místě velkého třešňového sadu a jeho tvůrcové zde chtějí demonstrovat stavební techniku a vývoj lidového domu od staveb primitivních po honosné statky; jednotlivé stupně vývoje dokládá stavbami z Čech i Moravy. Není to však koncepce definitivní. Položení muzea nedaleko známého archeologického naleziště nabízí i jiné řešení.

Zatímco severní Moravu, resp. její karpatskou část reprezentuje rožnovské Valašské muzeum v přírodě, nížinný a úrodný jihovýchod Moravy má svoji Strážnici. Nezůstalo jen u písní a tanců: na louky za zámeckým parkem se stěhují domy z Horňácka, drobné stavby z Kopanic i vinohradnické „búdy" z Dolňácka.

Slovenské múzeá v prírode

Slovenská cesta k múzeu v prírode sa v mnohom podobala na českú. Hlavnou motiváciou sa najmä v predvojnových rokoch stal zdravý patriotizmus. Významným strediskom všetkého úsilia bola Muzeálna slovenská spoločnosť so sídlom v Martine. Výstavbou skanzenu (tento termín sa vtedy používal) bol už v roku 1930 poverený národopisný odbor Spoločnosti. A hoci výsledok tohto úsilia zaradíme medzi nerealizované projekty, má svoje miesto v dejinách našich múzeí v prírode. Autorom projektu bol Karel Chotek, náš prvý profesor národopisu.

Návrh predpokladal zastúpenie všetkých typov ľudových stavieb zo Slovenska, ale aj z moravského Slovácka, ako aj obydlia Slovákov v zahraničí. Jednotlivé usadlosti mali obývať dedinčania z miesta pôvodnej stavby. Mali byť oblečení v kroji a venovať sa špecifickým prácam a remeslám svojho kraja a svoje výrobky predávať návštevníkom. Tak by sa konzervoval, ako doslova napísal Chotek, spôsob života ľudu.

Slovenský skanzen mal stáť na mieste nazývanom Opleto. Rátalo sa tu aj s jazerom, ktoré by vzniklo prehradením potoka. Pri hrádzi mali svoje miesto loďky rybárov a na jazere dom na koloch, teda dom z prehistorických časov. Počítalo sa však aj s plavárňou a v zime s korčuľovaním. Pri kostolíku sa mali konať ľudové slávnosti. Za projektanta a vedúceho výstavby navrhol Chotek Dušana Jurkoviča.

Za slovenský skanzen sa vtedy staval aj znalec slovenského ľudového umenia Josef Vydra a ešte pred vojnou a hneď po nej slovenský národopisec a múzejník Ján Geryk. Iný národopisec Vilém Pražák sa priklonil skôr k zriadeniu rezervácií, teda usadlostí a celých osád in situ, obývaných pôvodnými obyvateľmi.

Rovnako ako v Čechách i na Slovensku vojna nadlho prerušila túto perspektívu. Nová a rozhodujúca iniciatíva sa dostavila až v druhej polovici päťdesiatych rokov. A opäť dve rozdielne koncepcie, jedna od pamiatkárov, druhá od národopiscov, vyúsťujúce do názorového stretnutia v Rožnove (1958) a v Dolnom Smokovci (1959).

Z významných predstaviteľov slovenskej vedy a kultúry sa vtedy za skanzen vyslovili národný umelec Janko Alexy a národopisci Rudolf Bednárik a Ján Mjartan. Z nich práve posledný prispel k riešeniu rozporu jasným stanoviskom. Na rozdiel od pracovníkov pamiatkovej starostlivosti nezdôrazňoval natoľko umeleckú hodnotu domu; podľa Mjartana je niekedy minimálna. Dom v skanzene má predovšetkým dokumentovať svoju základnú funkciu, t. j. bývanie, ďalej prípravu stravy, rodinný život i zvyky a iné prejavy národnej špecifickosti. Ďalší vývoj sa našťastie uberal v Mjartanových intenciách.

Konkretizáciou idey dozrievajúcej niekoľko desaťročí sa stalo Múzeum slovenskej dediny v Martine. Je u nás jediným múzeom v prírode, reprezentujúcim ľudové staviteľstvo a spôsob života národa v jeho celistvosti, so všetkými kladmi i nedostatkami tejto idey. Jednotlivé slovenské regióny tu tvoria samostatné osady, ktoré budú v budúcnosti oživené ukážkami práce a zvykmi. V Jahodníckych hájoch pri Martine, kde toto múzeum vyrastá od šesťdesiatych rokov, vystavali dosiaľ osadu z Oravy a z Liptova a ďalšie stavby zo severozápadného Slovenska.

V šesťdesiatych a sedemdesiatych rokoch vznikol na Slovensku celý rad významných regionálnych múzeí v prírode. Najstaršiu národopisnú expozíciu na Slovensku nájdeme v Bardejove, v Šarišskom múzeu. Verejnosti bola sprístupnená už v roku 1965. Znalci ľudového umenia tu obdivujú najmä dva drevené kostoly východného rítu, ktoré pochádzajú z 18. storočia; jeden z nich sem bol premiestený už v roku 1936. Ďalší rozvoj múzea je obmedzený, lebo celý areál leží v oblasti (bazéne) liečebných prameňov. Najväčšou rozlohou sa môže pochváliť Múzeum kysuckej dediny vo Vychylovke. Rozsiahly areál múzea (143 ha), zaberajúci horské údolie a svahy okolo neho, vytvára vhodné podmienky na vyjadrenie sídelnej špecifiky Kysúc. Originálnou technickou pamiatkou, využívanou na prepravu návštevníkov, je úzkokoľajná železnica, pomocou ktorej sa v minulosti prepravovalo drevo. Aj skanzen na susednej Orave vyniká atraktívnym prostredím. Jeho tvorcovia našli preň miesto v neveľkom údolí horského potoka priamo pod štítmi Roháčov, pri obci Zuberec. Medzi unikáty sa tu zaraďuje zemianska usadlosť z Vyšného Kubína z roku 1752. Ľudové stavby ukrajinskej menšiny, žijúcej na východnom Slovensku, našli útočište v skanzene vo Svidníku, pri Múzeu ukrajinskej kultúry. Ich vysoké strechy sú zväčša pokryté šindľom. Osobité postavenie má Banské múzeum v prírode v Banskej Štiavnici. Nie je iba technickou pamiatkou, demonštruje aj technológiu baníckej práce, ako aj spôsob života baníkov za kapitalizmu.

Perspektívy

Overené je praxou, že čím rýchlejšie spejeme k modernému spôsobu života – so všetkými kladmi a nedostatkami, ktoré k tomuto dianiu patria, tým viac si vážime to, čo pomaly – s premenami prírody i spoločnosti – strácame. Tu záleží na vedení spoločnosti a na odborníkoch, ako tento vývoj usmernia. Práve socialistická spoločnosť má záujem i prostriedky na to, aby sa to dialo v mene kvality života.

Už sme si vysvetlili, kedy sa naša spoločnosť začala zaujímať o hodnoty tradičnej ľudovej kultúry a aké premeny tento záujem prekonal. Premeny záujmu boli vždy určované potrebami konkrétnej spoločnosti. Potrebami, ktoré podporovali ideológiu i hospodársku politiku vládnúcej triedy. Až potom to bol záujem spoločnosti o ochranu alebo aspoň dokumentáciu zanikajúcich hodnôt, v našom prípade folklóru, odevu, stavieb, prípadne ľudového výtvarného umenia.

Aké miesto má v tomto dianí múzeum v prírode, aká je jeho funkcia v súčasnej modernej spoločnosti? Jeho základná funkcia sa nemení: stáva sa opatrovateľom kultúrneho dedičstva nášho ľudu a špecifickou, atraktívnou formou zoznamuje návštevníkov so životom našich predkov. Jeho funkcia sa však rozširuje o nové významné úlohy. Vyplynuli zo skutočnosti, že v novobudovanej socialistickej spoločnosti tradičný spôsob života rýchlo zaniká, pretože stráca svoje funkčné opodstatnenie. Miznú pôvodné ľudové stavby, kroje, ľudová strava, zo života sa vytrácajú obyčaje, široká oblasť folklóru a ľudového umenia, ale aj minulý spôsob myslenia, minulé sociálne a výrobné väzby, ľudové slávnosti a ďalšie zložky ľudovej kultúry. Prežívajú len tie, ktoré sa prispôsobili novému systému hodnôt: pôvodné ľudové stavby sa využívajú ako rekreačné chalupy, ľudový nábytok sa stáva súčasťou moderného interiéru, tradičné textilné techniky, materiál i ornamenty slúžia na moderné obliekanie, niektoré tradičné jedlá a nápoje sa stávajú krajovými špecialitami, nastáva netušená renesancia folklóru, tradičný úžitkový predmet dostáva novú dekoratívnu funkciu a na ten účel sa nanovo vyrába. Sú to isto zdravé trendy vývoja a múzeum v prírode ich rozvoj plne podporuje.

No i tá základná funkcia opatrovateľa tradície a funkcia média, ktoré predstavuje našej spoločnosti obraz našej minulosti, sa v súčasnosti mení tak z hľadiska kvality, ako aj z hľadiska významu. V rokoch pred nástupom socializmu stále pretrvávala na vidieku tradičná poľnohospodárska a remeselnícka výroba a v obciach stálo veľa domov tradičnej podoby – a to platí aj o niektorých iných zložkách ľudovej tradície. Preto sa do skanzenu prevážali skôr vzácne a zaujímavé stavby a rovnaký prístup bol aj pri vybavovaní stavieb. Na druhej strane neboli také atraktívne remeselnícke a iné tradičné techniky. Mladý návštevník skanzenu dnes už nepozná starú dedinu. Predovšetkým pre neho a najmä pre budúce generácie musíme vytvárať pravdivý komplexný obraz našej minulosti, v ktorom práve bežné veci nesmú chýbať.

V tomto smere najďalej postúpilo rožnovské Valašské muzeum v přírodě. Jeho cieľom sa stala pravdivá rekonštrukcia, model valašskej dediny a malého mesta. Všetko podložil rozsiahly výskum ľudového staviteľstva na Valašsku. Iba tak sa mohla stanoviť typologická štruktúra valašskej dediny a mestečka, ako aj urbanistické kritériá. Taká modelová štruktúra napríklad určila, koľko má typická horská dedina veľkých sedliakov, koľko maloroľníkov, ktoré remeslá tu boli obvyklé, ako boli rozložené polia v dedine a pod.

Až potom sa mohlo začať s výberom konkrétnych stavebných objektov a ich zariadenia. Vedecky stanovený typ sa teda dokladá komplexnou prezentáciou spôsobu života konkrétnej rodiny v konkrétnom čase. Ako príklad poslúži mlyn postavený v múzeu v roku 1983. Štruktúrny model počítal s mlynom z podhorskej obce. Konkretizáciou tohto zámeru je výber a výstavba mlyna na vodný pohon, ktorý predstavuje konkrétne výrobné a sociálne väzby, ako boli dokumentované u rodiny Petřvalskovcov vo Veľkých Karloviciach v troch posledných desaťročiach 19. storočia.

Predsa však takej modelovej dedine a mestečku niečo chýba. Je to predovšetkým každodenná hospodárska činnosť každého druhu, starostlivosť o rodinu, ale aj spievanie, zvyky, slávnosti a i. Ak je však múzeum postavené podľa zásad konkrétnosti a komplexnosti, môžeme sa o demonštráciu týchto aktivít v múzeu pokúsiť. Tieto pokusy sa napokon uskutočňujú od začiatku existencie skanzenov a od toho času sa datuje aj nedôvera k takým pokusom. Výsledky niektorých skanzenov však túto skepsu čoraz viac potláčajú.

Najväčšia pozornosť právom patrí poľnohospodárstvu. V Rožnove sa usilujú o uzavreté pracovné cykly. Pastvinu premieňajú tradičným spôsobom na ornú pôdu a vysievajú do nej dnes už neznáme druhy obilnín: ikricu, špaldu, tengeľ, tatarku, bér a iné. Potom sa zberá za kosou, snopy obilia sa sušia na obilných koloch a napokon mlátia cepmi. Obilie sa odvezie do mlyna a z múky sa v starej peci pečie chlieb. Podobné okruhy vytvára aj salašnícka produkcia, na ktorej začiatku je ovčie mlieko a vlna. Prirátajme k tomu ešte kolekciu vyše sto starých odrôd ovocných stromov a ešte väčší počet rastlinných druhov okrasných kvetov, používaných na Valašsku, ako aj tzv. živé gazdovstvo na Matochovej usadlosti s plným stavom všetkých hospodárskych zvierat.

Druhý okruh aktivít patrí ľudovému remeslu a ľudovým umelcom. S múzeom ich spolupracuje vyše osemdesiat a okrem výrobkov na predaj predvádzajú svoju zručnosť početným návštevníkom múzea. Iniciatíva múzea na tomto poli pomáha udržať pri živote staré tradičné techniky. K potešujúcim skutočnostiam patrí zistenie, že sa s týmito technikami zoznamujú a naďalej ich rozvíjajú mladí ľudia.

Najväčšiu popularitu si získala tretia sféra aktivít, folklór, zvyky a všetko, čo k nim patrí. V zhode s obyčajovým kalendárom i s termínmi poľnohospodárskych prác a slávností sa v múzeu po celý rok konajú programy tradičného folklóru v podaní súborov ľudovej tvorivosti a autentických interpretov. Napríklad návštevníci múzea mohli v roku 1985 v rámci 4. Valašského roka vidieť okolo sedemdesiat programov. Začali sa fašiangami a jarným zvykoslovím a končili sa zimným jarmokom a koledou. K najväčším akciám tohto druhu patria Rožnovské slávnosti a Valašský jarmok.

Rožnovské múzeum tak plní odkaz svojho zakladateľa B. Jaroňka, ktorý si želal, aby sa skanzen stal živým múzeom. Napokon Rožnov nezostáva v tejto tendencii osamotený. O podobné aktivity sa už pokúšajú na Veselom kopci v obci Vysočina, v Strážnici, v Třebízi a aj v slovenských skanzenoch v Zuberci, vo Vychylovke a v Bardejovských kúpeľoch.

Tak múzeum v prírode zachraňuje, uchováva a niekedy aj ďalej rozvíja všetko hodnotné, čo sa z tradičnej ľudovej kultúry zachrániť dá. Pre tých starších sa stáva spomienkou, tí mladší v skanzene objavujú svoju minulosť, alebo – povedané slovami zakladateľa prvého skanzenu Artura Hazelia – poznávajú sami seba.

Jaroslav Štika

1 ZUBRNICE
2 TŘEBÍZ
3 KOUŘIM
4 PŘEROV NAD LABEM
5 VYSOČINA
6 STRÁŽNICE
7 ROŽNOV POD RADHOŠTĚM
8 MARTIN
9 NOVÁ BYSTRICA – VYCHYLOVKA
10 ZUBEREC – BRESTOVÁ
11 PRIBYLINA
12 STARÁ ĽUBOVŇA
13 BARDEJOVSKÉ KÚPELE
14 SVIDNÍK
15 BANSKÁ ŠTIAVNICA

Soustředění objektů lidové architektury Českého středohoří ZUBRNICE

Muzeum je vlastně celá vesnice i se železniční stanicí, k níž se z údolí Labe prodírá nedávno obnovená dráha. Uchované památky lidového stavitelství jsou charakteristické pro celé severní Čechy. Muzeum leží v dramatické krajině hraničních hor, jen několik desítek kilometrů od devastované krajiny severočeské uhelné pánve.

Ансамбль объектов народного зодчества из Чешских средних гор в с. Зубрнице. Музеем, в сущности, является вся деревня, включая железнодорожную станцию, к которой из долины Лабе проходит недавно восстановленная железная дорога. Сохранившиеся памятники народного зодчества характерны для всей северной Чехии. Музей расположен в драматической местности пограничных гор, лишь в нескольких десятках километров от опустошённой ныне местности северочешского угольного бассейна.

Die Konzentration von Objekten volkstümlicher Architektur des Böhmischen Mittelgebirges Zubrnice. Zum Museum zählt eigentlich das gesamte Dorf und der Zugbahnhof, zu dem sich die unlängst erneuerte Bahnstrecke aus dem Elbtal schlängelt. Die erhaltenen Denkmäler volkstümlicher Bauweise sind für ganz Nordböhmen charakteristisch. Das Museum liegt in einer dramatischen Landschaft angrenzender Berge, nur einige -zig Kilometer von der devastierten Landschaft des nordböhmischen Kohlebeckens entfernt.

Collection of folk architecture objects from the Bohemian Middle Mountains region at Zubrnice. Actually the whole village is a museum, including the railway station to which the recently re-established stretch penetrates from the Elbe valley. The preserved specimens of folk architecture are characteristic for the whole north of Bohemia. The museum lies in the dramatic landscape of the border mountains, only several tens of kilometres far from the devastated region of the North Bohemian coal basin.

I

1

2

I

3

Stavební konstrukce, ať již jde o zdivo (5), roubení (3) i hrázdění (1, 6), se zde vzájemně prolínají. Na návsi nás upoutá štít statku s domovním číslem 61 (4). Takové zdobení štítů je rozšířeno v celé severovýchodní části Čech. Do Zubrnice se přenesly i některé typické stavební objekty ze sousedních vsí. Patří mezi ně špýchar z Lochočic (1, 6) a studna na návsi (2) ze Střížovic u Českého Újezda. Je datovaná; na její kamenné obrubě najdeme letopočet 1695.

Строительные конструкции – кладка (5), крепление (3) и зарубка (1, 6) – здесь взаимно переплетаются. На деревенской площади привлечет наше внимание фронтон имения с номером дома 61 (4). Такого типа отделка фронтонов распространена во всей северо-восточной части Чехии. В с. Зубрнице были перенесены и некоторые типичные объекты строительства из соседних деревень. К ним относится амбар из с. Лохочице (1, 6) и колодец на деревенской площади (2) из с. Стршижовице под г. Чески-Уйезд. Он датирован – на его каменном бордюре мы находим дату 1695 г.

4

5

Die Baukonstruktionen durchdringen sich gegenseitig, ob es um Mauerwerk (5), Zimmerung (3) oder Schrämung (1, 6) geht. Auf dem Dorfplatz zieht ein Schild des Guts mit der Hausnummer 61 an (4). Solche Schildverzierungen sind im gesamten nordöstlichen Teil Böhmens verbreitet. Nach Zubrnice wurden ebenfalls einige typische Bauobjekte aus Nachbardörfern überführt. Dazu gehören der Speicher aus Lochočice (1, 6) und der Brunnen auf dem Dorfplatz (2) aus Střížovice bei Český Újezd. Dieser ist datiert; auf seiner Steineinfassung ist die Jahreszahl 1695 zu erkennen.

Types of construction, be it masonry (5), framework (3) as well as timber-work (1, 6) intermingle here. The village green will attract our attention because of the gable of the farmstead with house-number 61 (4). Such ornamentation of gables spread all over the north-eastern part of Bohemia. To Zubrnice, too, some typical architectonic objects from the neighbouring villages were transferred. They include the granary from Lochočice (1, 6) and the well on the village green (2) from Střížovice, part of Český Újezd. It is provided with a date; on its stone rim the inscription of 1695 can be found.

6

Národopisné muzeum
TŘEBÍZ

tvoří rovinná vesnice, typická pro úrodnou řepařskou oblast mezi Prahou, Krušnými horami a Českým středohořím. Jako muzejní expozice slouží pouze nejhodnotnější stavby na návsi. Dokládají způsob života a kulturní vyspělost zdejšího lidu v minulosti. Třebízská náves názorně dokládá, že stavební památka se může stát aktivní složkou života obce i v současnosti. Takovou je i rodný dům třebízského rodáka Václava Beneše Třebízského.

В этнографический музей Тршебиз входит деревня, расположенная на равнине, типичная для урожайной свекловодческой области между Прагой, Крушными горами и Чешскими средними горами. К экспозиции музея принадлежат только самые ценные постройки на деревенской площади. Они демонстрируют быт и культурный уровень местных жителей в прошлом. Деревенская площадь в с. Тршебиз является наглядным доказательством того, что памятник архитектуры может стать активным элементом жизни в современной деревне. Таким является и родной дом тршебизского уроженца Вацлава Бенеша Тршебизского.

Das Völkerkundemuseum Třebíz wird durch ein ebenes Dorf gebildet, das typisch für das fruchtbare Rübengebiet zwischen Prag, dem Erzgebirge und dem Böhmischen Mittelgebirge ist. Als Museumsstücke dienen nur die wertvollsten Bauten auf dem Dorfplatz. Sie belegen die Lebensweise und kulturelle Reife der hiesigen Menschen in der Vergangenheit. Der Třebízer Dorfplatz zeigt anschaulich, daß ein Baudenkmal aktive Komponente des Lebens einer Gemeinde in der Gegenwart sein kann. Dies trifft auch für das Geburtshaus des gebürtigen Třebízer, Václav Beneš, zu.

Ethnographic Museum at Třebíz is formed by a flat village, typical for the fertile sugar-beet region demarcated by Prague, the Ore Mountains and the Bohemian Middle Mountains. Only the most valuable buildings on the village green serve as the museum exposition. They attest the way of life and the cultural maturity of the local people in the past. The village green of Třebíz is an exemplary proof of the fact that an architectonic memorial can become an active part of the village life even in the present times. Such is the native house of Václav Beneš Třebízský, the writer who was born at Třebíz.

2

1

Nejbohatším ze všech byl statek Cífkův, stojící na návsi poblíže rybníka (1). Reprezentuje nejstarší zděnou lidovou architekturu Čech. Výstavný obytný dům Cífkova statku pochází ze 16. století, později však byl několikrát přestavěn (3). Do prostor Cífkova statku je umístěna expozice o vývoji zemědělství na Slánsku. Sousední usedlost číslo 2 má patrové hospodářské budovy, pocházející již z 19. století (2).

Самым богатым является имение Цифека, стоящее на деревенской площади вблизи от пруда (1). Оно демонстрирует старейший тип кирпичного народного зодчества Чехии. Благоустроенный жилой дом имения Цифека относится к XVI веку, однако, позднее он несколько раз перестраивался (3). На территории имения Цифека помещена экспозиция о развитии сельского хозяйства Сланской области. К соседнему имению № 2 относятся одноэтажные хозяйственные здания XIX века (2).

Das reichste aller Güter war das Cífkagut, das auf dem Dorfplatz neben dem Teich steht (1). Es präsentiert die älteste gemauerte volkstümliche Architektur Böhmens. Das Ausstellungswohnhaus des Cífkaguts stammt aus dem 16. Jahrhundert, später jedoch wurde es einige Male umgebaut (3). In den Räumlichkeiten des Cífkaguts wurde eine Exposition über die Entwicklung der Landwirtschaft im Gebiet um Slánsko eingerichtet. Das Nachbargut Nr. 2 hat Etagen- und Wirtschaftsgebäude, die aus dem 19. Jahrhundert stammen (2).

The richest farmstead of all was that owned by Cífka; it stands on the village green near the pond (1). It represents the oldest masonry folk architecture of Bohemia. The imposing living house of Cífka's farmstead originates from 16th century but it was re-built several times later on (3). The inner parts of Cífka's farmstead contain the exposition dealing with the development of agriculture in the Slaný region. The neighbouring estate No. 2 has two-storeyed homestead buildings originating already from 19th century (2).

2

3

2

1

2

3

Замыслом творцов экспозиции является стремление к максимальному оживлению интерьеров зданий. На кухне в имении Цифека до сих пор время от времени пекут хлеб и ватрушки (2), а в будущем планируются еще и дальнейшие демонстрации традиционного производства. К имению принадлежат и хлева с амбаром; они также относятся к XVI веку (1). К имению номер 10 примыкает маленькая избушка (3), демонстрирующая бедную жизнь т. наз. батраков, работавших в имении. На деревенской площади находится и лавка, оборудованная по образцу XIX века (4).

Das Anliegen der Schöpfer der Exposition besteht darin, so viel wie möglich das Interieur des Gebäudes zu beleben. In der Küche des Cífkaguts werden manchmal heute noch Brot und Kuchen gebacken (2) und in der Zukunft wird noch mit weiteren Beispielen traditioneller Produktion gerechnet. Zu dem Gut gehören ebenfalls Ställe mit einem Speicher; auch sie sind aus dem 16. Jahrhundert (1). Neben dem Gut Nr, 10 krümmt sich eine Ausgedingerhütte (3), die das notdürftige Leben der sog. Deputatarbeiter belegt. Zum Dorfplatz gehört außerdem ein Geschäft, das mustergemäß wie im 19. Jahrhundert ausgestattet ist (4).

Záměrem tvůrců expozice je co nejvíce oživit interiéry budov. V kuchyni Cífkova statku se ještě i dnes občas peče chléb a koláče (2) a v budoucnu tu počítají ještě s dalšími ukázkami tradiční výroby. Ke statku patří také chlévy se špýcharem; také ony pocházejí z 16. století (1). Pod statkem číslo 10 se krčí výměnkářská chalupa (3), dokládající bědný život tzv. deputátníků, kteří na statku pracovali. K návsi patří také obchod, vybavený podle vzoru z 19. století (4).

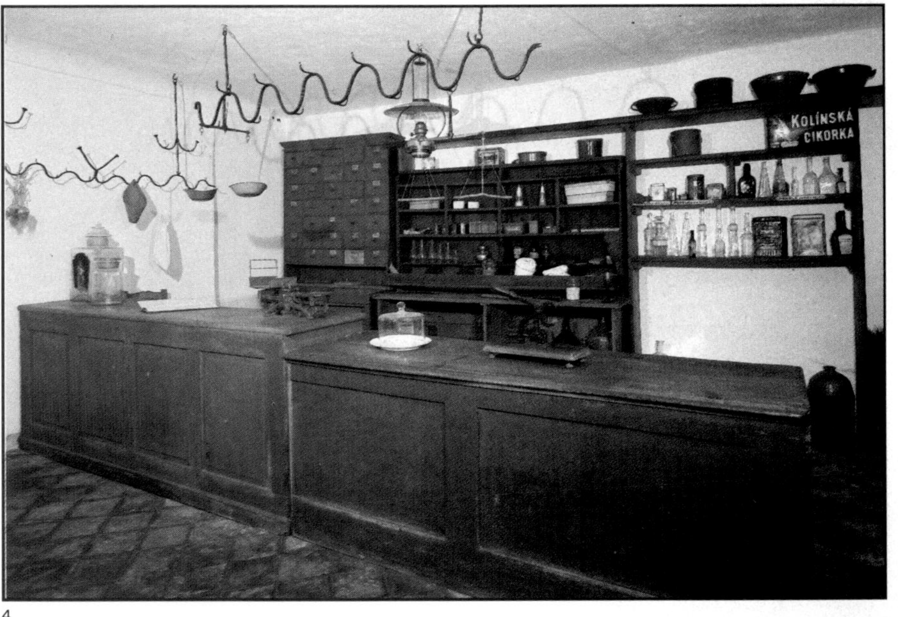

4

The exposition creators' intention has been as much as possible to enliven the interiors of the buildings. From time to time, bread and cakes are baked even nowadays in the kitchen of Cífka's farmstead (2) and further displays of traditional production are planned in future. The farmstead comprises also the stables with the granary; these, too, originate from 16th century (1). Huddled under the farmstead No. 10 stands the cottage for the retired (3) which demonstrates the miserable life of so called allowanced labourers who used to work in the farm. The village green is also complemented with a shop furnished according to the 19th century model (4).

5

2

1

2

3

4

K původním stavebním prvkům, zavádějícím nás do doby vzniku Cífkova statku, patří i okna staré sýpky (1, 2). Výměnek a statek číslo 2 vytvářejí charakteristickou zástavbu třebízské návsi (3). Patří k ní i zvonička a kostelík svatého Martina, postavený v 18. století (4). S obdivem si povšimneme, jak přirozeně jsou tyto stavby začleněny do urbanismu vsi i okolní přírody.

К исконным элементам строительства, вводящих нас в эпоху возникновения имения Цифека, относятся и окна старого амбара (1, 2). Дом старых хозяев и имение № 2 образуют характерную застройку деревенской площади села Тршебиз (3). К ней относится и небольшая колокольня и костел святого Мартина, построенный в XVIII веке (4). Здесь поражает нас естественность, с какой эти постройки вкючаются в урбанизм данной деревни и окружающей ее природы.

Zu den ursprünglichen Baukomponenten, die uns die Epoche der Entstehung des Cífkaguts näherbringen, gehören auch Fenster einer alten Speicheranlage (1, 2). Das Altenteil (Ausgedinge) und das Gut Nr. 2 bilden eine charakteristische Verbauung des Třebízer Dorfplatzes (3). Dazu gehören ebenfalls das Glockentürmchen und das Kirchlein (Martinskirche), das im 18. Jahrhundert erbaut wurde (4). Mit Bewunderung können wir registrieren, wie natürlich sich diese Bauten in die Architektur des Dorfes und der umgebenden Natur eingliedern.

Also the windows of the old granary (1, 2) lead us to the time of the foundation of Cífka's farmstead. The cottage of the retired and the farmstead No. 2 create the characteristic housing of the Třebíč village green (3). The little belfry and the little church of St. Martin built in 18th century (4) fit in there, too. We will notice with admiration in what natural way these buildings are incorporated within the urbanism of the village as well as the surrounding nature.

2

Muzeum vesnice KOUŘIM

vyrůstá ve velkém sadu na okraji města v charakteristické středočeské pahorkatině. Nedaleko odtud se nacházejí rozsáhlá prehistorická naleziště, dokládající život našich předků na úsvitu slovanského osídlení.

Музей деревни Коуржим возвышается в большом саду на окраине города в характерной среднечешской холмистой местности. Недалеко оттуда находятся обширные доисторические местонахождения, представляющие жизнь наших предков в самом начале славянского заселения.

Das Museum des Dorfes Kouřim wächst in einem großen Garten am Rande der Stadt, in einer charakteristischen mittelböhmischen Hügellandschaft empor. Nicht weit von hier befinden sich umfangreiche urgeschichtliche Fundstellen, die das Leben unserer Vorfahren zu Beginn der slawischen Ansiedlungen belegen.

Museum of the Village at Kouřim grows up in the large orchard on the outskirts of the town in the characteristic hilly landscape of Central Bohemia. Not far from here there are ample prehistoric finding places providing evidence of our ancestors' life on the dawn of Slavonic settlement.

3

1

2

3

4

Prozatím je zde nejvíce zastoupena lidová architektura ze středních Čech. Usedlost z Týřovic u Berouna (2) zastupuje charakteristické roubené stavby z malých vesniček kopcovité krajiny. Podobného rázu je i dům z Budče z horního Posázaví (1, 3). Stavebním dimenzím i hospodářské funkci usedlosti odpovídají i nevelké sýpky, komory a chlévy (4).

В самом большом количестве здесь пока представлена народная архитектура средней Чехии. Усадьба из с. Тыржовице-под-Бероунем (2) представляет характерные бревенчатые строения из маленьких деревушек холмистой местности. В подобном стиле построен и дом из с. Будеч верхнего Посазавья (1, 3,). Строительным размерам и хозяйственному назначению усадьбы соответствуют и небольшие амбары, чуланы и хлева (4).

Vorläufig ist hier die volkstümliche Architektur Mittelböhmens vertreten. Das Gehöft aus Týřovice bei Beroun (2) stellt charakteristische Zimmerbauten kleiner Dörfer in hügeliger Landschaft dar. Ähnlichen Charakter hat auch das Haus aus Budeč vom oberen Sázavaland (1, 3). Den Baudimensionen und der Wirtschaftsfunktion des Gehöftes entsprechen auch kleinere Speicher, Kammern und Ställe (4).

For the time being, the highest representation here is that of folk architecture from Central Bohemia. The estate from Týřovice near Beroun (2) represents the typical framework bouildings from the small villages of the hilly landscape. The house from Budeč from the upper stream of the the Sázava river (1, 3) displays a similar character, too. Building dimensions and production functions corresponding to an estate are found in smaller corn-lofts, lumber-rooms and stables (4).

3

1

2

3

Kouřimskému muzeu se daří instalace interiérů. K těm zdařilým patří i komora s nádobami a jiným tradičním zařízením na zpracování mléka (1) a světnice z domu z Budče dokládající způsob bydlení i lidové obyčeje, doložené lidovým obřadním pečivem (2). Neopomeňme též dřevěné arkádové sloupy v podsíni kovárny ze Starého Bydžova a jednu z nejstarších dochovaných hospodářských staveb, stodolu z Želejova na Jičínsku z roku 1660 (3).

Весьма удачным является устройство интерьеров музея в с. Коуржим. В особенности следует отметить интерьер чулана с бутылями и традиционными приборами для обработки молока (1), а также интерьер комнаты дома из с. Будеч, показывающий быт и народные обычаи (здесь представлены образцы народного обрядного печенья) (2). Следует отметить и деревянные колонны с аркадами в сенях кузницы из с. Стары-Биджов, а также одну из самых старых сохранившихся хозяйственных зданий – ригу из с. Желейов Йичинской области 1660 года (3).

Die Gestaltung des Interieurs des Museums in Kouřim ist gut gelungen. Zu den gediegenen gehören unter anderen die Kammer mit dem Geschirr und anderen traditionellen Einrichtungen für die Verarbeitung der Milch (1) sowie ein Stube aus dem Haus in Budeč, die die Wohnweise und Lebensbräuche darstellt, und zwar anhand von volkstümlichem Zeremoniengebäck (2). Man sollte keinesfalls die Arkadensäulen aus Holz im Vorhaus der Schmiede aus Starý Bydžov und eins der ältesten erhaltenen Wirtschaftsgebäude, die Scheune aus Želejov im Jičíner Gebiet aus dem Jahre 1660, übersehen (3).

The museum at Kouřim is well off with the interior installations. The successful ones comprise also the chamber with vessels and other traditional equipment for milk processing (1) and the room from the house from Budeč demonstrating the way of life as well as folk customs exemplified by folk ceremonial pastry (2). Let us not forget, either, the wooden arcade columns in the porch of the smithy from Starý Bydžov and one of the oldest preserved farming buildings, the barn from Želejov from the Jičín county from 1660 (3).

3

Polabské národopisné muzeum PŘEROV NAD LABEM

je vytvářeno lidovými stavbami přenesenými do jádra typické nížinné obce středočeského Polabí. V jeho blízkosti je i náves s rybníkem, zděnými statky a renesančním zámkem. Počátky muzea sahají až ke konci minulého století, k jeho rozvoji však došlo až v posledních letech.

Полабский этнографический музей Пршеров-на-Лабе представлен народными постройками, перемещенными в центр типичного населенного пункта среднечешского Полабья, расположенного на низменности. Недалеко находится и деревенская площадь с прудом, кирпичными имениями и замком в стиле Ренессанса. Музей был основан еще в конце прошлого века, однако, его развитие происходит только в настоящее время.

Das elbländische Völkerkundemuseum Přerov an der Elbe wird von Volksbauten gebildet, die in den Kern eines typischen Flachlandortes des mittelböhmischen Elblandes übergeführt wurden. In seiner Nähe befindet sich ebenfalls der Dorfplatz mit dem Teich, mit gemauerten Gütern und dem Rennaissanceschloß. Die Museumsanfänge reichen bis zum Ende des vergangenen Jahrhunderts. Zu seiner Entfaltung kam es jedoch erst in den letzten Jahren.

Elbe Region Ethnographic Museum at Přerov nad Labem is formed by folk buildings transferred into the nucleus of a typical lowlands locality of the Elbe region in Central Bohemia. In its vicinity lies the village green with a little pond, masonry farmsteads and a Renaissance mansion. The beginnings of the museum reach as far back as the end of the past century but its development has occurred only in recent years.

1

Základem muzea je tzv. staročeská chalupa pocházející z 18. století (1), s kamny a krásným kamnovcem ve světnici (2). Tento dům sloužil v minulosti také jako kovárna a úřadovna rychtáře. Světnice z Chvalovic je datovaná rokem 1785 (3).

Основу музея составляет т. наз. „старочешская изба" XVIII века (1) с печью и красивым баком для воды в комнате (2). В прошлом в этом доме располагалась кузница, а позднее – контора сельского старосты. Комната из с. Хваловице датирована 1785 годом (3).

Die Basis des Museums bildet eine sog. altböhmische Hütte, die aus dem 18. Jahrhundert stammt (1). In der Stube steht ein Ofen und ein Ofenkessel (2). Dieses Haus diente in der Vergangenheit zugleich als Schmiede und Amtssitz des Dorfschulzen. Die Stube aus Chvalovice wurde mit dem Jahr 1785 datiert (3).

The core of the museum is the so called Old Bohemian cottage originating from 18th century (1) with a stove and a beautiful stove pot in its sitting room (2). This house served in the past also as a smithy and the magistrate's office. The sitting room from Chvalovice is from 1785 (3).

2

3

1

Bohatství úrodného Polabí se odráží i v malovaném nábytku (3), v úrovni kuchyňského nádobí (1) a v dalších vystavených předmětech. Za domem z Chvalovic stojí chalupa přenesená z obce Draho (4), postavená roku 1766. V ní je dnes ukázka školní učebny (2). Úrodnost a bohatství stojí v příkrém kontrastu s nízkou životní úrovní domkářů a podruhů.

Богатства плодородного Полабья отражаются и в расписной мебели (3), в уровне кухонной посуды (1) и других предметов экспозиции. За домом из с. Хваловице стоит изба, построенная в 1766 г. и перемещенная сюда из населенного пункта Драго (4). В ней в наше время демонстрируется старое учебное помещение (2). Плодородная земля и богатство домов находятся в явном контрасте с низким жизненным уровнем малоземельных крестьян и батраков.

Der Reichtum des fruchtbaren Elblandes spiegelt sich in den bemalten Möbelstücken wieder (3), weiterhin im Niveau des Küchengeschirrs (1) und in weiteren ausgestellten Gegenständen. Hinter dem Haus aus Chvalovice steht eine Kate aus der Gemeinde Draho (4), die 1766 gebaut wurde. Heute befindet sich darin das Exemplar eines Schulraumes (2). Die Fruchtbarkeit und der Reichtum stehen im krassen Kontrast zu dem niedrigen Lebensniveau der Kätner und der Mietsleute.

The riches of the fertile Elbe region reflect in the decorated furniture (3), in the standard of the kitchen utensils (1) and in other exhibited objects. Behind the house from Chvalovice stands the cottage transferred from the settlement of Draho (4), built in 1766. A classroom is shown inside it nowadays (2). The fertility and wealth stand in a sharp contrast against the low living standard of cottagers and farm labourers.

2

3

4

4

1

2

3

Dům č. 13 na přerovské návsi s expozicí socializace zemědělství (1). Je se čím pochlubit, neboť i JZD Přerov nad Labem patří k nejlepším v kraji. Architektura selského baroka je doložena na dvou branách v expozičním areálu, a to u bývalé myslivny (2, 3).

В доме № 13 на пршеровской деревенской площади находится экспозиция социализации сельского хозяйства (1). Есть чем похвалиться, так как ЕСХК в Пршеров-на-Лабе относится к лучшим в области. Архитектура сельского барочного стиля представлена воротами на территории экспозиции, находящимися около бывшего охотничьего домика (2, 3).

Das Haus Nr. 13 auf dem Přerover Dorfplatz mit der Ausstellung der Sozialisierung der Landwirtschaft (1). Es gibt allen Grund sich zu rühmen, denn die LPG Přerov an der Elbe gehört zu den besten im Bezirk. Die Architektur des Bauernbarock wird durch zwei Tore im Ausstellungsgelände dargestellt. Sie stehen beim ehemaligen Jägerhaus (2, 3).

House No. 13 on the village green of Přerov with the exposition of the socialization of agriculture (1). There is a lot to be proud of as the Cooperative Farm at Přerov nad Labem belongs to the best ones in the district. Rustic baroque architecture is exemplified by two gates in the exhibition area, namely at the former game-keeper's lodge (2, 3).

4

Soubor lidových staveb a řemesel VYSOČINA

se rozkládá v několika malých osadách kopcovité krajiny Českomoravské vrchoviny: Svobodné Hamry, Dřevíkov, Možděnice, Veselý Kopec, Rváčov, Králova Pila. Jde tedy – podobně jako u Zubrnic a Třebízu – o využití původních staveb in situ, k nimž přibývají další stavební objekty.

Собрание крестьянских строений и ремесел Височина располагается в нескольких маленьких селениях холмистой местности Чешско-Моравской возвышенности: Свободне-Гамри, Држевиков, Можденице, Весели-Копец, Рвачов, Кралова-Пила. Значит, речь идет, подобно тому, как и в музеях Зубрнице и Тршебиз, об использовании в музейных целях исконных, неперенесенных построек, число которых увеличивается за счет дальнейших строительных объектов.

Das Ensemble der Volksbauten und des Handwerkes Vysočina teilt sich in mehrere kleine Ortschaften der Hügellandschaft der Böhmisch-Mährischen Höhe: Svobodné Hamry, Dřevíkov, Možděnice, Veselý Kopec, Rváčov, Králova Pila. Es geht demnach – ähnlich wie in Zubrnice und Třebíz – um die Ausnutzung ursprünglicher Bauwerke in situ, zu denen weitere Bauobjekte hinzukommen.

Collection of folk buildings and handicrafts at Vysočina is located in several small villages of the hilly country of the Bohemian-Moravian Uplands: Svobodné Hamry, Dřevíkov, Možděnice, Veselý Kopec, Rváčov, Králova Pila. The principle here – similarly as at Zubrnice and at Třebíz – is then the utilization of the genuine buildings in situ to which other architectonic objects are added.

1

2

Úly na okraji luk (1) a svahovité pastviny vytvářejí přirozené prostředí čtyřboké usedlosti přenesené na Veselý Kopec ze Sádku u Poličky. Patří k ní víceboká roubená stodola, která vznikla v 17. století (2). V údolí mezi olšemi je mlýn s olejnou a v pozadí ještě s pilou (3). Skromně prostřený stůl ve světnici sousedního domu přeneseného do muzea z Herálce (4).

Ульи на окраине лугов (1) и пастбища на склонах образуют естественную среду для четырехгранной усадьбы, перемещенной в Весели-Копец из с. Садек. К ней относится бревенчатая рига, построенная в XVII веке (2). В долине между ольхами стоит мельница с маслобойней и лесопильней (3). Скромно накрытый стол в комнате соседнего дома, перенесенного в музей из с. Гералец (4).

Die Bienenstöcke an den Rändern der Wiesen (1) und Hangweiden bilden eine natürliche Umgebung des vierkantigen Bauerngutes, das von Sádek bei Polička nach Veselý Kopec gebracht wurde. Zu diesem Gut gehört eine vieleckige gezimmerte Scheune, die aus dem 17. Jahrhundert ist (2). Im Tal zwischen den Erlen steht die Mühle mit einer Ölmühle und im Hintergrund eine Säge (3). Bescheiden gedeckter Tisch in der Stube des Nachbarhauses aus Heralec (4).

The beehives by the meadows (1) and pastures on the slopes create a natural environment for the four-sided estate transferred to Veselý Kopec from Sádek near Polička. Its part is the polygonal framework barn which was built in 17th century (2). In the valley, among the alder trees, there is a mill with an oil-press and a saw-mill in the background (3). A modestly laid table can be seen in the sitting room of the neighbouring house transferred to the museum from Herálec (4).

3

4

Cit a um řemeslníků reprezentuje vstup do veselokopeckého mlýna (1, 2). Jediné vodní kolo pohání moučné složení (3), stoupu na kroupy a varnu povidel (4), další kolo pohání stoupy v sousední lisovně oleje (6). Návštěvníci mohou uvidět mlýn a jeho složení v plné práci.

1

2

3

4

5

6

Чутье и умение ремесленников подтверждает вход в мельницу в Весели-Копец (1, 2). Одно лишь колесо приводит в движение жерновой состав (3), ступу для крупы и повидловарню (4), другое колесо приводит в движение ступы в соседнем устройстве для отжимания масла (6). Посетителям предоставляется возможность увидеть мельницу в полном действии.

Gefühl und Können der Handwerker repräsentiert der Eingang in die Mühle von Veselý Kopec (1, 2). Das einzige Wasserrad betreibt den Mahlgang (3), die Graupenstampfe und die Muskochanlage (4). Ein weiteres Rad betreibt die Ölpressestampfen nebenan (6). Die Besucher können die Mühle mit deren Konstruktion in voller Arbeit verfolgen.

The sensitivity and art of the craftsmen are represented by the entrance to the mill at Veselý Kopec (1, 2). A single water wheel drives the mill machinery (3), the groats stamp and the plum jam boiler (4), another wheel drives the crushers in the neighbouring oil-press (6). The visitors can watch the mill and its machinery in full operation.

5

1

V možděnické roubené sýpce byla zřízena kolářská dílna (1), v kopii domu ze Svratouchu dílna a obydlí tří generací truhlářů Žejdlíků (4). Místní kovář pracoval v upraveném špýcharu, který pochází z 18. století (2). Předností areálu Vysočina je kontakt se starými pamětníky tradičního řemesla, kterých je v tomto malebném koutu stále ještě dostatek.

В Мождеництком бревенчатом амбаре была устроена мастерская колесника (1), в копии дома из с. Свратоух – мастерская и жилище трех поколений столяров Жейдликов (4). Местный кузнец работал в приспособленном амбаре XVIII века (2). Преимуществом бсего музейного ансамбля „Височина" является его контакт со старыми свидетелями традиционных ремесел, которых в этом живописном уголке все еще много.

In dem gezimmerten Speicher von Možděnice wurde eine Wagnerwerkstatt eingerichtet (1), in der Nachbildung des Hauses aus Svratouch eine Werkstatt und Wohnstätte dreier Generationen der Tischler Žejdlík (4). Der örtliche Schmied arbeitete in einem hergerichteten Speicher aus dem 18. Jahrhundert (2). Der Vorzug des Geländes Vysočina besteht im Kontakt mit alten Baudenkmälern traditionellen Handwerks, die es in diesem malerischen Eck noch in Genüge gibt.

The framework corn-loft from Možděnice served for the establishment of wheelwright's workshop (1), the copy of a house from Svratouch provided place for the workshop and dwelling place of three generations of the Žejdlíks the joiners (4). The local blacksmith used to work in the adapted granary which originates from 18th century (2). The merit of the area at Vysočina is its contact with the old witnesses of traditional crafts who are still numerous enough in these picturesque parts.

2

3

4

1

2

Ve Svobodných Hamrech byl obnoven železářský hamr na spodní vodu (1), podle něhož původně dostala osada svůj název. Hamr patří k náročným technickým památkám a jeho uvedení do provozu patří k největším atrakcím Vysočiny. Vstupní část expozice na Veselém Kopci s kopií zvonice z Jeníkova (2).

В Свободне-Гамри реставрирована железоделательная мануфактура на грунтовой воде (1), по названию которой и названо селение. Она относится к трудным в техническом отношении памятникам и ее введение в строй – один из самых больших достижений музея Височина. Вход в экспозицию в с. Весели-Копец и копия колокольни из с. Еников (2).

In Svobodné Hamry wurde der Eisenhammer für das Grundwasser erneuert (1), nach dem ursprünglich die Ortschaft benannt wurde. Der Hammer gehört zu den komplizierten technischen Denkmälern und die Inbetriebnahme zu den größten Attraktionen von Vysočina. Eingangsteil der Exposition auf Veselý Kopec mit der Kopie des Glockenturmes aus Jeníkov (2).

At Svobodné Hamry the hammer-mill, which gave the genuine settlement its name, with bottom water drive (1), was renovated. The hammer-mill belongs to particular technical memorials and its setting into operation offers one of Vysočina's greatest attractions. The entrance part of the exposition at Veselý Kopec with a copy of the belfry from Jeníkov (2).

1

K búdám a vínu patří písnička, a to i v muzeu (1). Architektura lisoven a sklepů je velmi bohatá zejména v jihozápadní části Slovácka; reprezentují ji stavby z Vrbice (2). K ní přilehlé muzejní vinohrady klesají na rovinaté louky a přecházejí v soubor seníků z části obce Javorníka, zvané Lásky (3). Ve vinohradech se pěstují domácí původní odrůdy, které už sotva kde najdeme.

С винодельческими домиками и вином тесно связана песенка (1). Архитектура прессовых цехов и погребков очень богата, особенно в юго-западной части Моравской Словакии; ее представляют постройки из с. Врбице (2). Прилегающие к ним музейные виноградники спускаются на равнинные луга и переходят в комплекс сеновалов, происходящих из части населенного пункта Яворник, называемой „Ласки“ (3). В виноградниках выращивают исконные домашние сорта, которые уже почти нигде не встречаются.

Zu den Stübeln und dem Wein gehören Lieder und das auch im Museum (1). Die Architektur der Pressen und Keller ist sehr reichhaltig, vorwiegend im südwestlichen Teil von Slovácko; sie werden durch Bauten aus Vrbice repräsentiert (2). Die anliegenden Museumsweinberge grenzen an ebene Wiesen und gehen in ein Ensemble von Heuschobern über, aus einem Gemeindeteil von Javorník, genannt Liebe, stammend (3). Auf den Weinbergen werden heimische ursprüngliche Weinsorten angebaut, die man kaum noch anderswo findet.

The "booths" and wine are to be joined by a song, just as well in the museum (1). The architecture of winepresses and wine-vaults is fairly rich, especially in the south-west part of the Moravian-Slovak border; it is represented by the buildings from Vrbice (2). The adjacent museum vineyards descend to the flat meadows and give way to the collection of haylofts from a part of the Javorník settlement called Lásky (3). Genuine local varieties, which are scarcely to be found anywhere else, are grown in the vineyards.

2

3

6

1

2

3

4

Barevnost prosluněného Slovácka je cítit v celém životním prostředí a také i v těch nejchudobnějších světničkách horňácké dědiny Nová Lhota (1). Horňáčtí lidoví tkalci dodnes vynikají svým mistrovstvím (2). Kovárnu s celým zařízením přenesli do muzea z Lipova (3). Bětíkova chalupa z Podhradí na Luhačovicku je postavena z nepálených cihel, vepřovic. Její dvůr vymezuje patrová roubená sýpka z Pozlovic, typická pro celé Zálesí (4). V této části areálu se již projevuje vliv karpatské lidové kultury.

Красочность солнечной Моравской Словакии чувствуется во всей жизненной обстановке, а даже в самых бедных комнатках горняцкой деревни Нова-Лгота (1). Горняцкие народные ткачи до сих пор отличаются своим мастерством (2). Кузницу со всем ее оборудованием перенесли в музей из с. Липов (3). Изба Бетика из с. Подгради Лугачовицкой области построена из необожженного кирпича – самана. Во дворе – двухэтажный бревенчатый амбар из с. Позловице, типичный для всей области Залеси (4). В этой части музейного комплекса уже проявляется влияние карпатской народной культуры.

Die Farbigkeit des durch und durch sonnigen Slovácko ist in allen seinen Lebensphären zu spüren und demnach auch in den ärmsten Stuben von Nová Lhota, einem Horňácko-Dorf (1). Die Horňácker volkstümlichen Weber haben noch heute durch ihre Meisterarbeiten einen guten Namen (2). Die Schmiede mit der gesamten Einrichtung wurde aus Lipov ins Museum gebracht (3). Die Bětíkkate aus Podhradí bei Luhačovice wurde aus ungebrannten Ziegeln und Kotziegeln erbaut. Ihren Hof teilt ein gezimmerter Etagenspeicher aus Pozlovice, typisch für diese Gegend (4). In diesem Geländeteil dringt schon der Einfluß der karpatischen Volkskultur durch.

Chromatic richness of the sun-flooded Moravian-Slovak border can be felt in the whole living environment, even in the poorest little chambers at the Horňácko region village of Nová Lhota (1). The mastery of the folk weavers from the Horňácko region is prominent till nowadays (2). The smithy with all its equipment has been transferred to the museum from Lipov (3). Bětík's cottage from Podhradí in the Luhačovice region is built from unfired bricks, adobes. Its courtyard is demarcated by the two-storeyed framework corn-loft from Pozlovice which is typical for the whole region of Zálesí (4). This part of the area displays already the influence of the Carpathian folk culture.

1

2

Nejchudobnější kraj Slovácka, moravské Kopanice, reprezentuje Mikulincova usedlost z Vyškovce (3). Hodulíkova jizba dokládá, jak v této osadě žili někteří lidé až do poloviny našeho století (4). Stodoly se tu stavěly dál od obytných staveb (1) a kovárny spíše ve středu vesnic. V této kovárně pracoval Jan Veverka z Lipova (2).

Самую бедную часть Моравской Словакии – моравские Копаница, представляет усадьба Микулинца из с. Вишковец (3). Горница Годулика показывает, каким образом в этом селении жили некоторые люди до самой половины нашего века (4). Риги здесь строили подальше от жилых домов (1), а кузницы – скорее в центре деревень. В этой кузнице работал Ян Веверка из с. Липов (2).

Den ärmsten Bezirk im Gebiet Slovácko, mährisch Kopanice, repräsentiert das Mikulincer Bauerngut aus Vyškovec (3). Die Hodulíkstube demonstriert, wie in dieser Ortschaft einige Menschen bis in die erste Hälfte unseres Jahrhundert lebten (4). Die Scheunen baute man hier weiter von den Wohnstätten entfernt (1) und die Schmieden eher in die Dorfmitte. In dieser Schmiede arbeitete Jan Veverka aus Lipov (2).

The poorest part of the Moravian-Slovak border, Moravian Kopanice (slope fields) region, is respresented by Mikulinec's estate from Vyškovec (3). Hodulík's chamber exemplifies the way of life of some people from this settlement till the middle of our century (4). Barns used to be built farther off the living edifices here (1) while smithies used to be located rather in the village centres. This smithy used to be the working place of Jan Veverka from Lipov (2).

3

4

1

2

3

4

Hlína byla hlavním stavebním materiálem téměř na celém Slovácku. Většina domů postavených ve strážnickém muzeu byla původně z vepřovic (1). Rukou nanášené hliněné omítky mají citlivé tvary drobných nepravidelností s plastikou nebo malovanou výzdobou vstupních žuder (2, 3) nebo okenních otvorů (4). Tradice takového zdobení se na Slovácku udržuje doposud.

Глина являлась основным строительным материалом почти во всей Моравской Словакии. Большинство домов, находящихся в Стражницком музее, исконно построено из самана (1). В наносимой рукой глиняной штукатурке встречаются тонкие мелкие неровности, сводчатые пристройки у входов (2, 3) или оконные проемы (4) украшены пластикой или росписью. Традиция такого украшения сохраняется в Моравской Словакии и до наших дней.

Ton war vorrangiges Baumaterial fast im ganzen Gebiet von Slovácko. Der Großteil der Häuser, die im Strážnicer Museum aufgestellt wurden, waren ursprünglich aus Kotziegeln (1). Der von Hand aufgetragene Tonputz enthält empfindliche Formen kleiner Unebenheiten mit Plastik oder gemaltem Schmuck des Eingangsvorbaus (2, 3) oder der Fensteröffnungen (4). Die Tradition solcher Verzierungen hält sich im Gebiet Slovácko bis heute noch.

Clay used to be the principal building material almost all over the Moravian-Slovak border. Majority of houses erected in the museum at Strážnice had genuinely been built with adobes (1). Hand-laid plasters had sensitive shapes of minute irregularities with plastics or painted decorations of the entrance porches (2, 3) or window orifices (4). The tradition of such decoration is kept till nowadays in the Moravian-Slovak border.

Valašské muzeum v přírodě
ROŽNOV POD RADHOŠTĚM

vytváří model historické krajiny hornaté severovýchodní Moravy s expozicí Valašské dědiny, Dřevěného městečka a Mlýnské doliny. Je nejstarším muzeem v přírodě ve střední Evropě a nejrozsáhlejším u nás.

Валашский музей под открытым небом Рожнов-под-Радгоштем образует модель исторической местности гористой северо-восточной Моравии с экспозициями „Валашская деревня", „Деревянный городок" и „Мельничная долина". В Чехословакии это самый обширный и в средней Европе самый старый музей под открытым небом.

Das Walachenmuseum in der Natur Rožnov am Radegast bildet das Modell einer historischen Landschaft des gebirgigen nordöstlichen Mährens mit der Ausstellung des Walachendorfes, des Hölzernen Städtchens und des Mühlentales. Es ist das älteste Museum in der Natur in Mitteleuropa und das ausgedehnteste in der ČSSR.

Wallachian open-air Museum at Rožnov pod Radhoštěm creates a model of the historical countryside of the mountainous region of north-eastern Moravia with the exposition of the Wallachian Village, the Wooden Town and the Mill Dell. It is the oldest open-air museum in central Europe and the amplest one in this country.

7

1

2

3

4

5

V Dřevěném městečku je nejstarší stavbou Vaškova hospoda z rožnovského náměstí (1). V radnici vedle ní sídlil městský úřad (2). Pavlače měšťanských domů sloužily lázeňským hostům (3). K měšťanským zahradám patřily včelíny (4) a bokem od náměstí stával kostel. Za druhé světové války se v muzeu vystavěla kopie dřevěného kostela z Větřkovic (5).

Старейшей постройкой „Деревянного городка" является трактир Вашека из Рожновской площади (1). В ратуше рядом с ней находилось городское управление (2). Открытые галереи мещанских домов использовались курортниками (3). К садам мещан примыкали ульи (4) и в стороне от площади стоял костел. Во время второй мировой войны на территории музея построили копию деревянного костела из с. Ветршковице (5).

Die Wenzels Schenke ist im Hölzernen Städtchen das älteste Baudenkmal, am Rožnover Dorfplatz gelegen (1). Daneben, im Rathaus sitzt die Stadtbehörde (2). Die gangartigen Balkons der Bürgerhäuser dienten den Kurgästen (3). Zu den Bürgergärten gehörten Bienenhäuser (4), an der Seite des Platzes stand die Kirche. In der Zeit des zweiten Weltkrieges wurde im Museum die Kopie des hölzernen Kirchleins aus Větřkovice ausgestellt (5).

The oldest building in the Wooden Town is Vašek's tavern from the square of Rožnov (1). The adjacent town hall used to be the seat of the town authority (2). The porches of the burghers' houses used to serve spa guests (3). The beehives (4) pertained to the burghers' gardens and the church used to stand apart the square. The copy of the wooden church from Větřkovice (5) was built in the museum during World War II.

7

1

2

Vyspělou měšťanskou architekturu v Rožnově vytvářeli snad už od konce středověku roubením ze dřeva (1). Expozici Dřevěného městečka oživují nejen folklórní programy v amfiteátru (2), ale i ukázky rukodělných prací v expozicích (3, 4, 5, 6). V jediném roce je to někdy i sedmdesát programů tohoto druhu.

Высокоразвитая архитектура мещанских домов засвидетельствована в Рожнове еще в конце средневековья (1). Экспозиция „Деревянного городка" оживляется не только фольклорными программами в амфитеатре (2), но и демонстрациями рукоделий в экспозициях (3, 4, 5, 6). Иногда здесь в течение одного года можно увидеть до семидесяти программ такого типа.

Die reife bürgerliche Architektur in Rožnov wurde sicher schon seit Ende des Mittelalters durch Zimmerwerke aus Holz angewandt (1). Die Exposition des Hölzernen Städtchens beleben nicht nur Folkloreprogramme im Amphitheater (2), sondern ebenfalls Handarbeitsausstellungen (3, 4, 5, 6). In einem einzigen Jahr können es bis zu siebzig Programme dieser Art sein.

Mature civic architecture had been created in timber at Rožnov perhaps since the end of the Middle Ages (1). The exposition of the Wooden Town is enlivened not only by the folklore programmes performed in the amphitheatre (2) but also by demonstrations of handicraft works in the expositions (3, 4, 5, 6). Within a single year sometimes up to seventy programmes of this kind are presented.

3

4

5

6

7

1

2

Valašská dědina je živým areálem muzea – se salašnickým chovem ovcí (1), zemědělským hospodářstvím (2), pěstováním léčivých bylin a historických odrůd luštěnin, obilnin i ovocných stromů kolem přenesených roubených usedlostí (3). Mezi nimi zaujímá osobité místo chalupa z Prlova, jejíž obyvatelé poskytovali obětavou pomoc partyzánům v zimě 1944–45 (4, 5).

„Валашская деревня" – это живой музейный комплекс, где вокруг перенесенных бревенчатых усадеб можно познакомиться с пастбищным содержанием овец (1), с сельскохозяйственными работами (2), с выращиванием целебных трав, исторических бобов, зерновых растений и фруктовых деревьев (3). Среди всех объектов особое место занимает изба из с. Прлов, жители которой зимой 1944–45 гг. оказывали самоотверженную помощь партизанам (4, 5).

Das Walachendorf ist lebendiges Museumsgelände – mit einer Almschaafzucht (1), mit Landwirtschaft (2), mit Heilkräuteranbau und dem Anbau historischer Sorten von Hülsenfrüchten, Getreidesorten und Obstbäumen rund um die hergeführten gezimmerten Güter (3). Unter ihnen nimmt die Kate aus Prlov eine Sonderstellung ein, da die Bewohner der Kate den Partisanen im Winter 1944–45 aufopferungsvolle Hilfe leisteten (4, 5).

The Wallachian Village in the living area of the museum comprising chalet sheep-breeding (1), agricultural production (2), growing of medical plants and historical varieties of leguminous plants, cereals as well as fruit trees around the transferred timberwork estates (3). A special position among them is assumed by the cottage from Prlov the inhabitants of which were providing self-denying help to the partisans in the winter of 1944–45 (4, 5).

3

4

5

1

7

2

3

4

Ve vesnické části muzea pracuje větrný mlýn beraního typu z Kladník na Kelečsku (4). Sestrojil ho roku 1829 František Skopal. Obrovitá vrtule roztáčí palečné kolo na společné hřídeli, kolem něhož je čelisťová dřevěná brzda (1), ukončená ozdobně řezanou pákou (2). Rovněž moučnice je zdobená (3). Větrné mlýny se vyskytovaly především v okrajové části Valašska.

В деревенской части музея работает ветряная ударная мельница из с. Кладники (4), построенная в 1829 г. Франтишеком Скопалом. Могучий воздушный винт раскручивает цевочную шестерню на основном вале, вокруг которого – колодочный деревянный тормоз (1), заканчивающийся рычагом ручной декоративной резьбы (2). Хранилище для муки тоже украшено (3). Ветряные мельницы встречались прежде всего на окраине Валахии.

Im Dorfteil des Museums arbeitet eine widderartige Windmühle aus Kladníky im Kelečer Gebiet (4). Sie wurde 1829 von František Skopal zusammengestellt. Der Riesenpropeller wird durch ein Daumenrad auf gemeinsamer Welle in Rotation gebracht, die mit einer hölzernen Backenbremse (1) schmuckartig als geschnitzter Hebel endet (2). Auch der Mehlkasten ist verziert (3). Die Windmühlen traten vorwiegend im Randgebiet der Walachei auf.

The windmill od the ram type from Kladníky in the Kelč region (4) is working in the village part of the museum. It was constructed in 1829 by František Skopal. The huge propeller spins the thumb--wheel on the common shaft encompassed by the wooden jaw--brake (1) terminated by a decoratively carved lever (2). The meal-bench, too, is decorated (3). Windmills were to be found above all in the outer part of Wallachia.

Múzeum slovenskej dediny MARTIN

Leží vo zvlnenej kotline obklopenej hrebeňmi Malej a Veľkej Fatry. Vo svojej konečnej podobe obsiahne ukážky sídelných celkov zo všetkých regiónov Slovenska. Výstavba sa začala súborom z Oravy. Martinské múzeum v prírode je naším jediným celonárodným zariadením tohto druhu. S jeho otvorením sa počíta v roku 1992.

Музей словацкой деревни Мартин расположен в холмистой котловине, окруженной горным хребтом Малой и Большой Фатры. В своем окончательном виде он будет демонстрировать образцы комплексов народного зодчества изо всех регионов Словакии. Строительство началось с ансамбля из Оравы. Мартинский музей под открытым небом – единственное чехословацкое общенародное учреждение данного типа. Его открытие запланировано на 1992 г.

Das Museum des slowakischen Dorfes Martin liegt in einem gebirgigen Becken, umgeben von den Kämmen der Kleinen und der Großen Fatra. In seiner endgültigen Gestalt wird es Exemplare von Siedlungskomplexen aus der ganzen Region der Slowakei enthalten. Der Bau begann mit dem Ensemble aus Orava. Das Martiner Museum in der Natur ist die einzige nationale Anlage dieser Art in der ČSSR. Mit seiner Eröffnung rechnet man im Jahre 1992.

Slovak Village Museum at Martin lies in a corrugated hollow surrounded by the ridges of the Low Fatra and High Fatra mountains, respectively. In its final form it will comprise specimens of settlement wholes from all regions of Slovakia. The construction started with the collection from Orava. The Martin open-air museum is our only nation-wide institution of this kind. Its opening is planned for 1992.

1

2

3

4

Poschodové zrubové domy vyšnokubínskeho zemana z roku 1748 a mestského remeselníka z Veličnej z roku 1866 patria medzi unikáty ľudovej architektúry (1, 2). Dolnooravská izba z Jasenovej (3) charakterizuje ešte staršiu kultúrnu tradíciu než izba s jednoduchým nábytkom z hornooravského Hruštína (4).

Двухэтажные бревенчатые дома мелкопоместного дворянина из Вишни-Кубин (1748 г.) и городского ремесленника из с. Велична (1866 г.) принадлежат к числу уникальных объектов народного зодчества (1, 2). Дольноoравская комната из с. Ясенова (3) характеризует еще более старую культурную традицию, чем комната с простой мебелью из Горнооравской деревни Груштин (4).

Die gezimmerten Etagenhäuser des Vyšnokubiner Junkers aus dem Jahre 1748 und des bürgerlichen Handwerkers aus Veličná aus dem Jahre 1866 gehören zu den Unikaten der Volksarchitektur (1, 2). Die Dolnooravaer Stube aus Jasenová (3) charakterisiert eine noch ältere Kulturtradition als die Stube mit den einfachen Möbelstücken aus dem Hornooravaer Hruštín (4).

The two-storeyed timber houses of the squire from Horný Kubín from 1748 and of the town craftsman from Veličná from 1866, respectively, belong to the unique specimens of Slovak architecture (1, 2). The chamber in the Lower Orava region style from Jasenová (3) characterizes an even older cultural tradition than that represented by the chamber with simple furniture in the Upper Orava region style from Hruštín (4).

1

2

3

4

Kuchyňa s novším sporákom (3) a komora (1) bola pracoviskom gazdinej. Svahovitý terén umožňoval konštrukciu pavlače aj pri jednoduchých roľníckych domoch v Jasenovej (2). V oravskej časti expozície má svoje miesto aj drobná sakrálna stavba s kamennými reliéfmi z Bzín (4).

Кухня с печью более позднего времени (3) и чулан (1) были рабочим местом домохозяйки. Склонистая местность предоставляла возможность конструировать открытые галереи даже в простых крестьянских домах в с. Ясенова (2). Составной частью экспозиции из Оравы является и мелкое строение церковной архитектуры с каменными рельефами из с. Бзины (4).

Die Küche mit einem neueren Herd (3) und die Kammer (1) waren der Arbeitsplatz der Hausfrau. Das hangartige Terrain ermöglichte die Konstruktion der gangartigen Balkons auch bei einfachen Bauernhäusern aus Jasenová (2). Im Oravaer Ausstellungsteil haben auch kleine Sakramentbauten mit Steinreliefs aus Bziny (4) ihren Platz.

The kitchen with a newer range (3) and the closet (1) were the housewife's workplaces. The sloping terrain made it possible to construct porches even in simple peasant houses from Jasenová. The Orava part of the exposition assigned a proper place also to the minute sacral building with stone reliefs from Bziny (4).

1

2

Ploty, ovocné stromy a sýpky charakterizujú prostredie dolnooravskej dediny (1, 2). V radovej zástavbe z Liptova (3, 6) ukazuje murovaný dom z Vavrišova majstrovstvo liptovských murárov (6) a zrubový dom z Liptovskej Sielnice um tesárov (4). Dom z Vitálišoviec má šindľovú strechu (3) rovnako, ako aj niektoré humná (5).

Заборы, фруктовые деревья и амбары характеризуют среду Дольноoравской деревни (1, 2). В рядовой застройке из региона Липтов (3, 6) демонстрирует кирпичный дом из с. Вавришов мастерство липтовских каменщиков (6), а бревенчатый из с. Липтовска-Сиельница – способности плотников (4). Дом из с. Виталишовце (3), как и некоторые риги (5), имеет соломенную крышу.

3

4

5

6

Zäune, Obstbäume und Speicher charakterisieren das Milieu eines Dolnooravaer Dorfes (1, 2). Im Reihenbau aus Liptov (3, 6) zeigt ein gemauertes Haus aus Vavrišov das Meisterstück Liptover Maurer (6) und ein gezimmertes aus Liptovské Sielnice das Können der Tischler (4). Das Haus aus Vitališovce hat ein Strohdach (3), ähnlich wie einige Scheunen (5).

Hedges, fruit trees and corn-lofts characterize the environment of the village from the Lower Orava region (1, 2). In the row housing from Liptov (3, 6) the house from Vavrišov built in masonry shows the mastership of the Liptov bricklayers (6) and the framework house from Liptovská Sielnica shows the art of the carpenters (4). The house from Vitališovce has a thatched roof (3), the same as some barns (5).

Múzeum kysuckej dediny NOVÁ BYSTRICA – VYCHYLOVKA

patrí k najrozsiahlejším u nás. Horská lesnatá krajina Slovenských Beskýd s poľanami a terasovitými políčkami v areáli múzea charakterizuje mladé kopaničiarske osídlenie Kysúc. Súčasťou expozície je úzkokoľajná lesná železnica s úvraťovým stúpaním.

Музей Кисуцкой деревни Нова-Бистрица-Вихиловка относится к самым обширным в Чехословакии. Горная лесистая местность Словацких Бескид с полянами и маленькими полями, расположенными террасами на территории музея, характеризует молодое поселение Кисуц, размещенное на лесных вырубках. Составной частью экспозиции является лесная узкоколейная железная дорога с тупиковым подъемом.

Das Museum des Kysucer Dorfes Nová Bystrica-Vychylovka gehört zu den ausgedehntesten in der ČSSR. Die bergige bewaldete Landschaft der Slowakischen Beskyden mit ihren Hochebenen und terassenartigen Feldern im Museumsgelände wird von einer jungen Dorfortschaft, Kysuce, vervollständigt. Bestandteil der Exposition ist eine Schmalspurwaldbahn mit Steigung im Wendepunkt.

Kysuce Village Museum at Nová Bystrica-Vychylovka belongs to the largest ones in this country. The mountainous and woody countryside of the Slovak Beskides with clearings and little terrace fields on the museum premises characterize the recent settlement of the Kysuce region by peasants cultivating fields on slopes. Integral part of the exposition is narrow-gauge forest railway with dead-end system of ascent.

1

9

1

2

3

Živým prvkom je prevádzka úzkokoľajnej lesnej železnice (1), ktorá kedysi spájala Kysuce s Oravou. Klubinská píla v múzeu má stroj zo začiatku 20. storočia (2). Usadlosť s názvom Do Potoka (3) bola prenesená do múzea v prírode aj s ovocnými stromami a nad ňou boli upravené políčka i poľné cesty v rovnakom usporiadaní ako na pôvodnom mieste v obci Riečnica.

Живым элементом музея является и действующая узкоколейная лесная железная дорога (1), которая когда-то соединяла области Кисуце и Орава. В Клубинской лесопильне на территории музея находится машина начала XX века (2). Усадьба под названием „До потока" (3) была перемещена в музей даже с фруктовыми деревьями, а над ней были разработаны маленькие поля и проложены полевые дороги в таком же виде, в каком они находились на своем исконном месте, в населенном пункте Риечница.

Ein lebendes Element stellt auch der Verkehr der Schmalspurwaldbahn dar (1), die früher einmal Kysuce mit Orava verbunden hatte. Die Säge von Klubin besitzt die Maschinerie aus dem 20. Jahrhundert (2). Das Bauerngut mit der Bezeichnung „Zum Bach" (3) wurde in das Naturmuseum mit seinen Obstbäumen hergebracht. Und ein Stück darüber wurden die Feldstücke und Feldwege in gleicher Anordnung wie am ursprünglichen Platz in der Gemeinde Riečnica wieder angelegt.

An enlivening element is offered by the operation of the narrow-gauge forest railway (1) which used to connect the Kysuce and the Orava regions. The sawmill from Klubina in the museum has the engine from the beginning of 20th century (2). The estate named Do Potoka (To the Brook) (3) has been transferred to the museum together with the fruit trees and, over it, the little fields as well as field roads have been arranged in the same way as in their original places in the settlement of Riečnica.

Dolnooravský rínok vytvára model staršieho sídla (1, 2), na ktorom dominuje zemianska usadlosť z Vyšného Kubína, datovaná roku 1752 (2, 3, 6), sýpka zo Srňacieho z roku 1827 (4) a nad týmto súborom stavieb sa týči kópia zvonice, ktorá vznikla v Záskalí roku 1860 (5).

2

1

3

4

5

6

„Дольнооравский ринок" образует модель исторического селения (1, 2), над которым доминирует усадьба мелкопоместного дворянина из Вишни-Кубин, датированная 1752 годом (2, 3, 6) и амбар из с. Срняцие 1827 г. (4). Над этим комплексом возвышается копия колокольни, которая возникла в с. Заскали в 1860 г. (5).

Der Dolnooravský Ring bildet das Modell eines historisch älteren Sitzes (1, 2), an dessen einer Seite das Junkerngut aus Vyšný Kubín dominiert, datiert mit dem Jahr 1752 (2, 3, 6). Weiterhin der Speicher aus Srňacie von 1827 (4). Über dieses Ensemble erhebt sich die Kopie des Glockenturmes, der in Záskalí im Jahre 1860 entstand (5).

The Lower Orava region market-place creates the model of a historically older settlement (1, 2) the dominant of which is the squire's estate from Vyšný Kubín from 1752 (2, 3, 6), the corn-loft from Srňacie from 1827 (4), and protruding over this collection of constructions is the copy of the belfry which was built at Záskalí in 1860 (5).

1

2

3

4

5

Na dolnej Orave omazávali drevený zrub hlinou a bielili ho (1), naproti tomu v severnej časti regiónu zostával bez omietky, v zrube (4). Remeselníci v bývalom mestečku Veličná stavali domy s poloposchodím (1). V ich obydliach sa pamätá na reprezentáciu (2), nemenšiu dôležitosť však pripisovali dielni (3). Hornooravská časť na druhom brehu Studenej sa začína ukážkou Zamagurskej ulice (5).

В области нижней Оравы обмазывали деревянный сруб глиной, а затем белили (1), в то время как в северной части региона сруб оставался без штукатурки (4). Ремесленники бывшего городка Велична строили дома с полуэтажом (1). В их жилищах определено место для репрезентации (2), но немалое значение ими придавалось и мастерской (3). Горнооравская часть музея на втором берегу реки Студена начинается с демонстрации „Замагурской улицы“ (5).

An der unteren Orava wurden die Holzblockhütten mit Lehm verputzt und geweißt (1). Im nördlichen Regionsteil hingegen blieben sie ohne Putz, Blockbaute (4). Die Handwerker in der ehemaligen Stadt Veličná bauten Häuser mit Halbetage (1). In ihren Wohnstätten wird an Repräsentation erinnert (2). Der Werkstatt jedoch wurde keine geringere Bedeutung beigemessen (3). Der Teil vom Oravaoberlauf, am anderen Ufer der Studená, beginnt mit einem Exemplar der Zamagurská Straße (5).

In the Lower Orava region the log-cabins were smeared with clay and whitewashed (1), whereas in the northern part of the region they stayed without plaster inside (4). Craftsmen in the former town of Veličná used to build houses with mezzanins (1). Social prestige was remembered in their dwellings (2) but no less importance was attached to the workshop (3). The Upper Orava region part on the other bank of the Studená river starts with the exhibition of Zamagurská ulica (Zamagura Street) (5).

1

2

3

Najväčšie bohatstvo ľudovej architektúry v tvaroch striech, štítov, okien a portálov ukazujú stavby Zamagurskej ulice (4). Beskydské stavby majú starobylé valbové strechy; pozri šoltýstvo z Novoti (3). V dome z Oravskej Lesnej bola už modernejšia kuchyňa (2), a tá veľká z rabčického šoltýstva slúžila dokonca na bývanie (1).

Самое большое богатство народного зодчества представлено в формах крыш, фронтонов, окон и порталов зданий „Замагурской улицы" (4). Бескидские постройки характеризуются старинными вальмовыми крышами – см. здание сельского правления из с. Новоть (3). Кухня в доме из Оравска-Лесна уже более современная (2), а большая кухня в здании сельского правления с. Рабчице служила в качестве жилого помещения (1).

Den größten Reichtum der Volksarchitektur zeigen die Bauten der Zamagurská Straße in Form von Dächern, Schildern, Fenstern, Portalen. (4). Die Beskydenbauten haben ältertümliche Walmdächer; siehe das Schulzenhaus aus Novoť (3). Im Haus aus Oravská Lesná war schon eine moderne Küche (2). Die große Küche vom Rabčicer Schulzenhaus diente sogar als Wohnstätte (1).

4

The greatest treasure of folk architecture in the shapes of roofs, gables, windows and portals is shown in the constructions collected in Zamagurská ulica (4). The Beskides buildings have ancient hipped roofs as seen in the magistrate's office from Novoť (3). The house from Oravská Lesná had already been provided with a more modern kitchen (2), and the large kitchen from the magistrate's office at Rabčice was even used to live in (1).

Múzeum liptovskej dediny
PRIBYLINA

vyrastá medzi rozsiahlymi horskými lúkami pod Kriváňom a Liptovskými hoľami. Vytvára model niekoľkých dedín s panským sídlom a vodnými stavbami. Do prvej časti sa sústredili prevažne pamiatky zo zátopového územia priehrady Liptovská Mara.

Музей липтовской деревни Прибилина вырастает на обширных горных полянах под горами Кривань и Липтовске-Голе. Он представляет собой модель нескольких деревень с господской резиденцией и гидротехническими сооружениями. В первой части сосредоточены прежде всего памятники из паводковой территории плотины „Липтовска-Мара“.

Das Museum des Liptover Dorfes Pribylina ist zwischen weiten Bergwiesen unter dem Kriváň und den Liptovské hole gelegen. Es bildet das Modell einiger Dörfer mit Herrschaftssitz und Wasserbauten. Im ersten Teil sind vorwiegend Denkmäler aus dem Überschwemmungsgebiet der Talsperre Liptovská Mara konzentriert.

Liptov Village Museum at Pribylina grows up among the large mountain meadows under the mount of Kriváň and the Liptovské Hole mountain range. It creates the model of several villages with gentlemen's seat and water constructions. The first part has concentrated mostly memorable objects from the area flooded by the Liptovská Mara dam.

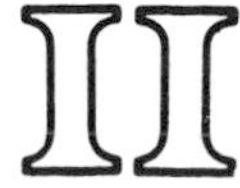

1

2

Niekoľko domov pochádza z Liptovskej Sielnice, dnes zatopenej vodami priehrady (2, 4). Dokladajú život malého mestečka chýrneho remeslom i vzdelanosťou. Svojou vysokou strechou dominuje nad celým areálom kópia neskorogotického kaštieľa z Parížoviec (3). Múzeum leží v ústí Račkovej doliny, takže priamo nad ním sa vypínajú štíty Západných Tatier.

Несколько домов происходит из с. Липтовска-Сиельница, в настоящее время затопленного водой плотины (2, 4). Они демонстрируют жизнь маленького городка, славящегося развитием ремесел и всеобщей образованностью. Высокая крыша копии поздне-готического здания из с. Парижовце доминирует над всем музейным комплексом (3). Музей расположен в устье „Рачковой долины", так что прямо над ним возвышаются пики Западных Татр.

Einige Häuser stammen aus Liptovská Sielnica, das heute durch das Wasser der Talsperre überschwemmt ist (2, 4). Sie stellen das Leben des kleinen, durch das Handwerk und die Bildung altbekannten Städtchens dar. Die Kopie des Spätgotikgebäudes aus Parížovce dominiert durch ihr hohes Dach im ganzen Areal (3). Das Museum liegt in der Mündung des Račektales, direkt darüber breiten sich die Gipfel der Westtatra (Západní Tatry) aus.

Several houses come from Liptovská Sielnica, now flooded by the waters of the dam (2, 4). They exemplify the life of the little town renowned for its crafts as well as civilization. The whole area is dominated by the high roof of the copy of the late-Gothic ditle castle from Parížovce (3). The museum lies in the mouth of the Račková dell so that the peaks of the Western Tatras are towering right above it.

3

4

Expozícia v prírode Okresného vlastivedného múzea STARÁ ĽUBOVŇA

leží na poľane pod stredovekým hradom. Na toto miesto sú prenesené stavebné pamiatky ľudovej architektúry okresu. Aj toto múzeum má svoj čas ešte pred sebou.

Экспозиция под открытым небом Районного краеведческого музея Стара-Лубовня располагается на поляне под средневековым укрепленным замком. Сюда перенесены памятники народного зодчества, находившиеся в регионе. У этого музея все будущее еще впереди.

Die in der Natur stehende Exposition des Kreisheimatkundemuseums Stará Ľubovňa liegt in einer Hochebene unter einer mittelalterlichen Burg. An diese Stelle wurden Baudenkmäler der Volksarchitektur des Kreises zusammengetragen. Auch dieses Museum hat seine Blütezeit noch vor sich.

Open-air exposition of the District Motherland Museum at Stará Lubovňa spreads over the clearing under a medieval castle. To this place the memorable specimens of folk architecture from the district have been transferred. This museum, too, is one of those the time of which is yet to come.

12

1

2

3

4

Múzeum v prírode pôsobí ako dedinka v podhradí (4). Chalupa z Veľkého Lipníka vznikla až v 20. storočí (1). Jej tradičné vybavenie sa používalo ešte donedávna. V kultovom kúte vidíme ikony, pretože sme v kraji s gréckokatolíckou alebo pravoslávnou liturgiou (2). Vo farebnosti textílií sa viac než inde na Slovensku uplatňuje červená (3).

Музей под открытым небом вызывает впечатление деревушки в окрестностях замка (4). Изба из с. Вельки-Липник возникла только в XX веке (1). Ее традиционное оборудование эксплуатировалось еще недавно. В ее культовом уголке видны иконы, так как мы находимся в области греко-римской или православной литургии (2). Что касается красочности текстильных изделий, здесь больше, чем в других местах Словакии встречается красный цвет (3).

Das Museum in der Natur macht den Eindruck eines Dörfchens unterhalb der Burg (4). Das Häuschen aus Velký Lipník entstand erst im 20. Jahrhundert (1). Dessen traditionelle Austattung wurde noch bis vor kurzer Zeit genutzt. In der Kultecke kann man Ikonen sehen, da dies eine Gegend der griechisch – orthodoxen bzw. rechtgläubigen Liturgie ist (2). In der Farbigkeit der Textilien wird hier mehr als anderswo in der Slowakei Rot verwendet (3).

The open-air museum performs as a little village in the castle's extramural settlement (4). The cottage from Velký Lipník was built as late as in 20th century (1). Its traditional furnishing was used until recently. In the cult corner we can see icons as we are in the country with Greek Catholic or Eastern rite liturgy (2). In the colour design of the textiles red is applied here more than anywhere else in Slovakia (3).

I2

Šarišské múzeum
BARDEJOVSKÉ KÚPELE

vzniklo na okraji kúpeľov v prostredí, charakteristickom pre malé dedinky vo Východných Beskydách. Taká je aj poloha usadlosti prenesenej z obce Kračunovce.

Шаришский музей Бардейовске-Купеле возник на окраине курорта в среде, характерной для маленьких деревень Восточных Бескид. Таково и местоположение усадьбы, перенесенной сюда из населенного пункта Крачуновце.

Das Šarišer Museum Bardejovské kúpele entstand am Rande eines Kurortes in einer Gegend, die in den Ostbeskyden charakteristisch für kleine Dörfchen ist. Dies trifft auch für die Lage des Gehöftes zu, das aus der Gemeinde Kračunovce überführt wurde.

Šariš Museum at Bardejovské kúpele (Bardejov Spa) has been founded on the outskirts of the spa in the characteristic environment of little villages in the Eastern Beskides. Such is also the position of the estate transferred from the settlement of Kračunovce.

1

V južných obciach regiónu omazávali zruby hlinou alebo stavali budovy priamo z hlinených nepálených tehál. Charakteristické šindľové strechy má napr. dom a sýpka z Hrabovej Roztoky (1, 4), ležiacej na juhovýchodných svahoch Vihorlatu. Z tej istej obce pochádza kadlub, ktorý slúžil ako obilná zásobnica (2). Za domom z Petrovej je rumpálová studňa (3). Na výrobu súkna slúžila valcha z Livova (5).

2

В южных населенных пунктах региона срубы обмазывали глиной, или же – строили прямо из глиняного необожженного кирпича. Характерные соломенные крыши можно увидеть, например, на доме и амбаре из с. Грабова-Розтока (1, 4), расположенного на юго-восточных склонах горного хребта Вигорлат. Из той же деревни происходит изложница, служившая когда-то хранилищем для зерна (2). За домом из с. Петрова находится колодец с воротом (3). Валяльная мастерская из с. Ливов была предназначена для производства сукна (5).

In östlichen Orten der Region wurden die Blockhütten mit Lehm verputzt oder es wurde direkt mit ungebrannten Tonziegeln gebaut. Charakteristische Strohdächer haben z. B. das Haus und der Speicher aus Hrabová Roztoka (1, 4), die an den Südosthängen des Vihorlat liegen. Aus dem gleichen Ort stammt das Modell, das als Getreidekamrat diente (2). Hinter dem Haus aus Petrová steht ein Haspelbrunnen (3). Zur Herstellung von Tuch wurde eine Walke aus Livov verwendet (5).

In the southern localities of the region, log-cabins used to be smeared with clay or built directly from adobes. Characteristic thatched roofs are e.g. those on the house and corn-loft from Hrabová Roztoka (1, 4) lying on the south-eastern slope of the mount of Vihorlat. From the same locality comes the vat which served as grain reservoir (2). Behind the house from Petrová there is a windlass well (3). For the production of cloth the fulling mill from Livov was used (5).

3

4

5

1

2

3

Za valchou stojí usadlosť z Malcova so zrubovým domom omazaným hlinou (1). Izba malcovského domu je zariadená v štýle života rodiny z prvej polovice 20. storočia (2). Pod posteľou je ďalšie výsuvné lôžko pre deti. Pod valchou je umiestený unikátny stroj na vodný pohon, ktorým sa v 18. storočí vŕtali drevené vodovodné rúry pre mesto Bardejov (3).

За валяльной мастерской расположена усадьба из с. Мальцов с бревенчатым домом, обмазанным глиной (1). Комната дома из с. Мальцов обставлена в стиле семейного быта первой половины XX века (2). Под кроватью находится вторая, выдвижная постель для детей. Под валяльной мастерской помещена уникальная машина на водяной тяге, с помощью которой в XVIII веке сверлили деревянные водопроводные трубы для города Бардейов (3).

Hinter der Walke steht ein Gehöft aus Malcov mit einem gezimmerten Haus, das mit Lehm verputzt ist (1). Die Stube des Hauses ist im Lebensstyl einer Familie aus der ersten Hälfte des 20. Jahrhunderts (2) eingerichtet. Unter dem Bett ist ein weiteres ausziehbares Bettchen für Kinder. Unterhalb der Walke ist eine unikate Maschine mit Wasserantrieb plaziert, mit dem im 18. Jahrhundert Holzwasserleitungen für die Stadt Bardejov gebohrt wurden (3).

Behind the fulling mill stands the estate from Malcov with a framework house smeared with clay (1). The sitting room inside the Malcov house is furnished according to the life style of the family from the first half of 20th century (2). Under the bed you can see another couchette to be pulled out for children. Under the fulling mill is placed a unique water-driven drilling machine which, in 18th century, was used to make wooden water pipes for the town of Bardejov (3).

1

2

3

K prostrediu lúk a sadov patrí včelín s klátovými i slamenými úľmi (1). Sýpky sa stavali najčastejšie nad pivnicami zapustenými do svahu, ako to ukazuje objekt prenesený z Malcova (2). Stavebným materiálom na severovýchodnom Slovensku bolo prevažne tvrdé bukové drevo. Na osmibokom humne pôvodom z obce Tarbaj vidno, ako dômyselne sa viazal zrub v rohoch (3).

От среды лугов и садов неотделим пчельник с соломенными и колодовыми ульями (1). Амбары чаще всего строились под погребами, встроенными в склон, как это видно на объекте, перенесенном сюда из с. Мальцов (2). Строительным материалом в северо-восточной Словакии являлось прежде всего твердое буковое дерево. На восьмигранном сарае, происходящем из с. Тарбай, видно, какую трудность представляла собой вязка сруба в углах (3).

Zur Umgebung der Wiesen und Gärten gehört ein Bienenhaus mit Bienenstöcken aus Klötzern und Stroh (1). Speicher wurden größtenteils auf Kellern gebaut, die in die Hänge eingepaßt wurden. So wie dies auch das Objekt aus Malcov zeigt (2). Als Baumaterial wurde in der Nordostslowakei vorwiegend hartes Eichenholz verwendet. An der achteckigen Scheune aus dem Ort Tarbaj ist zu sehen, wie schwer die Bindung eines Zimmerwerkes in den Ecken ist (3).

The environment of meadows and orchards is naturally complemented with bee-houses composed of beam and straw hives (1). Corn-lofts were most often built above cellars dug out in the slope as exemplified in the object transferred from Malcov (2). Construction material in north-eastern Slovakia was mostly hard beech wood. The octagonal barn from the settlement of Tarbaj demonstrates how difficult it was to join the timber in the corners (3).

Národopisná expozícia v prírode pri Múzeu ukrajinskej kultúry SVIDNÍK

leží na svahu nazývanom Kochanyj bereh. Z neho je výhľad po horskej krajine Východných Beskýd. Vzniká tam model dediny zo severného Zemplína a osady zo severného Šariša a Spiša, i s vodným mlynom, pílou a valchou.

Этнографическая экспозиция под открытым небом при „Музее украинской культуры Свидник" располагается на склоне, называемом „Коханый берег". Оттуда прекрасный вид на горную местность Восточных Бескид. Здесь же возникает модель деревни из северной части Земплинской области и селения из северной части Шаришской и Спишской областей – с водяной мельницей, лесопильней и валяльной мастерской.

Die Völkerkundeexposition in der Natur beim Museum der ukrainischen Kultur, Svidník, liegt am sog. Kochanyj bereh-Hang. Von hieraus hat man ein schönes Panorama auf die Berglandschaft der Ostbeskyden. Dort entsteht ein Modell eines Dorfes aus dem Norden Zemplín und eine Siedlung aus dem nördlichen Teil von Šariš und Spiš, mit Wassermühlen, einer Säge und einer Walke.

Ethnographic open-air exposition of Ukrainian Culture Museum at Svidník lies on the slope called Kochanyj bereh. From it the mountainous countryside of the Eastern Beskides can be scanned. The model of the northern Zemplín region village and of the northern Šariš region settlement is created there, comprising the water mill, sawmill and fulling mill.

14

1

2

3

4

Dom prenesený z obce Kečkovce bol vystavaný v roku 1905 (1). Okrem izby nad pivnicou (2) má bočnú obytnú komoru, predsieň, chliev, humno a kôlňu – všetko pod jednou strechou. V dome z Rešova je znázornená domáca výroba opálok (3). Usadlosť prenesená zo Snakova je tiež prikrytá jednou strechou, iba sýpka stojí z požiarnych dôvodov ďalej (4).

Дом, перенесенный из с. Кечковце был построен в 1905 г. (1). Кроме комнаты над погребом (2) здесь имеются боковой жилой чулан, сени, хлева, рига, сарай – все под одной крышей. В доме из с. Решов демонстрируется кустарное производство – плетение из лыка (3). Усадьба, перенесенная сюда из с. Снаков, также находится под одной крышей, только амбар стоит в целях противопожарной охраны в стороне (4).

Das Haus, aus der Gemeinde Kečkovce hierher gebracht, wurde im Jahre 1905 (1) gebaut. Außer der Stube über dem Keller (2) hat es eine Seitenwohnkammer, einen Flur, einen Stall, eine Scheune und einen Schuppen – alles unter einem Dach. In dem Haus aus Rešov wird die Heimproduktion von Flechtkorb demonstriert (3). Das Gahöft, das aus Snakov hergebracht wurde, bringt ebenfalls alle Lebensräume unter einem Dach unter, nur der Speicher steht aus Brandvorsichtsmaßnahmen abseits (4).

The house transferred from the settlement of Kečkovce was built in 1905 (1). Besides the sitting room above the cellar (2) it has a living chamber, a hall, a stable, a barn, and a shed – all under one roof. In the house from Rešov home production of wickerwork bowls is demonstrated (3). The estate transferred from Snakov is covered with the roof, too, only the corn-loft stands apart for fire-protection reasons (4).

I4

1

2

3

4

Celú usadlosť – odpredu až po holohumnicu vzadu – obklopujú kôlne vzniknuté predĺžením valbovej strechy (1, 3). Na sýpke sa výrazne uplatnila starobylá konštrukcia zrubovej klenby (3). V jednoducho vybavených izbách žiari červený textil, charakteristický pre ľudovú kultúru Ukrajincov (2). Trochu iné usporiadanie stavieb dokladá usadlosť z Rešova (4).

Всю усадьбу – спереди, до самого гумна сзади – облегают сараи, возникшие в результате удлинения вальмовой крыши (1, 3). У амбара очевидна древняя конструкция срубового свода (3). В комнатах с простой обстановкой резко выделяется красный текстиль, характерный для народной культуры украинцев (2). Немножко другое размещение строений встречается в усадьбе из с. Решов (4).

Die ganze Wirtschaft – von vorn bis hin zur Tenne – ist mit Schuppen umgeben, die durch die Verlängerung des Walmdaches entstanden sind (1, 3). Am Speicher kam die altherkömmliche Konstruktion des gezimmerten Gewölbes gut zur Anwendung (3). In den einfach ausgestatteten Stuben leuchtet rotes Textil, das für die Volkskultur der Ukrainer charakteristisch ist (2). Eine etwas andere Bauanordnung bezeigt das Gut aus Rešov (4).

The whole estate – from the front part to the threshing floor at the back – is encircled by sheds formed by the prolongation of the hipped roof (1, 3). The ancient construction of timber vaulting was applied substantially in the corn-loft (3). The rooms furnished in a simple way glare with red fabric characteristic for the folk culture of the Ukrainians (2). Slightly different arrangement of constructions is exemplified by the estate from Rešov (4).

14

Banské múzeum v prírode
BANSKÁ ŠTIAVNICA

nachádza sa neďaleko mesta v historickej baníckej zástavbe. Na strmých svahoch sa v rudných baniach stále ešte ťaží a zachovalo sa tu množstvo historických architektonických pamiatok. Múzeum zatiaľ vybudovalo časť technických stavieb a ukážky podzemnej ťažby.

Горный музей под открытым небом Банска-Штиявница находится недалеко от города, на территории исторической шахтерской застройки. В рудниках на крутых склонах все еще добывают руду. Здесь же сохранился целый ряд исторических памятников архитектуры. Пока в музее построены некоторые технические сооружения и открыта подземная демонстрация добычи руды.

Das Bergbaumuseum in der Natur, Banská Štiavnica, befindet sich unweit der Stadt, in historischer bergmännischer Verbauung. An steilen Hängen fördert man immer noch in Erzbergwerken. Hier blieben außerdem eine Reihe historischer architektonischer Denkmäler erhalten. Das Museum baute vorläufig einen Teil der technischen Bauwerke sowie unterirdische Exemplare der Förderung auf.

Mining open-air Museum at Banská Štiavnica finds itself near the town in the area of the historical mining housing. In the ore mines dug in the steep slopes the minng works are still under way and a number of historical architectonic memoriabilia has been preserved here. The museum has so far built a part of the technical constructions and the underground displays of mining.

1

V areáli technických stavieb dominuje banská klopačka (1) a ťažná veža prenesená zo šachty v Banskej Belej (2). Pod ňou je umiestený ťažný stroj pochádzajúci zo šachty Mária v Banskej Štiavnici (4). Múzeum sprístupnilo návštevníkom aj historickú štôlňu Bartolomej (3).

В ансамбле технических сооружений доминирует деревянная колокольня с часами (1), а также копер, перенесенный сюда из шахты в с. Банска-Бела (2). Под ним помещена подъемная машина, привезенная из шахты „Мария" в г. Банска-Штиявница (4). Музей открыл для посетителей и историческую штольню „Бартоломей" (3).

Auf dem Gelände der technischen Bauwerke dominiert ein Uhrturm (1) und ein Förderturm, der aus dem Schacht in Banská Belá (2) ist. Unter dem Turm steht eine Fördermaschine aus dem Schacht Mária in Banská Štiavnica (4). Das Museum machte den Besuchern ebenfalls den historischen Stollen Bartolomäus zugänglich (3).

The area of technical constructions is dominated by the mining knocker (1) and the head-gear tower transferred from the mine at Banská Belá (2). Under it is located the extracting engine originating from the Mária mine at Banská Štiavnica (4). The museum has made the historical gallery Bartolomej open to public (3).

2

3

4

1

2

3

4

V podzemnej expozícii sú ukážky stredovekej ručnej ťažby rudy (1) i súčasnej technológie s pneumatickým vrtákom (2) a kombajnom. Historický vývoj dokladá aj spôsob razenia chodieb, výdreva, koľaje a doprava vôbec (3). Na povrchu je inštalovaná stará ťažná veža z banskoštiavnickej šachty Mária (4).

В подземной экспозиции демонстрируется средневековая ручная добыча руды (1) и современная технология добычи с помощью пневматического сверла (2) и комбайна. Историческое развитие документируют также: способ проходки штреков, деревянная крепь, откаточный путь и транспорт вообще (3). На поверхности установлен старый копер из шахты „Мария" в г. Банска-Штиявница (4).

In der unterirdischen Ausstellung befinden sich Exemplare der mittelalterlichen manufakturellen Erzförderung (1) sowie gegenwärtige Technologien mit dem Pressluftbohrer (2) und der Kombine. Die historische Entwicklung demonstriert ebenso die Art und Weise des Stemmens eines Gandes, den Holzausbau, die Schienen und die Beförderung überhaupt (3). An der Oberfläche steht der alte Förderturm aus dem Schacht Mária in Banská Štiavnica (4).

The underground exposition demonstrates both medieval methods of manual extraction of ore (1) and contemporary technologies with a pneumatic drill (2) and combine extractor. The historical development is exemplified also by the methods od gallery breaking, timbering, rails and transport in general (3). On the surface is installed the old head-gear tower of the Mária mine from Banská Štiavnica (4).

Klopačka s hodinami a znakom dvoch kladív je symbolom baníctva na celom Slovensku. Privolávala pomoc pri banskom nešťastí, odmeriavala pracovný čas, oznamovala jeho začiatok i koniec.

Деревянная колокольня с часами и эмблемой с двумя молотками – символы горной промышленности во всей Словакии. Она звала на помощь при катастрофах на шахте, отмеряла рабочее время, объявляла о начале и конце работ.

Der Uhrturm mit Uhr und dem Zeichen zweier Hammer ist das Bergbausymbol in der ganzen Slowakei. Er alarmierte um Hilfe bei einem Berwerksunglück, maß die Arbeitszeit, gab ihren Beginn und ihr Ende an.

The knocker with a clock and the sign of two hammers is the symbol of mining all over Slovakia. It used to call in help in case if mine disasters, it measured the working time announcing both its beginning and end.

Soustředění objektů lidové architektury Českého středohoří v Zubrnicích

Místo: Zubrnice (okres Ústí n. L.) PSČ 403 24.
Spravující instituce:
Okresní vlastivědné muzeum, Ústí n. L. PSČ 400 00.
Výstavba schválena r. 1977, budování od r. 1977, zpřístupněno r. 1988.
Autor etnografické koncepce: PhDr. F. Ledvinka, autor architektonické studie:
ing. arch. J. Škabrada, CSc.
Expoziční areál dosud přesně nevymezen, jedná se o intravilán a část extravilánu obce, cca 30 ha.
Počet expozičních objektů v r. 1988: 12.
Expozice bude prezentovat lidovou kulturu období kapitalismu oblasti Českého středohoří prostřednictvím rekonstrukce historického jádra stávajícího sídla přenesením několika objektů z jiných obcí a památkovou obnovou místních domů na návsi.
Unikátní součástí expozice bude obnovení části zaniklé železniční tratě Ústí n. L. – Úštěk, roubený mlýn (1803) v katastru obce, špýchary z Lukova a Lochočic a dům č. 61.
Muzeum je otevřeno od 1. 5. do 31. 10. kromě pondělí denne od 9 do 17 hod.
Restaurace bude řešena v areálu expozice, nejbližší ubytování v Ústí n. L. a Úštěku.

Národopisné muzeum Třebíz

Místo: Třebíz (okres Kladno) PSČ 273 75.
Spravující instituce: Vlastivědné muzeum Slaný (provoz, odborná činnost, sbírky) a MNV Třebíz (výstavba a údržba objektů, správa). Výstavba schválena r. 1969, budování od r. 1969, veřejnosti zpřístupněno r. 1975.
Autoři etnografických studií:
L. Štěpánek, PhDr. V. Jiřikovská, CSc.,
autoři architektonických studií:
J. Nedvěd, ing. arch. J. Škabrada, CSc.,
autorka historické studie PhDr. J. Krotilová. Expoziční areál měří 32 ha.
Počet expozičních objektů v r. 1988: 24, počet dalších plánovaných expozičních objektů: 6.
Muzeum prezentuje lidovou kulturu Slánska (řepařská oblast severozápadní části středních Čech po okraj Českého středohoří) prostřednictvím úplné návesní obce Třebíz (převážně zděné stavby z kamene – opuky a pískovce, částečně hrázděné), jejíž jádro je rekonstrukcí historického životního prostředí dotvářenou několika přenesenými doplňujícími objekty. Unikátem je Cífkův statek ze 16.–19. stol., v jehož prostorách je prezentován způsob života v historických interiérech, vývoj zemědělství na Slánsku a ve zvláštních sálech jsou pořádány tematické výstavy. Další tři usedlosti expozice pocházejí z 18. stol. Rodný dům spisovatele Václava Beneše Třebízského je přístupný veřejnosti jako památník od r. 1904. Muzeum se podílí na pořádání Třebízských poutí (zpravidla 8. neděli po velikonocích) a pořádá další programy: ukázky lidové výroby, sušení ovoce, pečení v peci aj.
Muzeum je otevřeno od 1. 5. do 31. 10. denně mimo pondělí od 9 do 16 hod.
Návštěvnost v r. 1988 činila 11 000 osob.
Nejbližší ubytování a restaurace:
Slaný, Louny (9, 17 km).
Nejbližší občerstvení: hostinec v Třebízi.

Muzeum vesnice

Místo: Kouřim (okres Kolín) PSČ 281 61.
Spravující instituce:
Regionální muzeum Kolín, PSČ 280 00.
Výstavba schválena r. 1972, budování od r. 1972, zpřístupněno veřejnosti 1975.
Autorky etnografických koncepcí:
A. Pospíšilová, PhDr. M. Nováková,
autor architektonické studie:
ing. arch. P. Fuchs.
Expoziční areál měří 4 ha.
Počet expozičních objektů v r. 1987: 13, počet všech plánovaných expozičních objektů: 38.
Koncepce expozice nevyjasněna. Zpočátku do expozičního areálu byly přenášeny objekty ze zátopového území vodního díla Želivka, které byly zařazeny ve státním seznamu kulturních památek, se záměrem prezentace lidové kultury jižní části Středočeského kraje. V r. 1975 byla záchranná koncepce rozšířena ideovým záměrem SÚPPOP na území celé ČSR. Z ní se pak vycházelo při formování názorů vytvořit v Kouřimi muzeum stavebních technik bez ohledu na vzájemné ideové vztahy a vnitřní vybavení objektů.
Unikátem jsou polygonální stodoly z Durdic (1648) a z Želejova (1660), usedlost z Týřovic a rychta z Bradlecké Lhoty.
Muzeum je otevřeno denně mimo pondělí od 9 do 16 hod., od 1. 6. do 31. 9. do 17 hod.
Návštěvnost je asi 5 000 osob ročně.
Nejbližší ubytování a restaurace v Kouřimi, občerstvení na přilehlém koupališti.

Polabské národopisné muzeum v Přerově nad Labem

Místo: Přerov nad Labem (okres Nymburk) PSČ 289 16.
Spravující instituce: Polabské muzeum v Poděbradech (okresní muzeum pro okres Nymburk) PSČ 290 01.
Výstavba schválena r. 1979, budování od r. 1967, veřejnosti zpřístupněno r. 1967.
Autoři etnografických studií:
PhDr. H. Sedláčková, ing. I. Bernard,
autoři architektonické studie:
ing. arch. Koreček, ing. arch. Tichý.
Expoziční areál měří 1,8 ha.
Počet expozičních objektů v r. 1988: 32, počet dalších plánovaných expozičních objektů: 8.
Do muzea se přenášely památkové objekty lidové architektury středního Polabí (zejména z okresu Nymburk), jejichž existence na původním místě byla ohrožena. Základem muzea a prvním objektem byla tzv. staročeská chalupa (panská kovárna a později rychta z poloviny 18. století upravená kolem r. 1895). V ní jsou vystaveny národopisné sbírky.
Z bývalých panských staveb patří do muzea zděná myslivna (správní budova a depozitáře), tzv. bednárna s výstavním sálem a stará škola. Do sousedství na parkově upravenou náves byly od r. 1967 přeneseny chalupy z Draha a Chvalovic a další drobné objekty (špýchary, sušárna, studně, lidové plastiky apod.).
Od r. 1980 je realizován návrh zástavby na zahradách za bednárnou a myslivnou, kde budou do r. 1990 rekonstruovány usedlosti z Královéměstecka, Křinecka a okolí Nymburka. Mimo expoziční areál se nachází zděný statek č. 13 s barokním štítem a vjezdem s expozicí polabského zemědělství (síň tradic JZD).
Muzeum je otevřeno od 15. 4. do 30. 10. denně mimo pondělí od 14 do 16 hod.
Návštěvnost v r. 1988 činila 30 000 osob.
Nejbližší ubytování: hotel Polabí v Lysé n. L., nejbližší restaurace: motorest Kersko v Lysé n. L.
Nejbližší občerstvení: cukrárna proti národopisnému muzeu v Přerově n. L.

Soubor lidových staveb a řemesel Vysočina

Místo: obec Vysočina (okres Chrudim), pošta Hlinsko v Čechách, PSČ 539 01, sídlo správy v osadě Svobodné Hamry (obec Vysočina se nachází mezi Hlinskem v Čechách a Trhovou Kamenicí a zahrnuje osady Svobodné Hamry, Dřevíkov, Možděnice, Veselý Kopec a Rváčov, do expozičního areálu patří osada Králova Pila obce Všeradov).
Spravující instituce: Východočeské krajské středisko státní památkové péče a ochrany přírody v Pardubicích.
Výstavba schválena r. 1977, budování od r. 1969, zpřístupnění veřejnosti r. 1971, od r. 1988 rozšířen o řemeselnické chalupy v Hlinsku v Čechách.
Autoři etnografických studií:
L. Štěpán, PhDr. I. Vojancová, autoři architektonických studií:
L. Štěpán, ing. arch. L. Černík, ing. Z. Haken, ing. arch. J. Škabrada, CSc.
Expoziční areál v osadě Veselý Kopec měří 3,5 ha, celkově expoziční historická krajina se rozkládá cca na 9 km^2.
Počet expozičních objektů v r. 1988: 37, počet dalších plánovaných expozičních objektů 12.
Expozice prezentuje lidovou kulturu severní části Českomoravské vrchoviny (oblast výskytu roubených staveb) a zvláště tradiční lidovou techniku v širokých sídelních souvislostech. Unikátem je Králova Pila (mlýn s pilou), dům č. 4 z Veselého Kopce a čtrnáctiboká stodola ze Sádku (vše ze 17. století), 12 objektů z 18. století. V expozici se pořádají vánoční a jarní zvykoslovné akce, ukázky rukodělné výroby a chovu domácích zvířat.
Soubor je otevřen od 15. 4. do 31. 10. Svobodné Hamry denně mimo pondělí, od 9 do 16 hod., od května do září do 17 hod., v Možděnici mimo červenec a srpen jen v sobotu a neděli.
Návštěvnost v r. 1988 činila 129 000 osob.
Nejbližší ubytování:
hotely Záložna, Styl v Hlinsku v Čechách, nejbližší restaurace:
hotel Slavia v Trhové Kamenici.
Nejbližší občerstvení: v expozičním areálu na Veselém Kopci (od května do září).

Muzeum vesnice jihovýchodní Moravy

Místo: Strážnice (okres Hodonín) PSČ 696 62.
Spravující instituce:
Ústav lidového umění, Strážnice.
Výstavba schválena r. 1973, budování od r. 1974, zpřístupnění veřejnosti r. 1981.
Autoři etnografických studií:
doc. PhDr. V. Frolec, CSc., PhDr. J. Souček, PhDr. J. Tomeš, CSc., PhDr. J. Jančář, CSc.,
autor architektonické studie:
ing. arch. O. Máčel s kolektivem.
Expoziční areál měří 9,7 ha,
plánovaná výměra je 15 ha.
Počet expozičních objektů v r. 1987: 75, počet dalších plánovaných expozičních objektů: 20.
Expozice prezentuje lidovou stavební kulturu jihovýchodní Moravy prostřednictvím rekonstrukce ucelených sídelních tvarů. Zahrnuje lidové stavby obytného a hospodářského charakteru (z regionů

Moravské Kopanice, Luhačovické Zálesí, Horňácko, strážnické Dolňácko, v plánu je výstavba z Podluží, uherskobrodského, uherskohradišťského a kyjovského Dolňácka. Dále k expozici patří areály technických vodních staveb, lučního hospodářství a vinohradnický (24 sklepů a lisoven s ukázkou výsadby a pěstování odrůd vinné révy). V expozičním areálu se v průběhu léta (o sobotách a nedělích) konají pořady folklórních souborů nebo akce spojené s ukázkami výročních zvyků.
Muzeum je otevřeno od 1. 5. do 31. 10.,
v neděli od 10 do 18 hod.
a v dalších dnech mimo pondělí od 8 do 17 hod.
Návštěvnost v r. 1988 činila 32 354 osob.
Nejbližší ubytování: ve Strážnici autokempink ZO Svazarmu, hotel Černý orel a Interhotel Strážnice,
ve Veselí n. M. hotel Rozkvět,
nejbližší restaurace ve Strážnici Jarošovská pivnice a restaurace uvedených ubytovacích zařízení.
Nejbližší občerstvení: bufet Danaj, Strážnice, stánkové občerstvení
u vstupu do expozičního areálu.

Valašské muzeum v přírodě

Místo: Rožnov pod Radhoštěm (okres Vsetín) PSČ 756 61.
Spravující instituce: Valašské muzeum v přírodě, Rožnov p. R.
Dostavba schválena ve formě koncepčního rámcového libreta r. 1974, budování od r. 1923 v expozičním areálu Dřevěného městečka, od r. 1963 v expozičním areálu Valašské dědiny, zpřístupnění veřejnosti 1925.
Autoři studií pro řešení celku nebo expozičních areálu: Bohumír Jaroněk (výtvarný návrh zástavby), akad. arch. M. Podzemný, ing. arch. J. Sedláček, ing. A. Závada (architektonické), PhDr. J. Langer, CSc., PhDr. J. Štika, CSc. (etnografické), ing. J. Stromšík (provozní).
Expoziční areál měří 76 ha a je vyhlášen státem chráněnou zahradou a parkem.
Počet expozičních objektů v r. 1988: 77, dalších plánovaných expozičních objektů130.
Expozice prezentuje lidovou kulturu vesnického a maloměstského společenství regionu Valašska, jakož i tradiční lidové techniky z 18. až začátku 20. století prostřednictvím rekonstrukce sídel a jejich historického životního prostředí včetně pastvin, luk a polí s pěstováním historických odrůd zemědělských plodin a ovocných stromů, s chovem hospodářského zvířectva, zejména salašnickým chovem ovcí. Unikátem je stavba Valašské hospody ze 17. století, interiérová expozice fojtství, technické stavby na vodní pohon (s převedením jejich výrobní činnosti), dům z Lužné z 18. století, větrný mlýn, živé zemědělské hospodářství a řada historických plodin.
Muzeum otevřeno v jednotlivých areálech:
Dřevěné městečko: 1. 5.–15. 11. denně,
15. 12.–31. 3. v pondělí, středu, sobotu a neděli.
Valašská dědina: 15. 5.–30. 9.
Mlýnská dolina: 1. 4.–30. 9. Otvírací doba je od 8 do 17 hod., od května do srpna do 18 hod.
Návštěvnost v r. 1988 byla 595 000 osob.
Nejbližší ubytování: hotely v Rožnově p. R.: Rožnovan, Koruna, Tesla,
autokempinky TJ a Svazarm;
nejbližší stálá restaurace v expozičním areálu Dřevěného městečka.
Nejbližší občerstvení: v expozičních areálech.

Múzeum slovenskej dediny

Miesto: Martin – Jahodnícke háje, PSČ 036 01
Spravujúca inštitúcia: Etnografický ústav Slovenského národného múzea, Martin.
Koncepcia vytvorená 1965, začiatok stavby 1967, prvé sprístupnenie verejnosti 1983, po skončení ďalšej etapy bude znova sprístupnená 1992.
Autori etnografických štúdií:
koncepcia výstavby 1965
J. Boďa,
ing. arch. J. Turzo, CSc., PhDr. A. Polonec;
koncepcia výstavby a prevádzky 1971
PhDr. J. Kantár, CSc.;
projektová úloha expozície 1968
doc. PhDr. Š. Mruškovič, CSc.;
ideový zámer expozície 1974 PhDr. M. Benža, PhDr. S. Horváth, PhDr. I. Krištek, CSc.;
tematicko-urbanistické upresnenie koncepcie 1982 PhDr. S. Horváth, PhDr. I. Krištek, CSc.
Autori architektonických štúdií:
doc. ing. arch. D. Majzlík, CSc.,
ing. arch. J. Lichner, CSc., ing. arch. M. Bašo,
ing. arch. I. Puškár, CSc.;
urbanistická štúdia 1968
ing. arch. J. Turzo, CSc.
Expozičný areál meria 56,5 ha.
Počet expozičných objektov v r. 1987: 74.
Počet ďalších plánovaných objektov: 91 usadlostí a 152 jednotlivých objektov.
Expozícia prezentuje ľudovú kultúru lokálnych dedinských spoločenstiev z územia Slovenska z obdobia druhej polovice 19. a prvej polovice 20. storočia prostredníctvom rekonštrukcie sídel v súlade s etnografickými regiónmi (stavby hlinené, pletené, zrubové, murované) a ich historického prostredia. Unikátom je zemianska usadlosť z Vyšného Kubína (1748), zrubový kostol z Rudna a dom z Liptovskej Lúžnej. V expozícii sa usporadúvajú špeciálne programy pri príležitosti Medzinárodného dňa múzeí.
Návštevnosť v r. 1983 bola 11 000 osôb.
Najbližšie ubytovanie: Martin – hotel Turiec.
Najbližšie občerstvenie: bufet pred MSD.
Najbližšia stála reštaurácia: sídlisko Ľadoveň, cca 1 km od MSD.

Múzeum kysuckej dediny
Národopisná expozícia v prírode

Miesto: Nová Bystrica – Vychylovka (okres Čadca) PSČ 023 05.
Spravujúca inštitúcia: Kysucké múzeum, Palárikov dom, 022 01 Čadca.
Výstavba schválená v r. 1974, verejnosti sprístupnená prvá časť v r. 1981.
Autori etnografickej štúdie:
1974 – PhDr. J. Kantár, CSc.,
1979 – PhDr. A. Kocourková,
1984 – PhDr. M. Kiripolský, PhDr. A. Kocourková, PhDr. P. Maráky.
Autori architektonickej štúdie:
ing. arch. B. Dohnány, CSc. a kolektív (1976).
Architektonická spolupráca:
akad. arch. A. Goryczková (1984).
Expozičný areál má rozsah 143 ha,
jeho zastavaná časť cca 20 ha.
Areál je chránený rozsiahlym ochranným pásmom a rozkladá sa na území Chránenej krajinnej oblasti Kysuce (vyhlásená r. 1984).
Počet expozičných objektov v r. 1987: 22.
Počet všetkých plánovaných objektov: 67.
Expozícia usiluje o rekonštrukciu sídelnej krajiny a životného prostredia a prezentuje spôsob života a kultúru dedinského ľudu na Kysuciach z obdobia druhej polovice 19. a začiatku 20. storočia. Prevažná väčšina objektov je premiestená z rozličných kysuckých obcí (Riečnica, Harvelka, Klubina, Zborov nad Bystricou, Oščadnica, Korňa a perspektívne ďalšie). V areáli expozície je aplikovaná aj ochrana in situ pôvodných sezónnych pastierskych obydlí. V areáli a jeho tesnej blízkosti je obnovená časť trate úzkorozchodnej kysucko-oravskej železnice, ktorá sa bude využívať na dopravu návštevníkov a ukážky jazdy vlaku s parnou trakciou. K najzaujímavejším architektonickým detailom patrí archivoltový portál dverí obytného domu z Oščadnice z roku 1805, stropná maľba ľudového tvorcu v lodi kaplnky zo Zborova nad Bystricou, zdobené štíty viacerých obytných domov z Riečnice a ďalšie detaily. V interiéroch vybraných objektov sú inštalované pôvodné zariadenia získané zberom v obciach, z ktorých boli objekty do Múzea kysuckej dediny prevezené. V areáli expozície sa nepravidelne usporadúvajú ukážky ľudových výrobných techník a historických činností.
Múzeum je otvorené v sezóne od mája do októbra, denne okrem pondelka od 9.30 do 18. h. Návštevnosť v r. 1988: 14 000 osôb.
Najbližšie ubytovanie:
Stará Bystrica – turistická ubytovňa;
Čadca – hotel Lipa, horský hotel Husárik, turistická ubytovňa Športová hala;
Kysucké Nové Mesto – hotel Mýto,
hotel Závodný klub ROH ZVL.
Najbližšia reštaurácia: Nová Bystrica.
Najbližšie občerstvenie: v areáli expozície (krčma z Korne, SD Jednota Čadca).

Múzeum oravskej dediny

Miesto: Zuberec – Brestová (okres Dolný Kubín) PSČ 027 32.
Spravujúca inštitúcia:
Oravské múzeum, Dolný Kubín, PSČ 026 01.
Výstavba schválená r. 1967, začiatok výstavby r. 1968, sprístupnená verejnosti r. 1975.
Autor etnografickej štúdie:
PhDr. J. Langer, CSc.,
autor architektonickej štúdie:
ing. arch. M. Slováková.
Expozičný areál meria 20 ha.
Počet expozičných objektov v r. 1988: 76
Počet ďalších plánovaných objektov: dokončenie 2 usadlostí a postavenie 8 jednotlivých objektov.
Expozícia predstavuje ľudovú architektúru Oravy formou rekonštrukcie modelu sídla (zrubové stavby). Unikátom je neskorogotický kostol zo Zábreže (15.–18. storočie), zemianska usadlosť z Vyšného Kubína (1752), dom č. 57 z Čimhovej a ďalšie 3 objekty z 18. storočia. Na priestranstve pred múzeom sa koncom augusta usporadúvajú Podroháčske folklórne slávnosti (od r. 1975). V expozičnom areáli sa nepravidelne usporadúvajú ukážky folklóru, ľudových výrobných techník a iných historických činností prostredníctvom dedinských skupín a detských folklórnych súborov.
Múzeum je otvorené: denne okrem pondelka od mája do októbra od 8. do 15. h., od júna do augusta do 16. h.
Návštevnosť v r. 1988: 58 651 osôb.
Najbližšie ubytovanie:
Zuberec (zabezpečuje Slovakotour a TJ),
chaty Primula a Zverovka v Roháčoch,
najbližšia reštaurácia:

pred vstupom do múzea, Zuberec – Milotín, Roháče – chaty Primula a Zverovka.
Najbližšie občerstvenie: pred vstupom do múzea.

Múzeum liptovskej dediny

Miesto: Pribylina (okres Liptovský Mikuláš) PSČ 032 42.
Spravujúca inštitúcia:
Liptovské múzeum v Ružomberku, národopisné oddelenie v Liptovskom Hrádku PSČ 033 01.
Výstavba schválená v r. 1971, budovanie od r. 1972.
Autor etnografickej štúdie:
PhDr. J. Langer, CSc., PhDr. I. Zuskinová.
Autor architektonickej štúdie:
ing. arch. S. Dúbravec, CSc.
Expozičný areál meria: 25 ha.
Počet expozičných objektov v r. 1988: 31, počet ďalších plánovaných objektov 45.
Expozícia bude prezentovať ľudovú kultúru Liptova prostredníctvom vedeckej rekonštrukcie sídelného areálu s historickým jadrom, v ktorom sú obsiahnuté unikáty: kópia neskorogotického kaštieľa z Parížoviec, gotického kostola z Liptovskej Mary a gotického presbytára kostola z Liptovskej Sielnice, odkiaľ bol prenesený aj súbor usadlostí. Ďalšie zrubové objekty pochádzajú zo všetkých častí Liptova (18. a 19. storočie). Časť areálu s prenesenou ľudovou architektúrou bude slúžiť na ubytovanie turistov. V areáli bude vyriešené občerstvenie, na jeho okraji je hotel Esperanto s reštauráciou.

Expozícia v prírode
Okresného vlastivedného múzea
v Starej Ľubovni

Miesto: Stará Ľubovňa – pod hradom, PSČ 064 01.
Spravujúca inštitúcia:
Okresné vlastivedné múzeum, Stará Ľubovňa.
Výstavba schválená r. 1974, budovanie od r. 1977, sprístupnené verejnosti r. 1983.
Expozičný areál meria cca 10 ha.
Počet expozičných objektov cca 20.
Expozícia prezentuje ľudovú kultúru okresu Stará Ľubovňa formou prenesenia objektov zrubovej architektúry s vybavením ich interiérov. Unikátom je zrubový kostol z Matysovej (18. storočie).
Múzeum je otvorené okrem pondelka od 9. do 16. h.
Návštevnosť v r. 1988: 11 230 osôb.
Najbližšie ubytovanie v Starej Ľubovni, najbližšia reštaurácia koliba pod hradom.

Šarišské múzeum

Miesto: Bardejovské kúpele (okres Bardejov) PSČ 086 31.
Spravujúca inštitúcia:
Šarišské múzeum, Bardejov, PSČ 085 01.
Výstavba schválená 1961, budovanie v rokoch 1962–1972, sprístupnenie verejnosti r. 1965.
Autorka etnografickej štúdie:
prom. hist. B. Puškárová, CSc.,
autor architektonickej štúdie:
ing. arch. I. Puškár, CSc.
Expozičný areál meria 3,41 ha.
Expozičných objektov v r. 1988: 23.
Expozícia prezentuje ľudovú kultúru Šariša prostredníctvom prenesených reprezentujúcich objektov s interiérovým vybavením. Unikátom je vrták drevených vodovodných rúr na vodný pohon z Bardejova, drevené kostoly východného rítu zo Zboja (1706) a z Mikulášovej (1730) a zvonica z Jánoviec (1700). Väčšina domov pochádza z konca 19. storočia a charakterizuje obdobie kapitalizmu. V expozičnom areáli sa usporadúvajú kultúrne programy a ukážky ručnej výroby najmä na Medzinárodný deň múzeí a nepravidelne v priebehu letnej sezóny.
V priľahlej vile Rákoczi je národopisná expozícia a expozícia Ikony východného Slovenska.
Návštevnosť v r. 1988: 30 000 osôb.
Múzeum je otvorené denne okrem pondelka, od 8.15 do 12.00 a od 13.30 do 16.30 h. (Od októbra do apríla len do 15.00 h.)
Najbližšie ubytovanie:
hotel Minerál v Bardejovských kúpeľoch, najbližšia reštaurácia:
Minerál, Krištál a Kúpeľná dvorana.
Najbližšie občerstvenie: Expresso Srnka, Klub pacientov, Lahôdky – nákupné stredisko.

Národopisná expozícia v prírode
pri Múzeu ukrajinskej kultúry

Miesto: Svidník, PSČ 089 01.
Spravujúca inštitúcia:
Múzeum ukrajinskej kultúry, Svidník.
Výstavba schválená r. 1975, budovanie od r. 1975, sprístupnené verejnosti 1983.
Autor etnografickej štúdie:
PhDr. M. Sopoliga, CSc.,
architektonická štúdia:
Stavebná fakulta SVŠT Bratislava – vedúci práce doc. ing. arch. D. Majzlík, CSc., autor ing. arch. L. Jakubík. Expozičný areál meria 10 ha.
Počet expozičných objektov v r. 1988: 24, počet ďalších plánovaných expozičných objektov: 25.
Expozícia prezentuje ľudovú kultúru Ukrajincov žijúcich na severovýchodnom Slovensku prostredníctvom rekonštrukcie sídelného modelu (zrubové stavby) s interiérovým vybavením predstavujúcim obdobie kapitalizmu. Unikátom je zrubový kostolík z Novej Polianky (1766), vodný mlyn z Bogliarky.
V amfiteátri priľahlého letného kina sa od r. 1954 pravidelne koná folkloristický festival ukrajinského obyvateľstva v ČSSR.
Múzeum je otvorené od 1. 5. do 30. 10. okrem pondelkov od 9. do 16. h.
Návštevnosť v r. 1988: 10 100 osôb.
Najbližšie ubytovanie: hotel Dukla, najbližšia reštaurácia: hotel Dukla, hotel Pobeda, reštaurácia Verchovina.
Najbližšie občerstvenie: hotel Pobeda.

Banské múzeum v prírode
v Banskej Štiavnici

Miesto: Banská Štiavnica (2 km smerom na Levice), okres Žiar nad Hronom, PSČ 969 00.
Spravujúca inštitúcia:
Slovenské banské múzeum, Banská Štiavnica.
Výstavba schválená r. 1975, budovanie od r. 1965, sprístupnenie verejnosti r. 1974.
Autor ideového návrhu 1965:
ing. J. Bernáth, ideový zámer v spolupráci so špecialistami:
doc. ing. J. Boroška, CSc., ing. J. Cengel, doc. ing. J. Fabian, CSc., ing. M. Hock, ing. Š. Jankovič, ing. R. Magula, CSc., PhDr. J. Novák, PhDr. A. Polonec, CSc., ing. E. Kladivík, prof. ing. J. Puzder, CSc., prof. ing. A. Sopko, CSc., doc. ing. N. Szuttor, CSc., scenár 1969: PhDr. J. Vlachovič, CSc., V. Kollár, ing. M. Hock, ing. E. Kladivík, autor architektonickej štúdie:
ing. arch. O. Maděra, 1970.
Expozičný areál meria 20 ha.
Počet expozičných objektov v r. 1988: 16 a podzemná expozícia, počet ďalších plánovaných objektov: 33.
Expozícia prezentuje vývoj techniky a technológie hĺbkovej ťažby nerastov a životné prostredie baníkov v období kapitalizmu. Unikátom je podzemná expozícia šachty Ondrej s priestorovými dielmi zo 17.–19. storočia, v ktorých sú inštalované pôvodné nástroje a zariadenia používané v minulosti pri banských prácach. V novovyrazených banských dieloch je vystavená aj súčasná banská technika.
Múzeum je otvorené od mája do októbra denne okrem pondelka.
Návštevnosť v r. 1988: 50 100 osôb.
Najbližšie ubytovanie v Banskej Štiavnici: hotel Grand, najbližšia reštaurácia tamtiež.
Najbližšie občerstvenie: bufet v areáli múzea.

Další československá muzea
v přírodě,
která nejsou v publikaci obrazově zastoupena

V Humenném byla v roce 1983 otevřena Expozícia ľudovej architektúry, prezentující lidovou kulturu okresu Humenné v období kapitalismu. Od roku 1983 je ve výstavbě Slovenské poľnohospodárske múzeum v prírode v Nitre, které vytvoří rekonstrukci části sídla a areálů zemědělských staveb s návazností na zpracování produktů.
Dále se v České socialistické republice připravuje výstavba pošumavského muzea v přírodě v okrese Klatovy, zemědělská expozice v přírodě v části obce Příkazy (okres Olomouc), expozice v části obce Rymice (okres Kroměříž) má některé objekty již přístupné návštěvníkům, stejně tak jako hornická expozice v Příbrami – Březových Horách. V Ostravě – Petřkovicích bude vytvořeno muzeum hlubinného dolování uhlí z dolu Eduard Urx a blízké hornické kolonie Mexiko.
V Slovenské socialistické republice se připravuje výstavba regionálního muzea v přírodě Gemeru v Haliči, pro rozsáhlou oblast Pohroní ve Slovenské Ľupči a v Čiernom Balogu, při areálu folkloristických festivalů v Detvě soubor roubených staveb z rozptýleného osídlení okolí Zvolena a expozice Slovenského technického muzea s výrobními objekty na zpracování železa v Medzevu.

Ансамбль объектов народного зодчества из Чешских средних гор в с. Зубрнице.

Местонахождение: Зубрнице (район Усти-на-Лабе), индекс 403 24.
Управляющий центр: Районный краеведческий музей, Усти-на-Лабе, индекс 400 00.
Строительство одобрено и начато в 1977 г., музей открыт в 1988 г.
Автор этнографической концепции: д-р Ф. Ледвинка, автор архитектурного проекта: инж.-арх. Й. Шкабрада, канд. наук.
Территория экспозиции до сих пор точно не определена, речь идет о населенном пункте и его окрестностях, общая площадь 30 га.
Количество объектов в экспозиции в 1988 г.: 12.
Экспозиция реконструированного исторического центра данного населенного пункта, куда будут перенесены несколько объектов из других населенных пунктов и где будут восстановлены местные дома на площади, будет демонстрировать народную культуру эпохи капитализма района Чешских средних гор. Уникум экспозиции будет представлять восстановленная часть бывшей железной дороги Усти – Уштек, деревянная бревенчатая мельница (1803 г.), находящаяся на территории села, амбары из сел Луков и Лохочице, а также дом № 61.
Музей открыт с 1 мая по 31 октября ежедневно, кроме понедельника, с 9 до 17 часов.
Ресторан будет открыт на территории экспозиции, ближайшая гостиница находится в Усти-на-Лабе и Уштеке.

Этнографический музей Тршебиз

Местонахождение: Тршебиз (район Кладно), индекс 273 75.
Управляющий центр: Краеведческий музей в г. Сланы (экспозиции, научная деятельность, коллекции) и горсовет в Тршебизе (постройка и текущий ремонт объектов, дирекция).
Строительство одобрено и начато в 1969 г., музей открыт для посетителей в 1975 г.
Авторы этнографических очерков: Л. Штепанек, д-р В. Йиржиковска, канд. наук, авторы архитектурных проектов: Й. Недвед, инж.-арх. Й. Шкабрада, канд. наук, автор исторического очерка: д-р Й. Кротилова.
Площадь экспозиции: 32 га.
Количество объектов в экспозиции в 1988 г.: 24, количество запланированных объектов экспозиции: 6.
Музей демонстрирует народную культуру Сланской области (свекловодческий район северо-западной части средней Чехии до подножия Чешских средних гор) на примере всего населенного пункта (где преобладают сооружения: из камня, песчаного мергеля и песчаника, отчасти фахверк). Его центр возник вследствие реконструкции нескольких имеющихся и перенесенных сюда объектов и здесь же удалось создать историческую атмосферу того времени. Уникальным сооружением является имение Цифека от XVI – XIX вв., где в исторических интерьерах демонстрируется быт, развитие сельского хозяйства Сланской области и где в отдельных залах организуются тематические выставки. Следующие три крестьянских двора относятся к XVIII веку. В родном доме писателя Вацлава Бенеша Тршебизского установлен памятник, который открыт для посетителей с 1904 г. Музей принимает участие в организации народных гуляний (состоящихся, как правило, в восьмое воскресенье после пасхи) и сам организует и другие программы: демонстрация народных промыслов, сушка фруктов, выпечка в печи и др.
Музей открыт с 1 мая по 31 октября ежедневно, кроме понедельника, с 9 до 16 часов.
Посещаемость в 1988 году: 11 000 человек.
Ближайший ресторан и гостиница: Сланы, Лоуны (9, 17 км).
Ближайшая точка питания: в Тршебизе.

Музей деревни

Местонахождение: Коуржим (район Колин), индекс 281 61.
Управляющий центр: Региональный музей в Колине, индекс 280 00.
Строительство одобрено и начато в 1972 г., для посетителей музей открыт с 1975 г. Авторы этнографических концепций: А. Поспишилова, д-р М. Новакова, автор архитектурного проекта: инж.-арх. П. Фухс.
Площадь экспозиции: 4 га.
Количество объектов в экспозиции в 1987 г.: 13, общее количество всех запланированных объектов экспозиции: 38.
Концепция экспозиции до сих пор не выяснена. Вначале на территорию экспозиции были перенесены объекты из затопляемых земель гидросооружения „Желивка", которые внесены в список государством охраняемых памятников культуры, с целью демонстрации народной культуры южной части Среднечешской области. В 1975 году данная „защитная" концепция распространена на территорию всей ЧСР. Этой же концепцией позднее руководствовались при формировании взглядов на создание в Коуржиме музея видов строительной техники, независимо от взаимных идейных отношений и внутреннего оборудования объектов. Уникальными являются следующие постройки: полигональные сараи из с. Дурдице (1648 г.) и из с. Желейов (1660 г.), крестьянский двор из с. Тыржовице и здание сельского правления из с. Брадлецка-Лгота.
Музей открыт ежедневно, кроме понедельника, с апреля по октябрь, с 9 до 16 часов.
Средняя посещаемость музея: 5 000 человек в год.
Ближайший ресторан и гостиница – в г. Коуржим, ближайший буфет – в районе прилегающего бассейна для плаванья.

Полабский этнографический музей в Пршерове-на-Лабе

Местонахождение: Пршеров-на-Лабе (район Нымбурк), индекс 289 16.
Управляющий центр: Полабский музей в г. Подебрады (районный музей района Нымбурк), индекс 290 01.
Строительство одобрено в 1979 г., началось в 1967 г., для посетителей музей открыт в 1967 г.
Авторы этнографических очерков: д-р Г. Седлачкова, инж. И. Бернард, авторы архитектурного проекта: инж.-арх. Коречек, инж.-арх. Тихи.
Площадь экспозиции: 1,8 га.
Количество объектов в экспозиции в 1988 г.: 32, количество запланированных объектов экспозиции: 8.
В музей перемещались те памятники народного зодчества среднего Полабья (особенно из района Нымбурк), существование которых в исконном месте находилось под угрозой. Основой музея и первым его объектом явилась т. наз. старочешская изба (господская кузница и позднее здание сельского правления половины XVIII века, восстановленное около 1895 г.). В ней экспонируются этнографические коллекции. Из бывших господских сооружений к музею принадлежат: кирпичный охотничий дом (здание управления и депозита), т. наз. „бондарная мастерская" с выставочным залом и старая школа. Рядом, на деревенскую площадь со сквером, с 1967 г. перемещались избы из сел Драго и Хваловице и другие мелкие объекты (амбары, сушильня, колодец, народные пластики и т. п.). С 1980 года реализуется проект застройки в садах за „бондарной" и охотничьим домиком, куда до 1990 г. должны быть перенесены реконструированные крестьянские дворы из Кралове-местской, Кршинецкой областей и окрестностей Нымбурка. Вне территории экспозиции находится кирпичная усадьба № 13 с фронтоном и въездом в стиле барокко, где находится экспозиция полабского земледелия (зал традиций единого сельскохозяйственного кооператива).
Музей открыт с 15 апреля по 30 октября ежедневно, кроме понедельника, с 14 до 16 часов.
Посещаемость музея в 1988 году: 30 000 человек.
Ближайшая гостиница: „Полабье" в Лиса-на-Лабе, ближайший ресторан: „Керско" в Лиса-на-Лабе.
Ближайшая точка питания: кондитерская напротив этнографического музея в Пршерове-на-Лабе.

Собрание крестьянских строений и техники „Височина"

Местонахождение: населенный пункт Височина (район Хрудим), почта Глинско-в-Чехах, индекс 539 01, местопребывание управления в селении Свободне-Гамры (населенный пункт Височина находится между г. Глинско и Тргова-Каменице и включает селения Свободне-Гамры, Држевиков, Мождениц, Веселы-Копец и Рвачов, к территории экспозиции относится селение Кралова-Пила населенного пункта Вшерадов).
Управляющий центр: Восточночешский областной центр государственной охраны памятников и охраны природы в г. Пардубице.
Строительство одобрено в 1977 г., началось в 1969 г., для посетителей музей открыт в 1971 г.
Авторы этнографических очерков: Л. Штепан, д-р И. Воянцова, авторы архитектурных проектов: Л. Штепан, инж.-арх. Л. Черник, инж. З. Гакен, инж.-арх. Й. Шкадраба, канд. наук.
Площадь экспозиции: 3,5 га, в общем, исторический ландшафт занимает территорию 9 км^2.
Количество объектов в экспозиции в 1988 г.: 37, количество запланированных объектов экспозиции: 12.
Экспозиция демонстрирует народную культуру северной части Чешско-Моравской возвышенности (область, где находятся бревенчатые сооружения), в особенности традиционную народную технику в широких жилищных взаимосвязях. Уникальными сооружениями являются: т. наз. „Кралова Пила" (мельница с лесопильней), дом № 4 из селения Веселы-Копец, четырнадцатиугольный сарай из с. Садек (все от XVII века)

и 12 объектов XVIII века. В экспозиции организуются рождественские и весенние мероприятия фольклорного характера, демонстрируются ручное производство и животноводство.
Экспозиция открыта: с 15 апреля (в с. Свободне-Гамры с 1 мая) по 31 октября ежедневно, кроме понедельника; в с. Мождениџе – только по субботам и воскресеньям (кроме июля–августа).
Посещаемость музея в 1988 году: 129 000 человек.
Ближайшие гостиницы: „Заложна", „Стиль" в Глинско, ближайший ресторан: в гостинице „Славия" (Тргова-Каменице).
Ближайший буфет: на территории экспозиции в селении Веселы-Копец (открыт с мая по сентябрь).

Музей деревни юго-восточной Моравии

Местонахождение: Стражнице (район Годонин), индекс 696 62.
Управляющий центр: Институт народного искусства, Стражнице.
Строительство одобрено в 1973 г., началось в 1974 г., для посетителей музей открыт в 1981 г.
Авторы этнографических очерков: доц. д-р В. Фролец, канд. наук, д-р Й. Соучек, д-р Й. Томеш, канд. наук, д-р Й. Янчарш, канд. наук, автор архитектурного проекта: инж.-арх. О. Мачел и коллектив.
Площадь экспозиции: 9,7 га, запланированная площадь представляет 15 га.
Количество объектов в экспозиции в 1987 году: 75, количество запланированных объектов экспозиции: 20.
Экспозиция демонстрирует народное зодчество юго-восточной Моравии на примере реконструкции законченных комплексов крестьянских дворов, которые включают жилые и хозяйственные народные постройки (из регионов Моравске-Копаниџе, Лугачовицке-Залеси, из областей „Горняцко" и стражницкое „Долняцко"; кроме того, запланировано перемещение сооружений из „Подлужья" и из угерско-бродской, угерско-градиштьской и киёвской областей „Долняцко").
Экспозиция, далее, демонстрирует: гидротехнические сооружения, луговодство и виноградарство (24 винных погреба и прессовых цеха с демонстрацией посадки и выращивания сортов винограда). На территории экспозиции в летний период (по субботам и воскресеньям) проходят выступления фольклорных ансамблей или мероприятия, связанные с демонстрацией традиционных праздников.
Музей открыт с 1 мая по 31 октября – по воскресеньям с 10 до 18 часов, в остальные дни, кроме понедельника, с 8 до 17 часов. Посещаемость музея в 1988 году: 32 354 человек.
Ближайшая гостиница: автокемпинг первичной организации ДОСААФ в г. Стражнице, гостиницы „Черный орел" и „Интеротель" в г. Стражнице, гостиница „Розквет" в Весели-на-Мораве; ближайший ресторан: „Ярошовска пивнице" в г. Стражнице и рестораны в вышеприведенных гостиницах.
Ближайшая точка питания: буфет „Данай" в Стражнице; при входе на территорию экспозиции ларек.

Валашский музей под открытым небом

Местонахождение: Рожнов-под-Радгоштем (район Всетин), индекс 756 61.
Управляющий центр: Валашский музей под открытым небом, Рожнов-под-Радгоштем.
Генеральная концепция перестройки музея одобрена в 1974 г.; строительство музея проходит с 1923 года на территории экспозиции „Деревянный городок", с 1963 года – на территории экспозиции „Валашская деревня"; музей открыт для посетителей в 1925 году. Авторы всего проекта экспозиции или отдельных ее частей: Б. Яронек (художественный проект застройки), инж.-арх. М. Подземны, инж.-арх. Й. Седлачек, инж. А. Завада (архитектурное решение), д-р Й. Лангер, канд. наук, д-р Й. Штика, канд. наук (этнографическое решение), инж. Й. Стромшик (производственное решение).
Площадь экспозиции: 76 га. Она считается садом и парком, охраняемым государством.
Количество объектов в экспозиции в 1988 г.: 77, количество запланированных объектов: 130.
Экспозиция демонстрирует народную культуру деревень и провинций региона Валахии, а также виды традиционной народной техники XVIII – начала XX вв. – на примере реконструкции селений и воссоздания исторического быта, включая пастбища, луга и поля с выращиванием типичных для того времени сортов сельскохозяйственных культур и плодовых деревьев, с животноводством и, прежде всего, – с пастбищным содержанием животных. Уникальными являются сооружения: Валашский трактир XVII века, интерьерная экспозиция в доме сельского старосты, технические сооружения на водяной тяге (демонстрируется их производственная деятельность), дом из с. Лужна XVIII века, ветряная мельница, действующее ведение хозяйства и целый ряд исторических культур.
Время работы отдельных частей музея под открытым небом:
„Деревянный городок" – с 1 мая по 15 сентября ежедневно,
с 15 декабря по 31 марта – по понедельникам, средам, субботам и воскресеньям.
„Валашская деревня" – с 15 мая по 15 ноября
„Мельничная долина" – с 1 апреля по 30 сентября
Посещаемость музея в 1988 году: 595 000 человек.
Ближайшие гостиницы: „Рожнаван", „Коруна", „Тесла" в Рожнове, автокемпинги ДОСААФа и физкультурного единства; ближайший ресторан: на территории экспозиции „Деревянный городок".
Ближайшая точка питания: на территории экспозиций „Деревянный городок" и „Валашская деревня".

Музей словацкой деревни

Местонахождение: Мартин – Ягодницке-Гайе, индекс 036 01.
Управляющий центр: Этнографический институт Словацкого национального музея, Мартин.
Концепция музея создана в 1965 г., строительство началось в 1967 г.
Вся экспозиция будет вновь открыта после окончания следующего этапа – в 1992 г.
Авторы этнографических очерков: концепцию строительства в 1965 разработали: Й. Бодя, инж.-арх. Й. Турзо, канд. наук, д-р А. Полонец; концепцию строительства и хозяйственной части в 1961 г. – д-р Й. Кантар, канд. наук; проектную задачу экспозиции в 1968 г. – доц. д-р Ш. Мрушкович, канд. наук; идейный замысел экспозиции в 1974 г. – д-р М. Бенжа, д-р С. Горват, д-р И. Криштек, канд. наук; тематико-градостроительное уточнение концепции в 1982 г. – д-р С. Горват, д-р И. Криштек, канд. наук.
Авторы архитектурных проектов: доц. инж.-арх. Д. Майзлик, канд. наук, инж.-арх. Й. Лихнер, канд. наук, инж.-арх. М. Башо, инж.-арх. И. Пушнар, канд. наук, градостроительный очерк в 1968 г. инж.-арх. Й. Турзо, канд. наук.
Площадь экспозиции: 56,5 га.
Количество объектов в экспозиции в 1987 г.: 74; предполагается, что в будущем экспозиция будет включать всего 317 объектов.
Экспозиция демонстрирует народную культуру местных сельских общностей на территории Словакии эпохи второй половины XIX и 1 половины XX вв. – на примере реконструкции жилищ в соответствии с этнографическими регионами (глиняные, плетеные, бревенчатые, кирпичные сооружения) и воссоздания исторического быта. Уникальными являются: усадьба мелкопоместного дворянина из с. Вишни-Кубин (1748), бревенчатый костел из с. Рудно и дом из с. Липтовска-Лужна. На территории экспозиции организуются специальные программы по случаю Международного дня музеев.
Посещаемость в 1983 году: 11 000 человек.
Ближайшая гостиница: Мартин, гост. „Туриец".
Ближайшая точка питания: буфет перед музеем.
Ближайший ресторан: в поселке „Ладовень", приблизительно в 1 км от музея.

**Музей кисуцкой деревни
Этнографическая экспозиция
под открытым небом**

Местонахождение: Нова-Бистрица – Вихиловка (район Чадца), индекс 023 05.
Управляющий центр: Кисуцкий музей, дом Палариков, 022 01 Чадца.
Строительство одобрено в 1974 г., первая часть экспозиции открыта для посетителей в 1981 г.
Авторы этнографического очерка: 1974 г. – д-р Й. Кантар, канд. наук, 1979 г. – д-р А. Коцоуркова, 1984 г. – д-р М. Кирипольски, д-р А. Коцоуркова, д-р П. Мараки.
Авторы архитектурного проекта: инж.-арх. Б. Догнаны, канд. наук и коллектив (1976 г.).
Архитектурное сотрудничество: акад. арх. А. Горичкова (1984 г.).
Площадь экспозиции: 143 га, застроенная часть – приблизительно 20 га. Вокруг всей территории, которая входит в Область государством охраняемой местности Кисуцы (см. постановление от 1984 г.), располагается обширная защитная зона.
Количество объектов в экспозиции: 22 (в 1987 г.).
Количество всех запланированных объектов: 67.
Целью экспозиции является: восстановление жилищного ландшафта и окружающей среды, демонстрация быта и культуры крестьян кисуцкой области эпохи второй половины XIX – начала XX вв. Подавляющее большинство объектов перенесено сюда из различных кусуцких населенных пунктов (Риечница, Гарвелка, Клубина, Зборов-на-Бистрице, Ощадница, Корня и в перспективе и другие). На территории экспозиции охраняются и неперенесенные исконные сезон-

ные пастушеские жилища. В музее и в его непосредственной близости восстановлена часть железнодорожной линии узкоколейной кисуцко-оравской железной дороги, которая будет служить для перемещения посетителей, и, тем самым, будет демонстрироваться движение поездов с помощью паровой тяги. К самым интересным деталям относятся: архивольтовый портал двери жилого дома из с. Ощадница (1905 г.), роспись потолка народного художника в нефе часовни из с. Зборов-на-Бистрице, украшенные фронтоны нескольких жилых домов из с. Риечница и другие детали. В интерьерах выбранных объектов представляется исконная обстановка, предметы которой приобретены в результате сбора в тех населенных пунктах, откуда происходят объекты Музея кисуцкой деревни. На территории экспозиции нерегулярно организована демонстрация видов народной производственной техники и исторического быта.
Музей открыт во время сезона, т. е. с мая по октябрь ежедневно, кроме понедельника – с 9.30 до 18 часов.
Посещаемость музея в 1988 г.: 14 000 человек.
Ближайшая гостиница: Стара-Бистрица, туристская база; Чадца – гостиница „Липа", гостиница „Гусарик" в горах, туристская база „Шпортова гала"; Кисуцке-Нове-Место – гостиница „Мито" и гостиница профсоюзов „Заводни клуб ЗВЛ".
Ближайший ресторан: Нова-Бистрица.
Ближайшая точка питания: на территории экспозиции (корчма из с. Корня).

Музей оравской деревни

Местонахождение: Зуберец – Брестова (район Дольни-Кубин), индекс 027 32.
Управляющий центр: Оравский музей, Дольни-Кубин, индекс 026 01.
Строительство одобрено в 1967 г. и началось в 1968 г., для посетителей музей открыт в 1975 г.
Автор этнографического очерка: д-р Й. Лангер, канд. наук, автор архитектурного проекта: инж.-арх. М. Словакова.
Площадь экспозиции: 20 га.
Количество объектов в экспозиции в 1988 г.: 76.
Запланированные объекты: завершение строительства 2 усадеб и постройка 8 отдельных объектов.
Экспозиция представляет народную культуру Оравы на примере реконструкции модели жилища (бревенчатые сооружения). Уникальными являются: поздне-готический костел из с. Забреж (XV – XVIII вв.), усадьба мелкопоместного дворянина из г. Вишни-Кубин (1752 г.), дом № 57 из с. Чимгова и 3 дальнейших объекта XVIII в. На свободном пространстве перед музеем в конце августа устраивается „Подгорачский фольклорный праздник" (с 1975 г.). На территории экспозиции нерегулярно устраиваются демонстрации видов народной производственной техники и других исторических производств, а также демонстрации фольклора, в которых принимают участие крестьянские фольклорные группы и детские фольклорные ансамбли. Музей открыт ежедневно, кроме понедельника – с мая по октябрь.
Посещаемость в 1988 г.: 58 651 человек.
Ближайшие гостиницы и турбазы: в г. Зуберец – гост. „Милотин" (обеспечивает „Словакотур"), в районе горного хребта „Рогаче" – турбазы „Примула" и „Зверовка", ближайшие рестораны: у входа в музей и в вышеуказанных гостиницах и турбазах. Ближайший буфет: у входа в музей.

Музей липтовской деревни

Местонахождение: Прибилина (район Липтовски-Микулаш), индекс 032 42.
Управляющий центр: Липтовский музей в г. Ружомберок, этнографическое отделение в г. Липтовски-Градек, индекс 033 01.
Строительство одобрено в 1971 г. и началось в 1972 г.
Автор этнографического очерка: д-р Й. Лангер, канд. наук, г-р И. Зускинова, автор архитектурного проекта: инж.-арх. С. Дубравец, канд. наук.
Площадь экспозиции: 25 га.
Количество объектов в экспозиции в 1988 г.: 31, количество запланированных объектов: 45.
Экспозиция покажет народную культуру Липтова на примере реконструкции целого ансамбля жилищ с историческим центром, содержащим следующие уникальные сооружения: копию поздне-готического костела из с. Парижовце, готический костел из с. Липтовска-Мара и готическое пространство около главного алтаря из с. Липтовска-Сиельница, откуда перенесен и весь ансамбль усадеб. Другие бревенчатые объекты доставлены из разных частей Липтова (XVIII – XIX вв.). Часть экспозиции с перенесенным народным зодчеством будет служить для размещения туристов.
Питание будет обеспечено прямо на территории экспозиции, на ее окраине находится гостиница „Эсперанто" с рестораном.

Экспозиция под открытым небом Районного краеведческого музея в г. Стара-Лубовня

Местонахождение: Стара-Лубовня – под кремлем, индекс 064 01.
Управляющий центр: Районный краеведческий музей, Стара-Лубовня.
Строительство одобрено в 1974 г. и началось в 1977 г., для посетителей музей открыт в 1983 г.
Площадь экспозиции: 10 га.
Количество объектов в экспозиции: 20.
Экспозиция представляет народную культуру района Стара-Лубовня на примере перенесенных сюда объектов деревянной архитектуры и обстановки ее интерьеров. Уникальными являются: бревенчатый костел из с. Матысова (XVIII век).
Ближайшая гостиница находится в г. Стара-Лубовня, ближайший ресторан – бревенчатая хата под кремлем.
Посещаемость в 1988 году: 11 230 человек.
Музей открыт с мая по октябрь ежедневно, кроме понедельника, с 9 до 16 часов.

Шаришский музей

Местонахождение: Бардейовске-Купеле (район Бардейов), индекс 086 31.
Управляющий центр: Шаришский музей, Бардейов, индекс 085 01.
Строительство одобрено в 1961 г. и продолжалось с 1962 до 1972 гг., для посетителей музей открыт в 1965 году.
Автор этнографического очерка: дипломированный историк Б. Пушкарова, канд. наук, автор архитектурного проекта: инж.-арх. И. Пушкар, канд. наук.
Площадь экспозиции: 3,41 га.
Количество объектов в экспозиции в 1988 г.: 23.
Экспозиция показывает народную культуру Шариша на примере перенесенных типичных объектов с обставленным интерьером. В данной экспозиции представляют интерес: сверло деревянных водопроводных труб на водяной тяге из Бардейова, деревянные костелы восточного ритуала из с. Збой (1706 г.) и из с. Микулашова (1730 г.), а также колокольня из с. Яновце (1700 г.). Большинство домов относится к концу XIX века и характерно для эпохи капитализма. На территории экспозиции организуются культурные программы и демонстрируется ручное производство, особенно во время Международного дня музеев, а нерегулярно – во время летнего сезона. В прилегающем особняке „Ракоши" помещена этнографическая экспозиция и экспозиция „Иконы восточной Словакии".
Посещаемость музея в 1988 г.: 30 000 человек.
Музей открыт ежедневно, кроме понедельника, с 8.15 до 12.00, с 13.30 до 16.30 (с октября по апрель – до 15.00 часов).
Ближайшая гостиница: Бардейовске-Купеле, гост. „Минерал", ближайшие рестораны: „Минерал", „Криштал", „Купельна дворана".
Ближайшая точка питания: кафе „Срнка", „Клуб пациентов", торговый центр.

Этнографическая экспозиция под открытым небом при Музее украинской культуры

Местонахождение: Свидник, индекс 089 01.
Управляющий центр: Музей украинской культуры, Свидник.
Строительство одобрено в 1975 г. и началось в 1975 г., для посетителей музей открыт в 1983 г.
Автор этнографического очерка: д-р М. Сополига, канд. наук, архитектурный проект: Строительный факультет Политехнического института в Братиславе – руководитель работы: доц. инж.-арх. Д. Майзлик, канд. наук, автор: инж.-арх. Л. Якубик.
Экспозиция занимает площадь 10 га.
Количество объектов в экспозиции в 1988 г.: 24, количество запланированных объектов: 25.
Экспозиция демонстрирует народную культуру украинцев, живущих в северо-восточной Словакии, на примере реконструкции модели жилища (бревенчатые сооружения) и обстановки интерьеров периода капитализма. Уникальными являются следующие сооружения: небольшой бревенчатый костел из с. Нова-Полиянка (1766 г.) и водяная мельница из с. Боглиярка. В амфитеатре прилегающего летнего кинотеатра с 1954 г. регулярно проходит фольклорный фестиваль украинского населения, живущего в ЧССР. Музей открыт с 1 мая по 30 октября ежедневно, кроме понедельника.
Посещаемость в 1988 году: 10 000 человек.
Ближайшая гостиница: „Дукла", ближайшие рестораны: „Дукла", „Победа", „Верховина".
Ближайшая точка питания: в гостинице „Победа".

Горный музей под открытым небом в г. Банска-Штиявница

Местонахождение: Банска-Штиявница (в 2 км по направлению к г. Левице), район Ждияр-на-Гроне, индекс 969 00.
Управляющий центр: Словацкий горный музей, Банска-Штиявница.
Строительство одобрено в 1975 г. и началось в 1965 г. Для посетителей музей открыт в 1974 г.
Автор идейного проекта (1965 г.): Инж. Й. Бернат, идейный замысел при сотрудничестве специалистов: доц. инж. Й. Борошка, канд. наук, инж. Й. Ценгел, доц. инж. Й. Фабиан, канд. наук, инж. М. Гок, инж. Ш. Янкович, инж. Р. Магула, канд. наук, д-р Й. Новак, д-р А. Полонец, канд. наук, инж. Е. Кладивик, проф. инж. Й. Пуздер, канд. наук, проф. инж. А. Сопко, канд. наук, доц. инж. Н. Шуттер, канд. наук; авторы сценария (1969 г.): д-р Й. Влахович, канд. наук, В. Коллар, инж. Н. Гок, инж. Е. Кладивик; автор архитектурного проекта: инж.-арх. О. Мадера (1970 г.).
Площадь экспозиции: 20 га.
Экспозиция в 1987 г. включает 16 объектов и подземную экспозицию; количество запланированных объектов: 33.
Экспозиция отражает развитие техники и технологии подземной добычи ископаемых и представляет быт шахтеров периода капитализма.
Большой интерес вызывает подземная экспозиция в шахтах „Ондрей" и „Бартоломей" (XVII – XIX вв.), где экспонируются исконные орудия и устройства, которыми в прошлом пользовались шахтеры. Во вновь пробитых рудничных штреках экспонируется и современная шахтерская техника.
Музей открыт с мая по октябрь ежедневно, кроме понедельника.
Посещаемость в 1988 г.: 50 100 человека.
Ближайшая гостиница: Банска-Штиявница, гост. „Гранд", ближайший ресторан – там же.
Ближайшая точка питания: буфет на территории музея.

Другие чехословацкие музеи под открытым небом,
которые в публикации не сопровождаются фотодокументацией

В г. Гуменне в 1983 была открыта Экспозиция народного зодчества, демонстрирующая народную культуру района Гуменне периода капитализма. С 1983 г. строится Словацкий полеводческий музей под открытым небом в Нитре, в основе которого лежит реконструкция части жилищ и крестьянских дворов. В этом музее будет представлено одно из производств: обработка продуктов. Далее, в Чешской социалистической республике готовится строительство музея под открытым небом в области Шумавы (район Клатовы), земледельческая экспозиция под открытым небом в части населенного пункта Пршиказы (район Оломоуц); в экспозиции, образованной в части населенного пункта Римице (район Кромержиж), некоторые объекты уже открыты для посетителей, так же, как и в шахтерской экспозиции в г. Пршибрам-Бржезове-Горы. В Остраве-Петршковице будет создан музей подземной добычи угля на шахте „Эдуард Уркс" и в ближнем шахтерском рабочем поселке „Мексика".
В Словацкой социалистической республике готовится строительство: регионального музея под открытым небом в районе Гемера в Галиче; музея для обширной области Погронья в с. Словенска-Лупча, Чиерны Балог, далее в Детве – ансамбль бревенчатых сооружений из рассеянного поселения в окрестности г. Зволен – по соседству с местом, где проходят фольклорные фестивали и, наконец, экспозиция Словацкого технического музея с производственными объектами по обработке железа – в г. Медзево.

Die Konzentrierung der Bauobjekte der Volkskultur des böhmischen Mittelgebirges in Zubrnice

Ort: Zubrnice (Kreis Ústí an der Elbe) PLZ 403 24.
Verwaltungsinstitution: Heimatkundliches Kreismuseum, Ústí an der Elbe PLZ 400 00.
Baugenehmigung 1977, Baubeginn 1977, der Öffentlichkeit zugängig gemacht: 1988
Autor der ethnographischen Konzeption: PhDr. F. Ledvinka, Autor der architektonischen Studie: Ingenieurarchitekt J. Škabrada, CSc.
Das Ausstellungsgelände ist bisher nicht genau begrenzt, es handelt sich um ein Intravilan und einen Teil des Extravilans der Gemeinde, cca. 30 ha.
Anzahl der Ausstellungsobjekte im Jahre 1988: 12.
Die Ausstellung wird die Volkskultur der kapitalistischen Epoche im Gebiet des böhmischen Mittelgebirges präsentieren, und zwar durch Rekonstruktion des historischen Kerns des bestehenden Sitzes, die durch Überführung einiger Objekte anderer Gemeinden und durch Denkmalserneuerung öffentlicher Häuser auf dem Dorfplatz verwirklicht wird.
Unikater Bestandteil der Exposition wird die Wiederherstellung eines Teiles der untergegangenen Eisenbahnstrecke Ústí a. d. Elbe – Úštěk sein, sowie eine gezimmerte Mühle im Kataster der Gemeinde (1803), die Kornspeicher aus Lukov und Lochočice und das Haus Nr. 61.
Das Museum ist vom 1. 5. bis 31. 10. ausser montags täglich von 9 bis 17 Uhr geöffnet.
Ein Restaurant wird im Ausstellungsgelände realisiert. Die nächste Unterkunft befindet sich in Ústí an der Elbe und Úštěk.

Völkerkundemuseum Třebíz

Ort: Třebíz (Kreis Kladno) PLZ 273 75.
Verwaltungsinstitution: Heimatkundemuseum Slaný (Betrieb, fachliche Betreuung, Sammlungen) und Rat der Gemeinde Třebíz (Bau und Pflege der Objekte, Verwaltung).
Baugenehmigung: 1969, Baubeginn: 1969, der Öffentlichkeit zugänglich gemacht: 1975.
Autoren der ethnographischen Studien: L. Štěpánek, PhDr. V. Jiřikovská, CSc. Autoren der architektonischen Studie: J. Nedvěd, Ingenieurarchitekt J. Škabrada, CSc., Autorin der historischen Studie: PhDr. L. Krotilová.
Das Ausstellungsgelände misst 32 ha.
Anzahl der Ausstellungsobjekte im Jahre 1988: 24.
Anzahl weiterer geplanter Ausstellungsobjekte: 6.
Das Museum präsentiert die Volkskultur in Slánsko (Rübenanbaugebiet vom nordwestlichen Teil Mittelböhmens bis zum Rand des böhmischen Mittelgebirges (mittels der gesamten Dorfgemeinde Třebíz) vorwiegend gemauerte Bauten aus Stein, Pläuerkalkstein und Sandstein, teilweise Fachwerkbau), deren Kern, geprägt durch übergeführte Ergänzungsobjekte, die Rekonstruktion der historischen Umgebung darstellt. Einmalig ist das Cífekgut aus dem 16.–19. Jahrhundert, in dessen Räumlichkeiten die Lebensweise in historischen Interieurs präsentiert wird, wie auch die Entwicklung der Landwirtschaft im Gebiet um Slánsko. In abgesonderten Räumen werden thematische Ausstellungen veranstaltet. Weitere drei Bauerngüter stammen aus dem 18. Jahrhundert. Das Geburtshaus des Schriftstellers Václav Beneš Třebízský ist der Öffentlichkeit als Denkmal seit 1904 zugänglich. Das Museum beteiligt sich an der Veranstaltung der Třebízer Kirmes

(in der Regel am 8. Sonntag nach Ostern) und anderer Programme:
Ausstellung volkstümlicher Erzeugnisse, Obsttrocknen, im Backofen backen usw.
Das Museum ist vom 1. 5. bis 31. 10. täglich ausser montags von 9 bis 16 Uhr geöffnet.
Die Besucherzahl von 1988 betrug 11 000.
Nächste Unterkunft und Restaurant: Slaný, Louny (9, 17 km).
Nächster Imbiss: Geststube in Třebíz.

Dorfmuseum

Ort: Kouřim (Kreis Kolín) PLZ 281 61.
Verwaltungsinstitution: Regionales Museum Kolín, PLZ 280 00
Baugenehmigung: 1972, Baubeginn: 1972, der Öffentlichkeit zugänglich seit 1975.
Autoren der ethnographischen Konzeption: A. Pospíšilová, PhDr. M. Nováková, Autor der architektonischen Studie: Ing.-Arch. P. Fuchs, Das Ausstellungsgelände misst 4 ha.
Anzahl der Ausstellungsobjekte im Jahre 1987: 13. Anzahl aller geplanten Ausstellungsobjekte: 38.
Die Konzeption der Exposition ist nicht geklärt. Zu Beginn wurden in das Ausstellungsgelände Objekte aus dem Überschwemmungsgebiet des Wasserwerkes Želivka verlegt, die in das staatliche Verzeichnis für Kulturdenkmäler mit dem Ziel, die Volkskultur des südlichen Teiles des mittelböhmischen Bezirkes zu präsentieren, auf genommen wurden. 1975 wurde die Rettungskonzeption durch das ideologische Vorhaben SÚPPOPP auf dem Gebiet der gesamten ČSR verbreitet. Sie war Ausgangspunkt bei der Formierung der Anschauungen, in Kouřim ein Bautechnikenmuseum ohne Beachtung der gegenseitigen Verhältnisse auf ideelem Gebiet und der inneren Ausstattung der Objekte zu schaffen. Einzigartig sind polygonale Scheunen aus Durdice (1648) und aus Želejov (1660), das Gut aus Týřovice und das Gemeindehaus aus Bradlecká Lhota.
Das Museum ist von April bis Oktober täglich ausser montags von 9–16 Uhr geöffnet.
Die Besucheranzahl beträgt etwa 5 000 Personen pro Jahr.
Die nächste Unterkunft und Gaststätte sind in Kouřim, der nächste Imbiss im anliegenden Bad.

Elbländisches Völkerkundemuseum in Přerov an der Elbe

Ort: Přerov an der Elbe (Kreis Nymburk) PLZ 289 16.
Verwaltungsinstitution: Elbländisches Museum in Poděbrady (Kreismuseum für den Kreis Nymburk) PLZ 290 01.
Baugenehmigung 1979, Baubeginn 1967, der Öffentlichkeit zugängig gemacht: 1967.
Autoren der ethnographischen Studien: PhDr. H. Sedláčková, Ing. I. Bernard, Autoren der architektonischen Studie: Ing.-Arch. Koreček, Ing.-Arch. Tichý.
Das Ausstellungsareal misst 1,8 ha.
Anzahl der Ausstellungobjekte im Jahre 1988: 32, Anzahl weiterer geplanter Ausstellungsobjekte: 8.
Ins Museum wurden Denkmalobjekte der Volkskultur des mittleren Elblandes (vor allem aus dem Kreis Nymburk) gebracht, deren Existenz am ursprünglichen Ort gefährdet war. Grundstein und gleichzeitig erstes Objekt des Museums war das sog. altböhmische Häuschen (Herrschaftsschmiede und späteres Gemeindehaus aus der ersten Hälfte des 18. Jahrhunderts, 1895 wieder hergerichtet). Im Häuschen sind ethnographische Sammlungen untergebracht. Von den ehemaligen Herrschaftsbauten gehören zum Museum das Mauerwerk des Jägerhauses (Verwaltungsgebäude und Depositorien), das sog. Kastenhaus mit Ausstellungssaal und alter Schule. In die Nachbarschaft auf den neuhergerichteten Ring wurden seit 1967 Bauernhäuschen aus Draho und Chvalovice und weitere kleinere Objekte (Speicher, eine Trocknerei, Brunnen, Volksplastiken uä.) überführt. Seit 1980 wird der Verbauungsvorschlag auf den Gärten hinter dem Kastenhaus und Jägerhaus realisiert, wo bis 1990 Bauerngüter aus Králové městečko, Křinecko und der Umgebung Nymburks rekonstruiert werden sollen. Ausserhalb des Ausstellungsgeländes befindet sich das gemauerte Gut Nr. 13 mit Barockschild und Barockeinfahrt, in dem sich die Ausstellung der elbländischen Landwirtschaft (Tradionssaal der LPG) befindet.
Das Museum ist täglich vom 15. 4. bis 30. 10. ausser montags von 14 bis 16 Uhr geöffnet.
Die Besucherzahl betrug im Jahr 1988 30 000.
Nächste Unterkunft: Hotel Polabí in Lysá an der Elbe, nächstes
Restaurant: Motorest Kersko in Lysá a. d. Elbe.
Nächster Imbiss: Konditorei gegenüber dem Völkerkundemuseum in Přerov an der Elbe.

Ensemble der volkstümlichen Bauten und Technik Vysočina

Ort: Gemeinde Vysočina (Kreis Chrudim), Post Hlinsko in Böhmen, PLZ 539 01, Verwaltungssitz in der Ortschaft Svobodné Hamry (die Gemeinde Vysočina befindet sich zwischen Hlinsko in Böhmen und Trhová Kamenice und schliesst die Ortschaften Svobodné Hamry, Dřevíkov, Možděnice, Veselý Kopec und Rváčov ein, in das Expositionsareal gehört die Ortschaft Králová Pila der Gemeinde Všeradov). Verwaltungsinstitution: Ostböhmisches Bezirkszentrum für staatliche Denkmalpflege und Naturschutz in Pardubice.
Baugenehmigung: 1977, Baubeginn: 1969, der Öffentlichkeit zugängig gemacht: 1971.
Autoren der ethnographischen Studien: L. Štěpán, PhDr. I. Vojancová, Autoren der architektonischen Studien: L. Štěpán, Ing.-Arch. L. Černík, Ing. Z. Haken, Ing.-Arch. J. Škabrada, CSc.
Das Ausstellungsgelände in der Ortschaft Veselý Kopec misst 3,5 ha, die gesamte historische Ausstellungslandschaft hat ein Ausmass von 9 km^2 Fläche.
Anzahl der Ausstellungsobjekte 1988: 37,
Anzahl weiterer geplanter Ausstellungsobjekte: 12.
Die Ausstellung präsentiert die Volkskultur des nördlichen Teils der Böhmisch-Mährischen Höhe (Gebiet mit Zimmerwerken) und insbesondere die traditionsreiche Volkstechnik in weiten Siedlungszusammenhängen. Einzigartige Exemplare sind die Königssäge (Králová Pila) – als Mühle mit Säge, das Haus Nr. 4 aus Veselý Kopec und eine vierzehneckige Scheune aus Sádek (alles aus dem 17. Jahrhundert), 12 Objekte aus dem 18. Jahrhundert. In der Ausstellung werden Aktionen auf Weihnachts- und Frühjahrsbrauch basierend veranstaltet, sowie Vorführungen von Handwerksarbeiten und Zuchttieren realisiert.
Das Ensemble ist vom 15. 4. bis 31. 10. täglich ausser montags geöffnet. In Svobodné Hamry vom 1. 5. bis 31. 10., in Možděnice nur sonnabends und sonntags (ausser Juli und August).
Die Besucherzahl betrug 1988 129 000.
Nächste Unterkunft: die Hotels Záložná, Styl in Hlinsko in Böhmen, nächstes Restaurant: Hotel Slavia in Trhová Kamenice.
Nächster Imbiss: im Ausstellungsgelände auf dem Lustigen Hügel (Veselý Kopec) – von Mai bis September in Betrieb.

Dorfmuseum in Südostmähren

Ort: Strážnice (Kreis Hodonín) PLZ 696 62.
Verwaltungsinstitution: Volkskunstinstitut Strážnice.
Baugenehmigung: 1973, Baubeginn: 1974, der Öffentlichkeit zungig gemacht: 1981
Autoren der ethnographischen Studien: Doz. PhDr. V. Frolec, CSc., PhDr. J. Souček, PhDr. J. Tomeš, CSc., PhDr. J. Jančář, CSc., Autor der architektonischen Studie: Ing.-Arch. O. Máčel u. Koll. Das Ausstellungsgelände misst 9,7 ha, das geplante Ausmass beträgt 15 ha.
Anzahl der Ausstellungsobjekte im Jahr 1987: 75, Anzahl weiterer geplanter Ausstellungsobjekte: 20.
Die Exposition präsentiert die volkstümliche Baukultur Südostmährens durch Rekonstruktion ganzer Siedlungsformen. Sie schliesst Volksbauten mit Wohn- und Wirtschaftscharakter (aus den Regionen Moravské Kopanice, Luhačovické zálesí Horňácko, strážnické Dolňácko) ein. Geplant sind Objekte aus Podluží, aus der Gegend uherskobrodské Dolňácko, uherskohradišťské und kyjovské Dolňácko. Zur Exposition gehören weiterhin das Gelände der technischen Wasserbauten, der Wiesenwirtschaft und des Weinbergbesitzes (24 Keller und Kelterhäuser mit Beispielen für das Anpflanzen von Weinrebensorten). Im Ausstellungsgelände finden im Laufe des Sommers (an Sonnabenden und Sonntagen) Veranstaltungen mit Folkloreensemles oder Aktionen statt, die mit der Vorführung von Jubiläumsbräuchen verbunden sind.
Das Museum ist vom 1. 5. bis 31. 10. sonntags von 10 bis 18 Uhr und ausser montags täglich von 8 bis 17 Uhr geöffnet.
Die Besucherzahl von 1988 betrug 32 354.
Nächste Unterkunft: im Autocamp der GO Svazarm Strážnice, Hotel Schwarzer Adler (Černý orel) und Interhotel Strážnice, Hotel Rozkvět in Veselý an der Moravice.
Nächstes Restaurant in Strážnice – Jarošover Bierkeller und Restaurants der angeführten Übernachtungsobjekte.
Nächster Imbiss: Bufet Danaj, Strážnice, Kioskimbiss am Eingang des Expositionsareals.

Walachisches (Valašské) Freilichtmuseen

Ort: Rožnov am Radegast (Kreis Vsetín) PLZ 756 61.
Verwaltungsinstitution: Walachisches Museum in der Natur, Rožnov a. Radegast. Bauvollendung in Form eines Rahmenkonzeptionslibrettos aus dem Jahre 1974 genehmigt. Baubeginn 1923 auf dem Ausstellungsgelände des Hölzernen Städtchens (Dřevěné městečko), Baubeginn 1963 auf dem Gelände des Walachischen Dorfes (Valašská dědina), der Öffentlichkeit zugänglich seit 1925.
Autoren der Studien für die Lösung des Ganzen bzw. der Ausstellungsgelände: Bohumír Jaroněk (künstlerischer Entwurf für die Verbauung), Ing. Arch. M. Podzemní, Ing.-Arch. J. Sedláček, Ing. A. Závada (architektonisch), PhDr. J. Langer, CSc.,

PhDr. J. Štika, CSc., (ethnographisch), Ing. J. Stromšík (Durchführung). Das Ausstellungsgelände misst 76 ha und wurde durch den Staat zum Naturschutzgarten- und Park erklärt.
Anzahl der Ausstellungsobjekte 1988: 77.
weitere geplante Objekte: 130.
Die Ausstellung präsentiert die Volkskultur der Dorf- und Kleinstadtgemeinschaft der Walachischen Region, sowie die traditionsreiche Volkstechnik aus dem 18. Jahrhundert bis Anfang des 20. Jahrhunderts mittels Rekonstruktion von Wohnsitzen und deren historischer Umwelt einschliesslich Weiden, Wiesen und Felder mit dem Anbau historischer landwirtschaftlicher Nutzpflanzensorten und Obstbäume, vorrangig mit der Schaafzucht (almenwirtschaftsmässig). Einzigartig ist der Bau der Walachischen Gastwirtschaft aus dem 17. Jahrhundert, die Interieurausstellung einer Vogtei, technische Baufen mit Wasserantrieb (vorwiegend deren Arbeitsweise), ein Haus aus Lužná aus dem 18. Jahrhundert, eine Windmühle, lebende Landwirtschaft und ein Reihe historischer Pflanzen.
Das Museum ist auf den einzelnen Arealen wie folgt geöffnet:
Dřevěné městečko: vom 1. 5. bis 15. 11. täglich, vom 15. 12. bis 31. 3. montags, mittwochs, sonnabends und sonntags.
Valašská dědina: vom 15. 5. bis 30. 9.
Mlynská dolina: vom 1. 4. bis 30. 9.
Die Besucherzahl betrug 1988 595 000.
Nächste Unterkunft: Hotels in Rožnov am Radegast: Rožnovan, Koruna, Tesla, Autocamp des Sportbundes TJ und Svazarm; das nächste Restaurant befindet sich auf dem Ausstellungsgelände des Dörfchens Dřevěné městečko.
Nächster Imbiss: im Ausstellungsareal Dřevěné městečko und Valašská dědina.

Museum eines slowakischen Dorfes

Ort: Martin – Jahodnícke háje, PLZ 036 01.
Verwaltungsinstitution: Ethnographisches Institut des Slowakischen Nationalmuseums Martin.
Konzeption: im Jahre 1965 entwickelt, Baubeginn: 1967, erster Zugang der Öffentlichkeit: 1983, nach Beendigung der nächsten Etappe wird es wieder 1992 zugängig sein.
Autoren der ethnographischen Studien: Baukonzeption 1965 J. Boďa, Ing.-Arch. J. Turzo, CSc., PhDr. A. Polonec; Bau- und Betriebskonzeption 1971 PhDr. J. Kantár, CSc.; Entwurfsauftrag der Ausstellung 1968 Doz. PhDr. Š. Mruškovič, CSc.; Ideeller Plan der Ausstellung 1974 PhDr. M. Benža, PhDr. S. Horváth, PhDr. I. Krištek, CSc.; thematisch-urbanistische Konzeptionsbegrenzung 1982 PhDr. S. Horváth, PhDr. I. Krištek, CSc. Autoren der architektonischen Studien: Doz. Ing.-Arch. D. Majzlík, CSc., Ing.-Arch. J. Lichner, CSc., Ing.-Arch. M. Bašo, Ing.-Arch. I. Puškar, CSc.; urbanistische Studie 1968 Ing.-Arch. J. Turzo, CSc.
Das Ausstellungsgelände misst 56,5 ha.
Anzahl der Ausstellungsobjekte 1987: 74.
Insgesamt werden in der Ausstellung 317 Objekte zu sehen sein. Die Exposition präsentiert die Volkskultur lokaler Dorfgemeinschaften aus der Slowakei in der zweiten Hälfte des 19. Jahrhunderts und der ersten Hälfte des 20. Jahrhunderts mittels Rekonstruktion von Wohnsitzen in Übereinstimmung mit den ethnographischen Regionen (Tonbauten, Flechtwerk, Zimmerwerk, Mauerwerk) und deren historischer Umwelt. Einzigartige Exemplare sind ein Junkergut aus Vyšný Kubín (1748), das Zimmerwerk der Kirche in Rudno und ein Haus aus Liptovská Lužná. In der Exposition werden spezielle Programme aus Anlass des Internationalen Museentages veranstaltet.
Die Besucherzahl im Jahre 1983 betrug 11 000.
Nächste Unterkunft: Martin – Hotel Turiec.
Nächster Imbiss: Bufet vor dem MSD.
Nächstes ständiges Restaurant: Siedlung Ladoveň, cca. 1 km vom MSD.

Museum des Kysucer Dorfes
Völkerkundeausstellung
in der Natur

Ort: Nová Bystrica – Vychylovka (Kreis Čadca) PLZ 023 05.
Verwaltungsinstitution: Kysucer Museum, Palárikhaus, 022 01 Čadca.
Baugenehmigung: 1974, erster Teil der Öffentlichkeit zugängig gemacht: 1981.
Autoren der ethnographischen Studie: 1974 – PhDr. J. Kantár, CSc., 1979 – PhDr. A. Kocourková, 1984 – PhDr. M. Kiripolský, PhDr. A. Kocourková, PhDr. P. Maráky.
Autoren der architektonischen Studie: Ing.-Arch. B. Dohnány, CSc. und Kollektiv. Architektonische Zusammenarbeit: Ak. Arch. A. Goryczková (1984).
Das Ausstellungsgelände hat einen Umfang von 143 ha, sein verbauter Teil cca. 20 ha. Das Areal ist durch einen weitreichenden Schutzstreifen geschützt und erstreckt sich auf das Gebiet des Naturschutzgebietes Kysuce (Ernennung 1984). Anzahl der Ausstellungsobjekte: 22 (im Jahre 1984).
Anzahl aller geplanten Objekte: 67.
Die Ausstellung ist um die Rekonstruktion der besiedelten Landschaft und der Umwelt bemüht. Sie präsentiert die Lebensweise und Lebenskultur des Dorfvolkes in Kysuce in der Zeit der zweiten Hälfte des 19. Jahrhunderts und zu Beginn des 20. Jahrhunderts. Der überwiegende Teil der Objekte wurde aus verschiedenen Kysucer Gemeinden hergebracht (Riečnica, Harvelka, Klubina, Zborov an der Bystrica, Oščadnica, Korňa und weitere in der Perspektive). Im Ausstellungsgelände wird ebenso der Schutz in situ der ursprünglichen Saisonhirtenbehausung angewandt. Im Areal und dessen unmittelbarer Nähe wurde ein Teil der Trasse der Schmalspureisenbahn Kysucko – Orava erneuert, die für die Beförderung der Besucher und Vorführung der Dampflokfahrt genutzt wird. Zu den interessantesten architektonischen Details gehört das archivoltene Portal der Tür eines Wohnhauses aus Oščadnica aus dem Jahre 1805, die Deckenmalerei eines Volkskünstlers im Schiff der Kapelle aus Zborov an der Bystrica, verzierte Schilder mehrer Wohnhäuser aus Riečnica und andere Details. Die Interieurs auserwählter Objekte wurden mit ursprünglichen Einrichtungen durch Sammlung in den Gemeinden ausgestattet, aus denen diese ins Museum des Kysucer Dorfes überführt wurden. Auf dem Gelände der Ausstellung werden unregelmässig Vorführungen der Volksfertigungstechnik und historischer Betätigung veranstaltet.
Das Museum ist in der Saison von Mai bis Oktober täglich ausser montags von 9.30 bis 18 Uhr geöffnet.
Die Besucherzahl im Jahre 1988 betrug 14 000.
Nächste Unterkunft: Stará Bystrica – Touristenherberge; Čadca – Hotel Lipa, Berghotel Husárik, Touristenherberge, Sporthalle (Športová hala); Kysucer Neustadt (Nové Mesto) – Hotel Mýto, Hotel Závodný klub ROH ZVL.
Nächstes Restaurant: Nová Bystrica.
Nächster Imbiss: auf dem Ausstellungsgelände (Schenke aus Koreňa, SD Jednota Čadca).

Museum des Oravaer Dorfes

Ort: Zuberec – Brestová (Kreis Dolný Kubín) PLZ 027 32.
Verwaltungsinstitution: Oravaer Museum, Dolný Kubín, PLZ 026 01.
Baugenehmigung: 1967, Baubeginn: 1968, der Öffentlichkeit zugängig gemacht: 1975.
Autor der ethnographischen Studie: Ing.-Arch. M. Slováková.
Das Ausstellungsareal misst 20 ha.
Anzahl der Ausstellungsobjekte 1988: 76.
Anzahl weiterer geplanter Objekte: Beendigung zweier Bauerngüter und Errichtung 8 einzelner Objekte.
Die Ausstellung stellt die Volkskultur Oravas in Form von Rekonstruktion des Wohnsitzmodells dar (Zimmerwerk). Unikate sind die spätgotische Kirche aus Zábrež (15.–18. Jahrhundert), das Junkergut aus Vyšný Kubín (1752), das Haus Nr. 57 aus Čimhová und weitere 3 Objekte aus dem 18. Jahrhundert. Auf der Freifläche vor dem Museum werden (seit 1975) Ende August die Podroháčer Folklorefestspiele veranstaltet. Auf dem Ausstellungsgelände finden unregelmässig Vorführungen der Folklore, der Volksfertigungstechniken, und anderer historischer Tätigkeiten statt, die von Dorfgruppen und Kinderfolkloreensembles gezeigt werden.
Das Museum ist von Mai bis Oktober täglich ausser montags geöffnet. Die Besucherzahl im Jahr 1988 betrug 58 651.
Nächste Unterkunft: Zuberec (sichert Slovakotour), Herbergen Primula, Zverovka in Roháče, nächstes Restaurant: vor dem Eingang ins Museum, Zuberec – Milotín, Roháče – Herbergen Primula und Zverovka.
Nächster Imbiss: vor dem Museumseingang

Museum des Liptover Dorfes

Ort: Pribylina (Kreis Liptovský Mikuláš) PLZ 032 42.
Verwaltungsinstitution: Liptover Museum in Ružomberok, Völkerkundeabteilung in Liptovský Hrádok, PLZ 033 01.
Baugenehmigung: 1971, Baubeginn: 1972.
Autor der ethnographischen Studie: PhDr. J. Langer, CSc., PhDr. I. Zuskinová
Autor der architektonischen Studie: Ing.-Arch. S. Dúbravec, CSc.
Das Ausstellungsgelände misst 25 ha.
Anzahl der Ausstellungsobjekte 1988: 31,
Anzahl weiterer geplanter Objekte: 45.
Die Exposition wird die Volkskultur Liptovs mittels Rekonstruktion des Siedlungsgeländes mit historischem Kern präsentieren, in dem Unikate folgender Art vorhanden sind: die Kopie des spätgotischen Schlosses aus Parížovce, der gotischen Kirche aus Liptovská Mara und des gotischen Presbyteriums der Kirche aus Liptovská Sielnica, vonwo auch das Ensemble übergeführt wurde. Weitere Zimmerwerke stammen aus allen Teilen Liptovs (18. und 19. Jahrhundert). Der Teil des Areals mit der überführ-

ten Volksarchitektur wird als Unterkunft für Touristen dienen.
Auf dem Gelände wird die Frage des Imbisses gelöst, am Rand des Areals steht das Hotel Esperanto mit Restaurant.

Freilandexposition des Kreisheimatkundemuseums in Stará Ľubovňa

Ort: Stará Ľubovňa – unter der Burg, PLZ 064 01.
Verwaltungsinstitution: Heimatkundemuseum des Kreises Stará Ľubovňa.
Baugenehmigung: 1974, Baubeginn: 1977, der Öffentlichkeit zugängig gemacht: 1983.
Das Ausstellungsareal misst cca. 10 ha.
Anzahl der Ausstellungsobjekte: 20.
Die Exposition präsentiert die Volkskultur des Kreises Stará Ľubovňa. Dies wird durch Überführung der Objekte gezimmerter Architektur und deren Innenausstattung erreicht. Unikat ist das Zimmerwerk der Kirche aus Matysov (18. Jahrhundert).
Nächstes Quartier in Stará Ľubovňa, nächstes Restaurant – Almhütte unter der Burg.
Besucherzahl 1988: 11 230.
Das Museum ist ausser montags täglich von 9 bis 16 Uhr geöffnet.

Šarisches Museum

Ort: Bardejovské kúpele (Kreis Bardejov) PLZ 086 31.
Verwaltungsinstitution: Šarisches Museum, Bardejov, PLZ 085 01.
Baugenehmigung: 1961, Bau in den Jahren 1962–1972, der Öffentlichkeit zugängig gemacht: 1965.
Autorin der ethnographischen Studie: B. Puškárová, CSc.,
Autor der architektonischen Studie: Ing.-Arch. I. Puškár, CSc.
Das Ausstellungsgelände misst 3,41 ha.
Anzahl der Ausstellungsobjekte 1988: 23.
Die Ausstellung präsentiert die Volkskultur der Gegend Šariš mittels überführter Repräsentationsobjekte mit innerer Ausgestaltung. Ein Unikat ist ein Bohrer für Holzwasserleitungsrohren mit Wasserantrieb aus Bardejov, weiterhin sind es Holzkirchen des östlichen Ritus aus Zboj (1706) und aus Mikulášová (1730) und der Glockenturm aus Jánovce (1700). Die Mehrheit der Häuser stammt vom Ende des 19. Jahrhunderts und charakterisiert die Epoche des Kapitalismus. Auf dem Ausstellungsgelände finden Kulturprogramme und Handarbeitsausstellungen und zwar am Internationalen Museumstag statt, ausserdem auch unregelmässig im Laufe des Sommers. In der anliegenden Villa befindet sich eine Völkerkundeausstellung und eine Ikonenausstellung der Ostslowakei.
Die Besucherzahl 1988 betrug 30 000.
Das Museum ist ausser montags täglich 8.15, 12.00, 12.30, 16.30 Uhr (Oktober his April bis 15.00 Uhr) geöffnet.
Nächste Unterkunft: Hotel Minerál in Bardejovské kúpele, nächstes Restaurant: Minerál, Krištal und Kúpelná dvorana.
Nächster Imbiss: Expreso Srnka, Klub der Pazienten (Klub pacientov), Lahôdky – Einkaufszentrum.

Völkerkundeausstellung in der Natur beim Museum der ukrainischen Kultur

Ort: Svidník, PLZ 089 01.
Verwaltungsinstitution. Museum der ukrainischen Kultur Svidník.
Baugenehmigung: 1975, Baubeginn: 1975, der Őffentlichkeit zugängig gamacht: 1983.
Autor der ethnographischen Studie: M. Sopoliga, CSc., der architektonischen Studie: Fakultät für Bauwesen SVŠT Bratislava – Leiter der Arbeit Doz. Ing.-Arch. D. Majzlík, CSc., Autor Ing.-Arch. L. Jakubík.
Das Ausstellungsareal misst 10 ha.
Anzahl der Ausstellungsobjekte 1988: 24,
Anzahl der geplanten Ausstellungsobjekte: 25.
Die Ausstellung präsentiert die Volkskultur der Ukrainer, die in der Nordostslowakei leben. Dies wird durch die Rekonstruktion des Wohnsitzmodells (Zimmerwerk) mit innerer Ausstattung erreicht, die die Etappe des Kapitalismus darstellt. Unikate sind das gezimmerte Kirchlein aus Nová Polianka (1766), die Wassermühle aus Bogliarka. Im Amphitheater des anliegenden Sommerkinos findet seit 1954 regelmässig das Folklorefestival der ukrainischen Bevölkerung in der ČSSR statt.
Das Museum ist vom 1.5. bis 30.10. täglich ausser montags geöffnet. Die Besucherzahl betrug 1988: 10 000.
Nächste Übernachtungsmöglichkeit: Hotel Dukla, nächstes Restaurant: Hotel Dukla, Hotel Pobeda, Restaurant Verchovina. Nächster Imbiss: Hotel Pobeda.

Bergbaumuseum in der Natur in Banská Štiavnica

Ort: Banská Štiavnica (2 km in Richtung Levice), Kreis Žiar an der Hron, PLZ 969 00.
Verwaltungsinstitution: Slowakisches Bergbaumuseum Banská Štiavnica. Baugenehmigung: 1975, Baubeginn: 1965, der Öffentlichkeit zugängig gemacht: 1974.
Autor des ideellen Entwurfs 1965: Ing. J. Bernath, ideller Plan in Zusammenarbeit mit den Spezialisten: Doz. Ing. J. Boroška, CSc., Ing. J. Cengel, Doz. Ing. J. Fabian, CSc., Ing. M. Hock, Ing. Š. Jankovič, Ing. R. Magula, CSc., PhDr. J. Novák, PhDr. A. Polonec, CSc., Ing. E. Kladivik, Prof. Ing. J. Puzder, CSc., Prof. Ing. A. Sopko, CSc, Doz. Ing. N. Szutter, CSc., Szenarium 1969: PhDr. J. Vlachovič, CSc., V. Kollár, Ing. M. Hock, Ing. E. Kladivik, Autor der architektonischen Studie: Ing.-Arch. O. Maděra, 1970.
Das Ausstellungsareal misst 20 ha.
Anzahl der Ausstellungsobjekte 1987: 16 (+unterirdische Ausstellungen), Anzahl weiterer geplanter Objekte: 33.
Die Ausstellung präsentiert die Entwicklung der Technik und der Technologie der Tiefbauförderung von Mineralien und das Lebensmilieu der Bergleute in der Epoche des Kapitalismus. Unikat ist die unterirdische Exposition der Schächte Ondrej und Bartolomej mit räumlichen Abschnitten aus dem 17. his 19. Jahrhundert, in denen ursprüngliche Werkzeuge und Einrichtungen installiert wurden, die in der Vergangenheit bei bergmännischen Arbeiten benutzt wurden. In neuen Bergwerken ist auch die gegenwärtige Bergwerkstechnik ausgestellt.
Das Museum ist von Mai bis Oktober täglich ausser montags geöffnet. Die Besucherzahl betrug 1988: 50 100.
Nächste Unterkunft in Banská Štiavnica: Hotel Grand, nächstes Restaurant ebenda.
Nächster Imbiss: Bufet auf dem Museumsgelände.

Weitere tschechoslowakische Freilichtmuseum, die in der Publikation bildlich nicht vertreten sind

In Humenné wurde 1983 ein Ausstellungsgelände der Volksarchitektur eröffnet, das die Volkskultur des Kreises Humenné in der kapitalistischen Epoche präsentiert. Seit 1983 ist das Slowakische Feldwirtschaftsmuseum der Natur in Nitra im Bau, das durch die Rekonstruktion eines Teils der Siedlung und der Flächen der landwirtschaftlichen Bauten verwirklicht wird, die an die Verarbeitung der Produkte anknüpft.
Weiterhin ist in der Tschechoslowakischen Sozialistischen Republik der Bau des Böhmerwaldmuseums in der Natur, im Kreis Klatovy, geplant. Ebenso die landwirtschaftliche Exposition in einem Teil der Gemeinde Příkazy (Kreis Olomouc), die Exposition in einem Teil der Gemeinde Rymice (Kreis Kroměříž) steht mit einigen Objekten den Besuchern schon zur Verfügung, so auch die Bergbauexposition in Příbram – Březové Hory. In Ostrava – Petřkovice wird aus dem Bergwerk Eduard Urx und dem nahegelegenen Bergmannviertel Mexiko ein Museum gebildet, das den Tiefbau der Kohleförderung darstellt.
In der Slowakischen Sozialistischen Republik plant man bei Gemera in Halič den Bau eines Regionalmuseums in der Natur, weiterhin für das weitreichende Gebiet des Hronlandes in Slovenská Ľupča und Čierny Balog
In Detva soll ein Ensemble von Zimmerwerken, die aus der zerstreuten Siedlung in der Umgebung von Zvolen hergebracht werden, als Museum im Freien dienen. Eine geplante Exposition in Medzevo soll mit ihren Produktionsgegenständen zur Eisenbearbeitung das Slowakische Technische Museum präsentieren.

Collection of folk architecture objects from the Bohemian Middle Mountains region at Zubrnice

Location: Zubrnice (district of Ústí nad Labem), PSČ (postal direction number) 403 24.
Administering institution: Okresní vlastivědné muzeum (District Motherland Museum), Ústí nad Labem, PSČ 400 00.
Construction approved in 1977, building since 1977, opened for public in 1988.
Ethnographic conception author: PhDr. F. Ledvinka, architectonic study author: Ing. Arch. J. Škabrada, CSc.
Exposition area not precised yet, it concerns the built up part and partially the outskirts of the locality, c. 30 hectares.
Number of exposition objects in 1988: 12.
The exposition will present folk culture of the period of capitalism from the Bohemian Middle Mountains region through the reconstruction of the historical nucleus of the present-day settlement by the transfer of several objects from other localities and by the preservative renovation of the local houses surrounding the village green. Unique parts of the exposition will be a re-established stretch of the abolished railway line from Ústí nad Labem to Úštěk, the log-cabin mill (1803) on the locality cadastre, granaries from Lukov and Lochočice, and the house No. 61.
Museum opened from May 1 to October 31, daily except Mondays from 9 to 16 hrs.
Restaurant will be furnished on the exposition premises, nearest accomodation in Ústí nad Labem and at Úštěk.

Ethnographic Museum Třebíz

Location: Třebíz (district of Kladno), PSČ 273 75.
Administering institutions: Vlastivědné muzeum Slaný (Motherland Museum Slaný – operation matters, professional activities, collections) and Local National Committee Třebíz (building and maintenance of objects, administration).
Construction approved in 1969, building since 1969, opened for public in 1975.
Ethnographic studies authors: L. Štěpánek, PhDr. V. Jiřikovská, CSc., architectonic studies authors: J. Nedvěd, Ing. Arch. J. Škabrada, CSc., historical study author: PhDr. J. Krotilová.
Exposition area is 32 hectares.
Number of exposition objects in 1988: 24, number of further planned exposition objects: 6.
The museum presents folk culture from the Slaný region (the sugar-beet region of the north-west part of Central Bohemia to the border of the Bohemian Middle Mountains region) through the complete locality Třebíz with village green buildings mostly built in stone, limestone and sandstone, partially half-timbered) the nucleus of which is the reconstruction of the historical living environment with several complementary objects transferred into it. A unique part is Cífka's farmstead from 16th – 19th centuries in the rooms of which the way of life in historical interiors and the development of agriculture in the Slaný region are presented, and thematic exhibitions are held in special halls. Other three estates within the exposition originate from 18th century. The native house of Václav Beneš Třebízský the writer has been opened for public as a memorial since 1904. The museum takes part in the organization of Třebíz Fairs (as a rule on the eighth Sunday after the Easter every year) and prepares some other programmes: displays of folk production, fruit drying, baking in ovens, etc.
Museum opened from May 1 to October 31, daily except Mondays from 9 to 16 hrs.
Number of visitors in 1988 was 11.000.
Nearest accomodation and restaurant: Slaný, Louny (9 kms, 17 kms, respectively).
Nearest refreshment: inn at Třebíz.

Museum of the Village

Location: Kouřim (district of Kolín), PSČ 281 61.
Administering institution: Regionální muzeum Kolín (Regional Museum Kolín), PSČ 280 00.
Construction approved in 1972, building since 1972, opened for public in 1975.
Ethnographic conceptions authors: A. Pospíšilová, PhDr. M. Nováková, architectonic study author: Ing. Arch. A. Fuchs. Exposition area is 4 hectares.
Number of exposition objects in 1987: 13, number of all planned exposition objects: 38.
Exposition conception not yet clarified. At first the exposition premises were filled with objects transferred from the flooded territory of the Želivka dam which had been listed in the state survey of cultural relics with the intention to present folk culture from the southern part of the Central Bohemina region. In 1975, due to the intentions of the SÚPPOPP (State Office for Historical Monuments Care and Living Environment Protection), the preservation conception was broadened to cover the whole territory of the Czech Socialist Republic. This has resulted in the crystallization of opinions concerning the establishment, at Kouřim, of a museum of building techniques irrespective of the mutual appurtenance and interior furnishing of the objects. Unique parts are polygonal barns from Durdice (1648) and from Želejov (1660), the estate from Týřovice and the magistrate's house from Bradlecká Lhota. Museum opened from April to October, daily except Mondays from 9 to 16 hrs.
The annual number of visitors is c. 5.000.
Nearest accomodation and restaurant at Kouřim, refreshment at the adjacent swimming-pool.

Elbe Region Ethnographic Museum at Přerov nad Labem

Location: Přerov nad Labem (district of Nymburk), PSČ 289 16.
Administering institution: Polabské muzeum v Poděbradech (Elbe Region Museum at Poděbrady – the district museum for the Nymburk district), PSČ 290 01.
Construction approved in 1979, building since 1967, opened for public in 1967.
Ethnographic studies authors: PhDr. H. Sedláčková, Ing. I. Bernard, architectonic study authors: Ing. Arch. Koreček, Ing. Arch. Tichý.
Exposition area is 1.8 hectares.
Number of exposition objects in 1988: 32, number of further planned objects: 8.
The museum has served for the transfer of protected objects of folk architecture from the central Elbe region (mostly from the Nymburk disctrict), the existence of which on their original places was threatened. The basis of the museum and its first object was co called Old Bohemian cottage (manorial smithy and later the magistrate's seat from the middle of 18th century adapted towards 1895). Ethnographic collections are exhibited in it. Former manorial buildings belonging to the museum comprise the game-keeper's lodge built in masonry (the administrative edifice and depositories), so called coopery with the exhibition hall, and the old school. In its vicinity, the village green adapted as a park has been since 1967 occupied with cottages transferred from Draho and Chvalovice and with other smaller objects (granaries, a drying kiln, fountains, folk sculptures, etc.). Since 1980 the museum has been realizing the construction plan in the gardens behind the coopery and the game-keeper's lodge where by 1990 will have been reconstructed estates from the Městec Králové and Křinec regions and from the environs of Nymburk. On the outskirts of the exposition premises is situated the masonry farmstead No. 13 with a baroque gable and gateway with the exposition of agriculture in the Elbe region (the cooperative farm's Hall of Traditions).
Museum opened from April 15 to October 31, daily except Mondays from 14 to 16 hrs.
Number of visitors in 1988 was 30.000.
Nearest accomodation: hotel Polabí at Lysá nad Labem, nearest restaurant: pull-up Kerako at Lysá nad Labem.
Nearest refreshment: sweetshop opposite the ethnographic museum at Přerov nad Labem.

Collection of Folk Buildings and Technical Equipment at Vysočina

Location: the village of Vysočina (district of Chrudim), post office Hlinsko v Čechách, PSČ 539 01, seat of administration at Svobodné Hamry (the village of Vysočina lies between Hlinsko v Čechách and Trhová Kamenice and comprises the settlements of Svobodné Hamry, Dřevíkov, Možděnice, Veselý Kopec and Rváčov, a part of the exposition premises is the settlement Králova Pila of the village of Všeradov).
Administering institution: Východočeské krajské středisko státní památkové péče a ochrany přírody v Pardubicích (East Bohemia Regional Centre of the State Care of Historical Monuments and Nature Protection in Pardubice).
Construction approved in 1977, building since 1969, opened for public in 1971.
Ethnographic studies authors: L. Štěpán, PhDr. I. Vojanová, architectonic studies authors: L. Štěpán, Ing. Arch. L. Černík, Ing. Z. Haken, Ing. Arch. J. Škabrada, CSc.
Exposition area at the settlement of Veselý Kopec is 3.5 hectares, on the whole the historical countryside of the exposition spreads over the area of c. 9 sq. kms.
Number of exposition objects in 1988: 37, number of further planned exposition objects: 12.
The exposition presents folk culture of the northern part of the Bohemian-Moravian Uplands (the area of occurrence of log-cabin buildings) and especially it presents the traditional folk technical equipments in their broader settlement context. Unique parts are Králova Pila (a mill with a sawmill), the house No. 4 from Veselý Kopec and the barn of fourteen sides from Sádek (all from 17th century), 12 objects from 18th century. The exposition gives place to performances of Christmas and spring customs based on the combination of words and action, to displays of hand-made products and domestic animals breeding exhibitions.
Collection opened from April 15 to October 31, at Svobodné Hamry from May 1, daily except Mondays, at Možděnice except July and August only on Saturdays and Sundays.

Number of visitors in 1988 was 129.000.
Nearest accomodation: hotels Záložna, Styl at Hlinsko v Čechách, nearest restaurant: hotel Slavia at Trhová Kamenice. Nearest refreshment: in the exposition area at Veselý Kopec (from May to September).

Museum of the South-East Moravian Village

Location: Strážnice (district of Hodonín), PSČ 696 62.
Administering institution: Ústav lidového umění (Folk Art Institute), Strážnice.
Construction approved in 1973, building since 1974, opened for public in 1981.
Ethnographic studies authors: Doc. PhDr. V. Frolec CSc., PhDr. J. Souček, PhDr. J. Tomeš, CSc., PhDr. J. Jančář, CSc., architectonic study author: Ing. Arch. O. Máčal et al.
Exposition area is 9.7 hectares, planned area is 15 hectares. Number of exposition objects in 1987: 75, number of further planned exposition objects: 20.
The exposition presents folk building culture of south-east Moravia through the reconstruction of integral settlement formations. It comprises folk buildings of residential and production character (from the regions of Moravské Kopanice, Luhačovické Zálesí, Horňácko, Strážnice, Dolňácko; according to the plan, further buildings will be added from Podluží and Dolňácko (lowlands) parts of the Uherský Brod, Uherské Hradiště and Kyjov districts, respectively). The exposition also comprises technical and water buildings, equipments connected with the utilization of meadows and vineyard keeping (24 wine-cellars and wine-press rooms with demonstration of planting and growing of vine varieties). During summer the exposition premises give place to performances of folklore ensembles or to actions connected with demonstration of annual customs.
Museum opened from May 1 to October 31, on Sundays from 10 to 18 hrs, on other days except Mondays from 8 to 17 hrs.
Number of visitors in 1988 was 32.354.
Nearest accomodation: at Strážnice the caravan site Autokempink ZO Svazarm, hotel Černý orel and Interhotel Strážnice, at Veselí nad Moravou hotel Rozkvět, nearest restaurant: Jarošovská pivnice at Strážnice and the restaurants of the aforesaid accomodation facilities.
Nearest refreshment: buffet Dunaj at Strážnice, a refreshment stall is being prepared by the entrance into the exposition area.

Wallachian open-air Museum

Location: Rožnov pod Radhoštěm (district of Vsetín), PSČ 756 61. Administering institution: Valašské muzeum v přírodě (Wallachian open-air Museum), Rožnov pod Radhoštěm.
Finishing construction approved in the form of the conception script outline in 1974, building since 1923 in the exposition area of The Wooden Town, since 1963 in the exposition area of The Wallachian Village, opened for public in 1925.
Authors of studies concerning the design of the whole museum or its exposition areas: Bohumír Jaroněk (creative design of dislocation), Ing. Arch. M. Podzemný, Ing. Arch. J. Sedláček, Ing. A. Závada (architectonic studies), PhDr. J. Langer, CSc., PhDr. J. Štika, CSc. (ethnographic studies), Ing. J. Stromšík (operation matters study).
Exposition area is 76 hectares and it has been decreed a state protected garden and park.
Number of exposition objects in 1987: 76, further planned exposition objects: 130.
The exposition presents folk culture of the village and town communities from the Wallachian region as well as traditional folk technical equipment from 18th till the beginning of 20th centuries through the reconstruction of settlements and their historical living environment including pastures, meadows and fields with the growing of historical varieties of agricultural produce and fruit trees, with the breeding of domestic animals, especially the chalet sheep-breeding. Unique parts are the edifice of the Wallachian pub from 17th century, interior exposition in the magistrate's house, water-driven technical buildings (their productive activity is performed), the house from Lužná from 18th century, a wind mill, working farmstead with a number of historical agricultural produce items.
Opening hours of the museum in individual areas:
The Wooden Town: from May 1 to November 15 every day, from December 15 to March 31 on Mondays, Wednesdays, Saturdays and Sundays
The Wallachian Village: from May 15 to September 30
The Mill Dell: from April 1 to September 30
Number of visitors in 1988 was 595 000. Nearest accomodation: hotels at Rožnov pod Radhoštěm: Rožnovan, Koruna, Tesla, caravan sites of TJ and Svazarm; nearest permanent restaurant in the exposition area of The Wooden Town.
Nearest refreshment: in the exposition areas of The Wooden Town and The Wallachian Village, respectively.

Slovak Village Museum

Location: Martin – Jahodnícke háje, PSČ 036 01.
Administering institution: Etnografický ústav Slovenského národného múzea (Ethnographic Institute of the Slovak National Museum), Martin.
Conception constituted in 1965, construction started in 1967, first opened for public in 1983, after the completion of further stage reopening for public will be in 1992.
Ethnographic studies of the authors: construction conception from 1965 J. Boďa, Ing. Arch. J. Turzo, CSc., PhDr. A. Polonec; construction and operation matters conception from 1971 PhDr. J. Kantár, CSc.; exposition project from 1968 Doc. PhDr. Š. Mruškovič, CSc.; exposition idea and intention elaborated in 1974 by PhDr. M. Benža, PhDr. S. Horváth, PhDr. I. Krištek, CSc.; precision of the conception from the thematic and urban points of view from 1982 PhDr. S. Horváth, PhDr. I. Krištek, CSc.
Architectonic studies authors: Doc. Ing. Arch. D. Majzlík, CSc., Ing. Arch. J. Lichner, CSc., Ing. Arch. M. Bašo, Ing. Arch. I. Puškár, CSc.; urban study from 1968 Ing. Arch. J. Turzo, CSc. Exposition area is 56.5 hectares.
Number of exposition objects in 1987: 74, total number of exposition objects will be 317.
The exposition presents folk culture of the local village communities from the territory of Slovakia from the period of the second half of 19th century and the first half of 20th century through the reconstruction of settlements in accordance with the ethnographic regions (clay houses, wickerwork dwellings, log-cabins, masonry buildings) and their historical environments. Unique parts are the squire's estate from Vyšný Kubín (1748), the log church from Rudno, and the house from Liptovská Lužná Special programmes are organized in the exposition on the occasion of the International Day of Museums.
Number of visitors in 1983 was 11.000.
Nearest accomodation: Martin – hotel Turiec.
Nearest refreshment: buffet in front of the museum.
Nearest permanent restaurant: settlement Ladoveň, c. 1 km from the museum.

Kysuce Village Museum
Ethnographic open-air Exposition
Location: Nová Bystrica – Vychylovka (district of Čadca), PSČ 023 05.
Administering institution: Kysucké múzeum (Kysuca Muzeum), Palárikov dom, 022 01 Čadca.
Construction approved in 1974, first part opened for public since 1981.
Ethnographic study authors: 1974 – PhDr. J. Kantár, CSc., 1979 – PhDr. A. Kocourková, 1984 – PhDr. M. Kiripolský, PhDr. A. Kocourková, PhDr. P. Maráky.
Architectonic study authors: Ing. Arch. B. Dohnány, CSc. et al. (1976).
Architectonic collaboration: Acad. Arch. A. Goryczková (1984).
Exposition area is 143 hectares, its part with buildings is c. 20 hectares.
The area is surrounded by an ample protective zone and it spreads on the territory of the Protected Countryside Region of Kysuce (decreed in 1984).
Number of exposition objects in 1987: 22.
Total number of planned objects: 67.
The exposition aspires to the reconstruction of the settled countryside and living environments and it presents the way of life and the culture of village people in Kysuce region from the second half of 19th century and the beginning of 20th century. The majority of objects are transferred from various villages of the Kysuce region (Riečnica, Harvelka, Klubina, Zborov nad Bystricou, Oščadnica, Korňa, and from others in prospect). The exposition area applies also the protection in situ of original seasonal dwelling-places for shepherds. A part of the track of the narrow-gauge railway line from Kysuce-Orava region has been re-established within the area and its close vicinity to be used for the transport of visitors and to demonstrate train traffic with steam traction.
The most interesting architectonic details comprise the archivolt portal of the door of the residential house from Oščadnica from 1805, the vaulting painting by a folk artist in the nave of the small village chapel from Zborov nad Bystricou, the decorated gables of several residential houses from Riečnica, and other details. The interiors of selected objects are furnished with the original installations obtained by means of collection in the villages from which come the objects transferred to Kysuce Village Museum. The exposition area gives place to irregular displays of folk production technologies and historical activities.
Museum opened in season from May to October, daily except Mondays from 9.30 to 18 hrs.
Number of visitors in 1988: 14.000.
Nearest accomodation: Stará Bystrica – tourist lodge; Čadca – hotel Lipa, mountain hotel Husárik, tourist lodge Športová hala; Kysucké Nové Mesto – hotel Mýto, hotel Závodný klub ROH ZVL.
Nearest restaurant: Nová Bystrica.
Nearest refreshment: In the exposition area (folk tavern from Korňa catered for by the consumer's cooperative Jednota Čadca).

Orava Village Museum

Location: Zuberec – Brestová (district of Dolný Kubín), PSČ 027 32.
Administering institution: Oravské múzeum (Orava Museum), Dolný Kubín, PSČ 026 01.
Construction approved in 1967, building started in 1968, opened for public in 1975.
Ethnographic study author: PhDr. J. Langer, CSc., architectonic study author: Ing. Arch. M. Slováková.
Exposition area is 20 hectares.
Number of exposition objects in 1988: 76, number of further planned objects: termination of 2 farmsteads and building of 8 individual objects.
The exposition presents folk architecture of Orava region in the form of the settlement model reconstruction (log buildings). Unique parts are late-Gothic church from Zábrež (15th – 18th centuries), the squire's estate from Vyšný Kubín (1752), the house No. 57 from Čimhová, and other 3 objects from 18th century. The space in front of the museum gives place to Podroháče Folklore Festivals held annually (since 1975) by the end of August. The exposition area gives place to irregular displays of folklore, folk production technologies and other historical activities performed by village groups and children's folklore ensembles.
Museum opened daily except Mondays from May to October.
Number of visitors in 1988 was 58.651.
Nearest accomodation: Zuberec (provided by Slovakotour), chalets Primula and Zverovka at Roháče, nearest restaurant: in front of the entrance into the museum, Zuberec – Milotín, Roháče – chalets Primula and Zverovka.
Nearest refreshment: in front of the entrance into the museum.

Liptov Village Museum

Location: Pribylina (district of Liptovský Mikuláš), PSČ 032 42.
Administering institution: Liptovské múzeum v Ružomberku, národopisné oddělení v Liptovskom Hrádku (Liptov Museum at Ružomberok, Ethnographic Department at Liptovský Hrádok), PSČ 033 01.
Construction approved in 1971, building since 1972.
Ethnographic study author: PhDr. J. Langer, CSc., PhDr. I. Zuskinová architectonic study author: Ing. Arch. S. Dúbravec, CSc.
Exposition area is 25 hectares.
Number of exposition objects in 1988: 31, number of further planned objects 45.
The exposition will present folk culture of the Liptov region through the scientific reconstruction of the settlement area with its historical nucleus which contains unique parts: the copy of the late-Gothic monastery from Parížovce, the Gothic church from Liptovská Mara and the Gothic presbytery of the church from Liptovská Sielnica from which also a collection of estates has been transferred. The other woodwork objects come from all parts of the Liptov region (18th and 19th centuries). One part of the area into which folk architecture has been transferred will serve for the accomodation of tourists.
Refreshment will be provided in the area; neigbouring it is hotel Esperanto with a restaurant.

Open-air exposition of the District Motherland Museum at Stará Ľubovňa

Location: Stará Lubovňa – under the castle, PSČ 064 01.
Administering institution: Okresné vlastivedné múzeum (District Motherland Museum), Stará Lubovňa.
Construction approved in 1974, building since 1977, opened for public in 1983.
Exposition area is c. 10 hectares.
Number of exposition objects: 20.
The exposition presents folk culture of the Stará Lubovňa district through the transfer of woodwork architecture objects with their interior furnishings. A unique part is the woodwork church from Matysová (18th century).
Nearest accomodation at Stará Lubovňa, nearest restaurant the shepherd cottage under the castle.
Number of visitors in 1988 was 11.230.
Museum opened except Mondays from 9 to 16 hrs.

Šariš Museum

Location: Bardejov Spa (district of Bardejov), PSČ 086 31.
Administering institution: Šarišské múzeum (Šariš Museum), Bardejov, PSČ 085 01.
Construction approved in 1961, building since 1962 to 1972, opened for public in 1965.
Ethnographic study author: graduated historian B. Puškárová, CSc.
Architectonic study author: Ing. Arch. I. Puškár, CSc.
Exposition area is 3.41 hectares.
Number of exposition objects in 1988: 23.
The exposition presents folk culture of the Šariš region through the transfer of representative objects with their interior furnishings. Unique parts are the water-driven drilling machine, from Bardejov, to make wooden water pipes, the wooden churches of the Eastern rite from Zboj (1706) and Mikulášová (1730), and the belfry from Jánovce (1700). The majority of the houses originate from the end of 19th century and characterize the period of capitalism. The exposition area gives place to cultural performances and displays of handicraft production, especially on the occasion of the International Day of Museums, and irregularly during the summer season. The adjacent villa of Rákocsi contains an ethnographic exposition and the exposition Icons of East Slovakia.
Number of visitors in 1988 was 30.000.
Museum opened except Mondays from 8.15 to 12 hrs and from 12.30 to 16.30 hrs (from October to April to 15 hrs).
Nearest accomodation: hotel Minerál at Bardejov Spa.
Nearest restaurant: Minerál, Krištál and Kúpelná dvorana.
Nearest refreshment: espresso Srnka, Klub pacientov, Lahôdky the shopping centre.

Ethnographic open-air exposition of Ukrainian Culture Museum

Location: Svidník, PSČ 089 01
Administering institution: Múzeum ukrajinskej kultúry (Ukrainian Culture Museum), Svidník.
Construction approved in 1975, building since 1975, opened for public in 1983.
Ethnographic study author: PhDr. M. Sopoliga, CSc., architectonic study: Faculty of Construction of the Slovak Technical University in Bratislava – team leader Doc. Ing. Arch. D. Majzlík, CSc., author Ing. Arch. L. Jakubík.
Exposition area is 10 hectares.
Number of exposition objects in 1988: 24, number of further planned exposition objects: 25.
The exposition presents folk culture of the Ukrainians living in north-east Slovakia through the settlement model reconstruction (woodwork buildings) with interior furnishings representing the period of capitalism. Unique parts are the wooden church from Nová Polianka (1766) and the water mill from Bogliarka. In the amphitheatre of the adjacent summer cinema regular annual folklore festivals of the Ukrainian population in the CSSR have been held since 1954.
Museum opened from May 1 to October 31 except Mondays.
Number of visitors in 1988 was 10.000.
Nearest accomodation: hotel Dukla, nearest restaurant: hotel Dukla, hotel Pobeda, restaurant Verchovina.
Nearest refreshment: hotel Pobeda.

Mining open-air Museum at Banská Štiavnica

Location: Banská Štiavnica (2 kms in the direction of Levice), district of Žiar nad Hronom, PSČ 969 00.
Administering institution: Slovenské banské múzeum (Slovak Mining Museum), Banská Štiavnica.
Construction approved in 1975, building since 1965, opened for public in 1974.
Author of the idea and intention from 1965: Ing. J. Bernáth, idea and intention in the collaboration with specialists: Doc. Ing. J. Boroška, CSc., Ing. J. Cengel, Doc. Ing. J. Fabian, CSc., Ing. M. Hock, Ing. Š. Jankovič, Ing. R. Magula, CSc., PhDr. J. Novák, PhDr. A. Polonec, CSc., Ing. E. Kladivík, Prof. Ing. A. Sopko, CSc., Doc. Ing. N. Szuttor, CSc., script from 1969: PhDr. J. Vlachovič, CSc., V. Kollár, Ing. M. Hock, Ing. E. Kladivík, architectonic study author: Ing. Arch. O. Maděra, 1970.
Exposition area is 20 hectares.
Number of exposition objects in 1988: 16 and the underground exposition, number of further planned objects: 33.
The exposition presents the development of technical equipment and technology of depth extraction of minerals and the living environment of miners in the period of capitalism. A unique part is the underground exposition in the Ondrej and Bartolomej Mine with working places from 17th – 19th centuries with the installation of the original implements and devices used in the past in mining works. In the new mined out workings also contemporary mining technical devices are exhibited.
Museum opened from May to October, daily except Mondays.
Number of visitors in 1988 was 50.100.
Nearest accomodation at Banská Štiavnica: hotel Grand, nearest restaurant at the same place.
Nearest refreshment: buffet within the museum area.

Other Czechoslovak open-air museums
which are not represented in pictures in the publication

At Humenné the Exposition of Folk Architecture presenting folk culture of the Humenné district in the period of capitalism was opened in 1983. Slovak Agricultural open-air Museum at Nitra, which will present the reconstruction of the parts of settlements and areas of agricultural buildings related to produce processing, has been constructed since 1983. Besides that, in the Czech Socialist Republic, the construction of Bohemian Forest open-air Museum in the district of Klatovy and an agricultural exposition in nature in a part of the Příkazy village (district of Olomouc), respectively, are being prepared, while some of the objects of the exposition in a part of the Rymice village (district Kroměříž) are already open to public same as the mining exposition at Příbram – Březové Hory. At Ostrava – Petřkovice
a museum of coal mining will be established from the Eduard Urx Mine and the near-by miners' colony called Mexico.
In the Slovak Socialist Republic the construction of regional open-air museum is being prepared at Gemer, at Halič, and for the ample territory around the Hron River at Slovenská Lupča and Čierny Balog; a collection of woodwork buildings from the dispersed settlement in the surroundings of Zvolen will be constructed to join the area of folklore festivals at Detva, and the exposition of Slovak Technical Museum with production objects for iron processing will be constructed at Medzev.

ČESKOSLOVENSKÁ MUZEA V PŘÍRODĚ

Úvodný text Jaroslav Štika, texty k fotografiám a katalóg múzeí Jiří Langer.
Preklady Eva Mrhačová-Kučerová (ruština), Elvíra Hanzlíková (nemčina) a Miroslav Janoušek (angličtina).
Fotografie Milan Fabĺan, Miroslav Kukačka, Miloš Polášek a Petr Sikula.
Preklad do slovenčiny Peter Mišák.
Prebal, väzbu a grafickú úpravu navrhol Bohuslav Blažej.

Vydalo Vydavateľstvo Osveta, n. p., Martin
v koprodukcii s nakladateľstvom Profil Ostrava roku 1989
ako svoju 3184. publikáciu.
Zodpovední redaktori Milan Fabian (Osveta) a Jiří Štefanides (Profil).
Výtvarní redaktori Robert Brož (Osveta) a Václav Beránek (Profil).

301-09/18. Vydanie 1. Náklad 10 000 slovenská mutácia, 20 000 česká mutácia.
Počet strán 176. AH 32,62 (textu 9,47; obrázkov 23,15). VH 32,86. Vytlačili
Tlačiarne SNP, štátny podnik, závod Neografia, Martin. SÚKK 1562/I-88

ISBN 80-217-0039-4 Kčs 79,– 85.8